Japan, Australia and Asia-Pacific Security

The threats to security in East Asia have been serious and constant since the end of World War II. This book provides a comprehensive account of the evolution of one key axis of regional stability, defence contacts between Japan and Australia, tracing the relationship between the two countries from the early post-war period to the post-9/11 present. Most works on Japan–Australia relations focus on the economic nexus, which is not surprising given that this has been the most salient aspect of post-war bilateral ties. But while trade and investment remains the dominant feature of the Australia-Japan relationship, defence and security ties have assumed increasing importance since the mid-1990s, and especially since the terror attacks on New York and Washington and the ensuing US-led war on terror. With problems such as North Korea's nuclear program and the China–Taiwan standoff constantly threatening regional stability, Canberra and Tokyo have sought to strengthen bilateral relations, and all indications are that this relationship is likely to grow in the future. This book traces the post-war evolution of the relationship between Japan and Australia in the broader context of Asia-Pacific security, and addresses regional, sub-regional and transnational issues. Particular attention is given to how the US, the UN and the events of 9/11 have had an impact on bilateral defence contacts and regional security dynamics.

Brad Williams is a postdoctoral research fellow in the Department of Political Science, National University of Singapore. He received his doctorate from Monash University, and his research interests include international relations of the Asia-Pacific region, Japanese politics and foreign policy, and post-communist politics, with particular reference to Russia.

Andrew Newman is an Assistant Counsellor (Nuclear Science and Technology) in the Australian Embassy in Washington. He received his doctorate from Monash University, and his research interests include international security, terrorism, international relations and American politics and foreign policy.

Routledge Security in Asia Pacific series
Series Editors
Leszek Buszynski, International University of Japan, and William Tow,
University of Queensland

Security issues have become more prominent in the Asia Pacific region
because of the presence of global players, rising great powers, and confident middle powers, which intersect in complicated ways. This series puts
forward important new work on key security issues in the region. It
embraces the roles of the major actors, their defence policies and postures
and their security interaction over the key issues of the region. It includes
coverage of the United States, China, Japan, Russia, the Koreas, as well as
the middle powers of ASEAN and South Asia. It also covers issues relating
to environmental and economic security as well as transnational actors and
regional groupings.

Japan, Australia and Asia-Pacific Security

Edited by
**Brad Williams and
Andrew Newman**

Routledge
Taylor & Francis Group

LONDON AND NEW YORK

First published 2006
by Routledge
2 Park Square, Milton Park, Abingdon, Oxon, OX14 4RN

Simultaneously published in the USA and Canada
by Routledge
711 Third Avenue, New York, NY 10017

Routledge is an imprint of the Taylor & Francis Group, an informa business

Transferred to Digital Printing 2008

First issued in paperback 2012

Typeset in Times New Roman by Taylor & Francis Books

British Library Cataloguing in Publication Data
A catalogue record for this book is available from the British Library

Library of Congress Cataloging in Publication Data
Japan, Australia and Asia-Pacific security / edited by Brad Williams and
Andrew Newman.
p. cm. – (Routledge security in Asia Pacific series)
Includes bibliographical references and index.
ISBN 0–415–38139–8 (alk. paper)
1. National security–Japan. 2. National security–Australia. 3. National
security–Pacific Area. 4. Australia–Relations--Japan. 5.
Japan–Relations–Australia. I. Williams, Brad, 1969– II. Newman,
Andrew 1971– III. Series.
UA845.J3153 2006
355'.03109520994–dc22
2005030670

ISBN13: 978-0-415-38139-0 hardback
ISBN13: 978-0-415-64936-0 paperback

Contents

Contributors

Desmond Ball is a professor in the Strategic and Defence Studies Centre of the Australian National University, of which he previously served as head from 1984 to 1991. He is also a founding member of the Steering Committee of the Council for Security Cooperation in the Asia-Pacific (CSCAP). Among numerous other books and articles, he has recently published monographs *Death in Balibo, Lies in Canberra* (with Hamish McDonald, Allen and Unwin 2000) and *The Boys in Black: The Thahan Phran (Rangers), Thailand's Para-military Border Guards* (White Lotus 2004).

C. W. Braddick is Convenor of the International Relations of Northeast Asia at the Australian National University and Professor of International Political History at Musashi University, Tokyo. He is the author of *Japan and the Sino-Soviet Alliance, 1950–1964* (St Antony's/Palgrave Macmillan 2004), as well as numerous articles on Japanese politics and foreign relations.

John Bruni is Adjunct Lecturer in Strategic Studies in the Centre for Asian Studies at the University of Adelaide, and has worked on Australian defence and regional security issues in various capacities for over eighteen years. Dr Bruni is the author of *On Weapons Decisions: How Australia Chooses to Arm Itself (1963–96)* (Southern Highlands Publishers 2002).

Katsumi Ishizuka is a lecturer in the Department of International Business Management, Kyoei University, Japan. His research focuses on UN peacekeeping operations. He is the author of *Ireland and International Peacekeeping Operations 1960–2000: A Study of Irish Motivation* (Frank Cass 2005).

Purnendra Jain is Professor and Head of Asian Studies at the University of Adelaide in Australia. He is the author, editor and co-editor of ten books and has published more than four dozen book chapters and scholarly articles in international journals. His most recent book is *Japan's Subnational Governments in International Affairs* (Routledge 2005).

Andrew Newman is an honorary research fellow with the School of Political and Social Inquiry, Monash University. He has consulted for several US think-tanks on weapons proliferation issues and has published articles on arms control/proliferation in journals such as *The Nonproliferation Review*, *Strategic Studies*, and *Contemporary Security Policy*. He is currently Assistant Counsellor for Nuclear Science and Technology at the Australian Embassy, Washington DC.

Naoko Sajima is an associate professor at Senshu University in Japan. From 1987 to 2001 she worked for the Japan Defense Agency (JDA). In 2005 she was awarded the fifteenth Cum-Sophia Award for the *Concise Encyclopaedia of Security Affairs*, of which she was chief editor.

Alison Tokita is Associate Professor of Japanese Studies in the School of Languages, Cultures and Linguistics, Monash University, and current president of the Japanese Studies Association of Australia. An established teacher and researcher in Japanese culture, she is currently involved in a project examining the reception of Japanese popular culture in Asia, its effect on Asian attitudes towards Japan, as well as Japan's awareness of the importance of its relations with Asia.

William T. Tow is Professor of International Security in the Department of International Relations, The Australian National University. He is the author of many books and articles on Asian security politics (including *Asia-Pacific Strategic Relations – Seeking Convergent Security*, Cambridge University Press 2001). He is Editor of the *Australian Journal of International Affairs*.

Russell Trood is a Liberal senator from Queensland in the Australian parliament. At the time of preparing his contribution to this book, Senator Trood was Associate Professor of International Relations in the Department of International Business and Asian Studies at Griffith University.

David Walton is a lecturer in the School of Humanities, University of Western Sydney. He is the author of several book chapters and journal articles on Australia-Japan relations. David's current projects include 'Economic diplomacy in Australia-Japan relations, 1986–1990' (with Geoff Miller).

Brad Williams is postdoctoral fellow in the Department of Political Science, National University of Singapore and an honorary research fellow with the School of Political and Social Inquiry, Monash University. He has published several articles on the international relations of the Asia-Pacific region in journals such as *Europe-Asia Studies*, *East Asia: An International Quarterly*, *The Pacific Review* and *The Nonproliferation Review*.

David Wright-Neville is a senior lecturer and co-convenor of the Global Terrorism Research Unit in the School of Political and Social Inquiry, Monash University. He has worked as a senior intelligence analyst for the Australian government. His current research focuses on the relationship between globalisation and political violence, especially in Southeast Asia and the Indian sub-continent.

Foreword

Alison Tokita

It gives me great pleasure to see the publication of this volume entitled *Japan, Australia and Asia-Pacific Security*. The volume had its origins in a symposium held by the Japanese Studies Centre (JSC) at Monash University in February 2004, on the theme 'The New Security: Japanese and Australian Cooperation in Creating Asia-Pacific Regional Security', for which the keynote speaker was Mr Yasushi Akashi (former undersecretary general of the United Nations). Mr Akashi spoke on 'Hard and soft approaches to security in the Asia-Pacific region: Japan's role and contribution to regional peace'. The symposium was sponsored by the Consulate General of Japan in Melbourne.

The symposium formed part of a project on regional security and Australia-Japan cooperation in the age of global terror, an outcome of a long-running series of symposiums on Australia-Japan relations run by the JSC. The broad aim of the project was to document and analyse the present level of joint activity, and to identify potential areas of cooperation between Japan and Australia in regional security.

Despite strong residual anti-Japanese sentiments following on the negative experiences of the Pacific War, since the 1970s Australia has developed and maintained a very high level of interest in Japan. This is reflected not only in the growth of trade, tourism, investment and grassroots exchange of people, but also in the growth of Japanese language teaching and Japanese studies in Australian educational institutions. The 'Australia-Japan Conference for the 21st Century', held in Sydney in April 2001, reaffirmed the strength of the relationship, and a number of initiatives for creative partnership emerged from this conference, including in the domain of higher education, economic partnership and security. Furthermore, the November 2002 Australia-Japan Conference for a Creative Partnership in Tokyo emphasised the need for Australia and Japan to explore possible bilateral cooperative security activities, including to promote broader regional cooperation on transnational issues, while noting the progress already made, including the draft 'Action Plan' proposed during former director general of the Japan Defence Agency Nakatani Gen's visit to Australia in August 2002.

However, it must be acknowledged that Australia's sights seem to have shifted away from Japan in recent years, especially since 11 September 2001, to have a stronger focus on the United States. At the same time, the emerging stature of China as a superpower is also serving to take Japan off the national horizon.

One of the most urgent issues facing both Australia and Japan is the security of the Asia-Pacific region: East Timor, Indonesia, North Korea, the Solomon Islands, Papua New Guinea, and the pervasive threat of terrorism. At the same time, the difficulty of border controls in the face of movements of refugees and others also threatens to destabilise nation states in the region. Drugs and international crime are an ongoing concern requiring international cooperation. The concept of 'New Security' recognizes that military strategy alone cannot meet the security needs of the region. To be effective, states must consider human security – religion, mass poverty, border questions – and enlist corporate social responsibility.

Japan and Australia have been participating in joint military training exercises for several years. As the two most highly developed democracies in the region, with significant common interests and similar relationships towards Asia, it can be anticipated that there is considerable potential for dialogue about greater cooperation in contributing towards regional security. This cooperation could include peacekeeping operations, ODA, and anti-terrorism strategies.

Both Japan and Australia have been involved – to a large degree because the primary security agreement of each has been with the United States since 1952 – in conflict resolution in Cambodia, Afghanistan, East Timor and Iraq. Yet there is little understanding on the part of the general public in Australia of Japan's contribution in such situations.

In his address, Mr Yasushi Akashi emphasised the close links between Australia and Japan, including security collaborations. He argued that the more effective long-term way to combat terrorism was the 'soft' approach of economic and social means, to eradicate poverty, hunger and injustice, and to guarantee democracy and human rights. In the context of the still at-times ambiguous relationship between Australia and Japan, and the more problematic relationship between Japan and Asia, we would do well to remember, he insisted, that post-war Japan adopted the so-called peace constitution, whose Article 9 committed Japan to a non-military global strategy, and was responsible for the focus on economic development. At the same time, Japan makes a significant contribution to world peace through the 'soft' means of financial contribution to the UN, and through its ODA.

Mr Akashi also talked, however, about being 'confronted with a series of new questions'. Since 1992, Japan has sent Self Defense Forces to a number of UN peacekeeping missions, which is perceived by many Asian countries as being the thin end of the wedge of a remilitarised Japan. Mr Akashi is not a pacifist in the narrow sense of the term; he would 'like to see a more politically forthcoming attitude from the Japanese government', but at the same time he insisted that the 'Japanese people are so much afraid of Japan becoming a military power', thus neatly expressing the ambivalence, indeed the dilemma, of Japan's situation concerning military power.

Whereas Japan's Asian neighbours, especially Korea and China, are highly suspicious and distrustful of Japan, despite loving Japan's popular culture, and oppose Japan being given a permanent seat on the UN Security Council, Australia has moved from deep antipathy immediately after the Pacific War, to a position of not only having a vibrant economic relation, and active cultural and citizen exchanges with Japan, but also to the point of collaboration in security endeavours and military exercises. This is a remarkable change over sixty years, and a relationship which will have much to celebrate and build on in 2006, which has been designated as the Year of Australia-Japan exchanges.

The relation between Australia and Japan exists in the shadow of the relation of each to the United States, with whom each has a vital security treaty. As Mr Akashi commented in his address: 'both Japan and Australia are trying to come closer to Asian countries, but . . . in times of crisis our passion for the United States is stronger'. This could be seen as a mutual dependency on the United States, and thus a hindrance to a fully autonomous engagement on the north-south axis. Nevertheless, the many opportunities to engage, not only in joint military exercises and security operations, but also in working shoulder-to-shoulder in areas of conflict such as, most recently, in Iraq, point to the likelihood of increasing common interests in regional security and increasing collaboration between the two countries.

I would like to express my deep appreciation to the Consulate General of Japan in Melbourne, especially the Consul General Mr Masaaki Miyashita, and Consul Katsunori Ashida, for making it possible to invite Mr Akashi, and to bring in a number of speakers from interstate to explore these issues in the symposium. The project brings together a number of leading scholars in the field, with Mr Akashi, who does not only debate issues, but has lived the issues in his work as peace negotiator and representative of the United Nations, in a number of conflict situations. I would also like to thank Brad Williams for his work as project researcher, and to him and Andrew Newman for undertaking to edit this volume of papers.

Alison Tokita
Former Director of the Japanese Studies Centre and Associate Professor of Japanese Studies, Monash University, Melbourne, July 2005

Abbreviations

ABM	Anti-Ballistic Missile Treaty
ADF	Australian Defence Force
ANZUS	Australia, New Zealand, United States
APEC	Asia-Pacific Economic Cooperation
ARF	ASEAN Regional Forum
ASDF	Air Self Defense Force, Japan
ASEAN	Association of Southeast Asian Nations
ASEM	Asia-Europe Meeting
ASIS	Australian Secret Intelligence Service
ASPAC	Asian-Pacific Council
ATBM	Anti-Tactical Ballistic Missile
AUSMIN	Australia-US Ministerial Meeting
BMD	Ballistic Missile Defence
CSBM	Confidence and Security Building Measures
CSCAP	Council for Security Cooperation in the Asia Pacific
DEA	Department of External Affairs, Australia
DIO	Defence Intelligence Organisation, Australia
DSD	Defence Signals Directorate, Australia
DSP	Defense Support Program
EASR	East Asia Strategy Report
ECAFE	Economic Commission for Asia and the Far East
ELINT	Electronic Intelligence
FPDA	Five Power Defence Arrangements
GSDF	Ground Self Defence Force, Japan
IAEA	International Atomic Energy Agency
IMINT	Imaging Intelligence
INTERFET	International Force East Timor
IPMT	International Peace Monitoring Team
JANZUS	Japan plus ANZUS
JDA	Japan Defense Agency
JIO	Australian Joint Intelligence Organisation
LDP	Liberal Democratic Party
LRMP	Long-Range Maritime Patrol Aircraft

MSDF	Maritime Self Defense Force, Japan
MOFA	Ministry of Foreign Affairs, Japan
MRBM	Medium-Range Ballistic Missile
MTCR	Missile Technology Control Regime
NASDA	National Space Development Agency, Japan
NIDS	National Institute for Defense Studies, Japan
NSC	New Security Concept, China
ODA	Official Development Assistance
ONA	Office of National Assessments, Australia
OPK	Ocean-Peacekeeping Operations
OSIS	Ocean Surveillance Information System, US Navy
PKF	Peacekeeping Forces
PKO	Peacekeeping Operations
PLA	People's Liberation Army, China
PMG	Peace Monitoring Group
PRC	Peoples' Republic of China
PSI	Proliferation Security Initiative
RAAF	Royal Australian Air Force
RAN	Royal Australian Navy
RGS	Relay Ground Station
RIMPAC	'Rim of the Pacific' (military exercises)
RMA	Revolution of Military Affairs
RMSI	Regional Maritime Security Initiative
SBIRS	Space-Based Infra-Red System (satellites)
SEWS	Shared Early Warning System
SDF	Self Defense Forces, Japan
SEATO	Southeast Asia Treaty Organisation
SIGINT	Signals Intelligence
SLOCs	Sea Lines Of Communication
STAR	Second Secure Trade in the APEC Region
UN	United Nations
UNCI	UN Commission for Indonesia
UNCOK	UN Commission on Korea
UNMISET	United Nations Mission of Support in East Timor
UNTAET	United Nations Transitional Administration in East Timor
UNTAC	United Nations Transitional Authority in Cambodia
UNTEA	UN Temporary Executive Authority in West Irian
USFJ	US Forces in Japan
WMD	Weapons of Mass Destruction
WNG	West New Guinea
WPNS	Western Pacific Naval Symposium

Introduction

The US and UN in Australia-Japan defence and security cooperation

Brad Williams and Andrew Newman

While overshadowed by the flourishing bilateral trade and investment link-ages that have developed during the post-war period, defence and security[1] have been important factors shaping Australia-Japan relations since the late nineteenth century. A salient feature of the Australia-Japan defence and security nexus has been the involvement of the great powers of the day: the British and the United States. The former were influential throughout much of the pre-World War II period before the collapse of empire, while the latter has had a particularly profound impact during the Cold War period and beyond.

Shocked at the extent to which Japan had fallen behind the Western powers scientifically, technologically and economically during the isola-tionist Tokugawa period, the founders of the new Meiji state embarked upon a program of rapid modernisation designed to close this gap and avoid the threat of colonisation. Under the banner of 'rich nation, strong army' (*fukoku kyōhei*), Japan soon rose to a position of prominence in East Asia, as evidenced by its victories in the Sino-Japanese War (1894–5) and the Russo-Japanese War (1904–5) – the latter representing the first defeat of a Western great power by an Asian nation.

Seeking to counter the threat of Russian expansionism and safeguard its interests in the Far East, the British sought cooperative relations with Japan, which was similarly wary of the Russian threat and wanted to protect its gains in Korea. This congruence of interests led to the signing of the Anglo-Japanese Alliance in 1902 – an agreement that remained in effect until 1923. This alliance facilitated an event that is perhaps unknown to most students of the military and diplomatic history of Australia and Japan. In response to a request from the British government during the First World War, a Japanese naval vessel, the *Ibuki*, provided escort for Australian and New Zealand forces bound for Egypt.[2] Moreover, as a non-fighting ally of the British, Japan played a similar role to Australia in the Pacific by seizing control of German territories, although there is no evidence to suggest a coordinated approach to this task.

However, it should be noted that direct Australia-Japan defence coopera-tion was tenuous at best during this period and that Australians were wary of a Japanese threat. This was not so much a concern about Japan's military capabilities as a fear of cultural invasion by Asian immigrants into Anglo-Saxon society. Australian fears were accentuated by the country's geographic distance from Europe and subsequent feelings of cultural isolation. A desire to counter the so-called 'yellow peril' was manifested in the 1901 Immigration Act and the White Australia policy – the latter only repudiated in 1973. This policy was a source of much angst to the Japanese, who saw themselves as racially superior to the other Asian peoples.

As an interesting side story, security concerns regarding Japan were the trigger for the establishment of a Japanese language program in Australia in 1917. The program, which was based at Sydney University under the stewardship of James Murdoch, was primarily intended to provide a select core of military personnel with a language capability sufficient for translating documents and deciphering Japanese communications. Today, the study of the Japanese language – the most popular foreign language taught in Australian schools – is used for the more benign purposes of facilitating economic and cultural ties and promoting mutual understanding.

From the 1930s to the end of the Second World War, the nature of the Japanese threat to Australia was transformed from immigration influx to possible military invasion. The bombing of Darwin, midget submarine attacks on Sydney Harbour, as well as the protracted and bloody campaign to halt Japan's southward advance in the jungles of New Guinea and the Coral Sea, served as reminders to Australians at the time of the gravity of the danger posed by Japan. Revelations at war's end surrounding the deaths of large numbers of Australian POWs resulting from cruel and inhumane treatment at the hands of their Japanese captors engendered a deep-seated hostility among Australians that would shape public attitudes toward Japan for many years.

At the end of the war, Australia's major foreign policy objective was to guard against possible future aggression, notably from Japan.[3] During the US-led occupation of Japan, the Australian government, backed by hostile public opinion, sought to impose a 'hard' peace on the vanquished. For Australians, Japan had launched a brutal war of aggression that brought untold suffering to the people of many countries in the region and, as a result, would be made to pay. This hardline attitude was congruent with the early US occupation objectives of democratising, demilitarising and disempowering Japan to ensure that it would no longer be capable of threatening regional peace and security again.

This policy proved to be short-lived. The emerging ideological rivalry for global dominance between the two superpowers, the United States and the Soviet Union, forced the former to reassess fundamentally its objectives *vis-à-vis* Japan; Japan would now be transformed into an economically robust bastion of democracy designed to help restrict the spread of communism in East Asia. Allowing Japan to fulfil this role would require the Allies to seek a more benevolent, or a 'soft' peace. The Australian and New Zealand governments, in particular, were fearful of both the communist threat and possible future Japanese belligerence, and subsequently sought security guarantees from the US as a precondition for agreeing to peace treaty terms with Japan. On 15 September 1951, representatives from forty-eight countries signed the San Francisco Peace Treaty, which went into effect in April the following year. The US concomitantly concluded a security treaty with Japan and entered into a trilateral pact with Australia and New Zealand. ANZUS was the price the US paid for Canberra and Wellington's acceptance of the terms outlined in San Francisco.[4] Japan and Australia were now incorporated into the US containment strategy in Asia.

Lingering war memories and animosity diminished the likelihood of Australia entering into any mutual defence arrangement with Japan following the latter's restoration of sovereignty in 1952. Instead, both countries were indirectly allied through their respective security treaty arrangements with the US. In a theme taken up by some of the contributors to this volume, this marked the beginning of Japan and Australia's role as the 'northern and southern anchors' of the US alliance system in East Asia.[5] This is not to say there was a total absence of Australia-Japan defence and security cooperation during this time and that this was entirely derivative of both countries' politico-military ties with the US.[6] David Walton's chapter highlights an emerging pragmatism within sections of the Australian government that resulted in an emphasis on developing networks of key government officials from both countries who were particularly concerned about regional security issues such as the *Konfrontasi* between Malaysia and Indonesia from 1962 to 1965. Australian officials had become increasingly cognizant of the importance to national interests of Japanese information on issues not only related to Indonesia but also mainland China and Vietnam.

Despite its wariness regarding a possible resurgence of Japanese military power in the 1950s and 1960s, the Australian government came to the realisation that it would be necessary for Japan to undertake a limited rearmament program in order to defend against communist aggression. Australia's position was that this gradual expansion of Japanese defence capabilities should take place within the framework of the US alliance. Canberra also sought to establish closer political ties with Japan, whose economy was experiencing rapid development and was thirsting for raw materials to fuel this growth. While Japan was no longer seen as an isolated threat, there were fears it could become one if allied with countries such as the People's Republic of China[7] – an important market for Japanese businessmen and economic planners. This created incentives for Australia to integrate Japan into regional political and security structures, which is exemplified by Canberra's important role in persuading Tokyo to join the Asian-Pacific Council (ASPAC). Despite the failure of the council, Chris Braddick observes in his chapter that the ASPAC project was the first step toward the development of an 'Asia-Pacific regional consciousness: an identity shared by Australia and Japan'.

Some might be surprised by the degree of Australia-Japan defence and security cooperation that has developed since the 1970s. Des Ball's chapter outlines a vast range of bilateral activities, which include intelligence exchanges, reciprocal visits by senior officials, security dialogue, joint military exercises and Australian support for Japan's space program. Ball also highlights the 'coincidental and mutually reinforcing rather than coordinated' attempts by both countries to institutionalise multilateral security cooperative mechanisms such as the ASEAN Regional Forum (ARF) and Council for Security Cooperation in the Asia-Pacific. Importantly, during a July 2001 session of the ARF in Hanoi, Australian and Japanese officials began to discuss privately the notion of developing a new trilateral security dialogue with the US.[8] As Purnendra Jain and John Bruni's chapter highlights, the parties concerned were eager to emphasise the informal nature of this dialogue.

The re-emergence of conservative rule in Australia and Japan in the mid-1990s saw a further strengthening of both countries' politico-military alliances with the US, as well as bilateral defence and security cooperation. Upon taking office in 1996, Prime Minister Howard vowed to place renewed emphasis on relations with the US, which he asserted had become stagnant as a result of Labor's push towards establishing multilateral security arrangements in Asia. On a symbolic level, this policy reorientation was first evident when Australia was the lone regional voice that spoke out in support of the US deployment of two aircraft carrier battlegroups to the Taiwan Straits during Taiwan's first-ever democratic elections.

The 1996 Joint Declaration on Security signed by President Clinton and Prime Minister Hashimoto and the 1997 US-Japan Defense Guidelines paved the way for greater defence cooperation between the two countries. The Joint Declaration and Defense Guidelines stated that Tokyo would offer logistical support for US forces operating in 'areas surrounding Japan'. Both documents not only clarified the nature of Japanese assistance to the US military, but also deemed 'the definition of these areas would be determined by "situational" rather than "geographic" imperatives, suggesting the potential inclusion of Taiwan and the South China Sea in the alliance's scope'.[9] In a move ostensibly designed to counter the North Korean missile threat but most likely directed at a rising China, both countries also agreed to cooperate in an ongoing study of theatre missile defence (TMD). The Japanese government announced its decision to join the TMD research program in September 1998, one month after Pyongyang's launch of a *Taepodong* ballistic missile that had passed directly over northern Japan.[10]

This period also witnessed an expansion in the scope of Australia-Japan security relations. Both countries concluded a Joint Declaration on the Australia-Japan Partnership and the Australia-Japan Partnership Agenda, in May 1995 and August 1997 respectively.[11] A notable feature of the Joint Declaration and Partnership Agenda is their reference to the United Nations (UN). From a Japanese perspective, both documents contain written declarations of Australian support for one of Tokyo's longstanding foreign policy objectives: securing a permanent seat on an expanded UN Security Council. They also call for increased cooperation in various UN international peace building and peacekeeping operations (PKO), discussed in greater detail in Katsumi Ishizuka's chapter. PKO represent an important foreign policy tool for Tokyo, allowing it to dispatch military personnel abroad to meet its obligations as a regional power contributing to international peace and security, without overly alarming and causing its Asian neighbours to fear that Japan is again treading down the path towards militarism. By cooperating in this regard, Australia is, in a sense, helping Japan in its bid to become a 'normal' country.

While some in Japan may see expanding multilateral diplomacy as providing 'a balance against the country's US-focused bilateralism [and even] a hedge against abandonment by the American security guarantor',[12] there are no doubts that Washington continues to be the primary reference point for Japanese foreign and security policies. Prime Minister Koizumi openly declared where his nation's loyalties would lie when, in January 2004, he emphasised the overwhelming importance for Japan to show that it was a 'trustworthy ally', because if ever Japan were to come under attack it would be the US, not the UN or any other country, that would come to its aid.[13] Similarly, Australia's close allegiance to the US was demonstrated in a statement Prime Minister Howard made on 14 September 2001, in which he invoked the ANZUS Treaty, which calls for mutual assistance in the event of an armed attack on one of the parties.[14]

Both prime ministers' comments have, of course, been made against the backdrop of the US-led 'war on terror' following on from the September 11 terrorist attacks on New York and Washington DC. The threat posed by international terrorism has given new impetus to expanded defence and security cooperation between Australia, Japan and the US. Specifically, Australia and Japan have made military contributions to Operation *Enduring Freedom*, designed to overthrow Afghanistan's Taliban regime and deny Al Qaeda a main base of operations for its terrorist activities,[15] and the US campaign in Iraq. Such action by Canberra and Tokyo may be considered 'mutually reinforcing rather than coordinated', a theme Des Ball and Purnendra Jain and John Bruni explore in greater detail in their chapters.

On 19 October 2001, the Japanese Diet approved anti-terror legislation authorising Japan's Self Defense Forces to provide military support to the 'war on terror'. While backtracking on some of its earlier promises of military assistance, the Japanese government decided to deploy a non-*Aegis* destroyer to collect intelligence, minesweepers and supply ships to the Indian Ocean, committed C-130 transport aircraft to fly US military equipment and personnel to locations in the Asia-Pacific region and, in a one-time operation, transported Thai troops to a country near the Afghan border as part of its contribution to *Enduring Freedom*.[16] The Australian government deployed 1,500 defence force personnel, including elite SAS troops, to

Afghanistan. Australia and Japan were the only countries in East Asia to make a military contribution to the Afghan campaign.

The notion of indirect collaboration between Australia and Japan in support of US anti-terror objectives has again been evident during the war in Iraq and the first eighteen months of the subsequent reconstruction and security phase of the US-led occupation. After an initial period of ambiguity before the war, resulting largely from insufficient public support and opposition from Arab oil suppliers, the Japanese government moved to support the US when it launched its invasion. Japanese assistance to Operation *Iraqi Freedom* consisted of medical and financial support, as well as 1,000 non-combat military personnel to assist in humanitarian relief and reconstruction in southern Iraq. This represented the first time Japanese military units have been deployed abroad outside the UN framework.

Facing similar domestic political divisions, the Howard government ordered 2,000 defence force personnel to the Persian Gulf upon receiving a call from President Bush informing it of the commencement of hostilities. Unlike Japan, Australian forces participated in combat operations with HMAS *Anzac* providing fire support to British commandos and SAS troops neutralising the Iraqi missile threat in the western part of the country. HMAS *Darwin* conducted hundreds of searches of vessels in the Persian Gulf suspected of transporting illicit cargo, and HMAS *Kanimbla* provided a command and control platform for Coalition naval forces.

Both countries' active participation in the US-led 'war on terror' has not only served to highlight the previously unforeseen areas of defence cooperation, but is also indicative of the extent to which Australian attitudes toward Japan have moved beyond wartime animosity and enmity. For instance, Brad Williams and Andrew Newman shed light on Australia-Japan cooperation aimed at preventing the spread of weapons of mass destruction, their delivery systems and related materials. They note the various Australian government efforts to realise Japanese participation in military interdiction exercises staged in the Coral Sea in September 2003 under the banner of the Proliferation Security Initiative. That Japanese security forces were operating along Australia's coast without any discernible public backlash in Australia was a symbolically important aspect of the exercises.

Perhaps the most significant indicator of the positive transformation of Australian attitudes toward Japan was Canberra's decision in February 2005 to respond to a request by Prime Minister Koizumi and deploy 450 troops to protect Japanese military engineers involved in reconstruction projects in southern Iraq. Regarding his decision to respond to Tokyo's request, Prime Minister Howard cited the importance of the Japanese presence in Iraq in terms of the fight against terrorism and emphasised that 'Working alongside and in partnership with a close regional ally and partner such as Japan is very important from Australia's point of view.'[17]

There is general agreement amongst the contributors that Australia-Japan defence and security cooperation is strengthening, even if the scope is limited.

As Ball highlights, cooperation is likely to derive from a 'coincidence of interests and partnership in multilateral activities' rather than genuinely bilateral dynamics. This may take various forms, including further joint peace-keeping operations, as suggested by Katsumi Ishizuka, greater participation in regional security arrangements, deeper intelligence-sharing or, as David Wright-Neville notes, efforts to combat terrorism within East Asia. However, Jain and Bruni caution that any move to formalise defence links 'would have grave regional implications'. For this reason, cooperation is likely to remain largely informal – a 'shadow alliance' or 'smokescreen' with, in William Tow and Russell Trood's words, US regional strategy acting as the 'independent variable'.

Notes

1 According to Robyn Lim, defence is concerned with the threat of invasion. Security, on the other hand, 'means the ability of a state to conduct its affairs free from threats, intimidation or other pressures that might unacceptably constrain its policy choices'. R. Lim, 'Australia's stake in Asia Pacific regional security', in P. King and Y. Kibata (eds) *Peace Building in the Asia Pacific Region*, St Leonards NSW: Allen & Unwin, 1996, p. 76.

2 N. Sajima, 'Japanese security perceptions of Australia', chapter in this volume.

3 A. Rix, *The Australia-Japan Political Alignment: 1952 to the Present*, London: Routledge, 1999, p. 147.

4 Ibid., p. 148.

5 See also Rawdon Dalrymple, 'Japan and Australia as anchors: do the chains still bind?' in King and Kibata, *op. cit.*, pp. 38–9.

6 Des Ball notes in his chapter in this volume the difficulty of distinguishing between purely bilateral Australia-Japan activities and the activities that result from both countries' respective relations with the US.

7 Rix, *op. cit.*, pp. 156–7.

8 P. Jain, 'Turning to a new chapter on defence', *Advertiser*, 1 August 2001, cited in Jain and Bruni's chapter in this volume.

9 T. J. Christensen, 'China, the U.S.-Japan alliance and the security dilemma in East Asia', in G. J. Ikenberry and M. Mastanduno (eds) *International Relations Theory and the Asia-Pacific*, New York: Columbia University Press, 2003, p. 34. Ralph Cossa notes that this phrase denoted contingencies on the Korean Peninsula. R. A. Cossa, 'Japan-South Korea summit may calm Asian fears', *Honolulu Star-Bulletin*, 21 June 1996, http://starbulletin.com/96/06/21/editorial/ viewpoint.html (accessed 27 April 2005).

10 *Asahi Shimbun* (evening edn) 21 September 1998, p. 1.

11 A copy of the texts can be found at http://www.mofa.go.jp/region/asia-paci/ australia/join _ au.html and http://www.dfat.gov.au/geo/japan/partnership_ agenda. html, respectively. It should be noted that the Joint Declaration was signed by Japanese Prime Minister Murayama Tomiichi and his Australian counterpart Paul Keating.

12 R. Drifte, *Japan's Quest for a Permanent Security Council Seat: A Matter of Pride or Justice?*, Basingstoke: Macmillan/St Antony's Press, 2000, p. 3.

13 *Asahi Shimbun*, 28 January 2004, http://dna.asahi.com (accessed 4 February 2005).

14 R. Garran, 'PM invokes defence pact to back US action', *The Australian*, 15 September 2001, http://elibrary.bigchalk.com (accessed 4 May 2005).

15 Only the Australian forces participated in combat operations in Afghanistan.

16 B. Williams, 'Japan, North Korea and the "war on terror"', in M. Vicziany, D.

Wright-Neville and P. Lentini (eds) *Regional Security in the Asia Pacific: 9/11 and After*, Cheltenham: Edward Elgar, 2004, pp. 230 and 244 n1.

17 L. Dodson and T. Allard, 'Nation split as PM sends more troops', *Sydney Morning Herald*, 23 February 2005, http://elibrary.bigchalk.com (accessed 9 May 2005). During talks with Prime Minister Koizumi in Tokyo in March 2005, Australian foreign minister Alexander Downer stated that '55 per cent of Australians oppose the move' to deploy more troops to Iraq to protect Japanese forces. 'Australia tells Japan political risks taken in Iraq deployment', *Radio Australia*, 22 March 2005, cited in *BBC Monitoring Asia Pacific*, 22 March 2005, http://elibrary.bigchalk.com (accessed 9 May 2005). It is most likely that the position of the Australian public stems specifically from its general opposition to the deployment of more troops to Iraq rather than the specific nature of their mission.

1 Australia-Japan and the region, 1952–65

The beginnings of security policy networks

David Walton

Introduction

Japan has loomed large in post-war Australian foreign and economic policies. At the regional level the relationship with Japan has become since the 1960s Australia's longest, arguably most important and trouble-free bilateral relationship. The rapid improvement in bilateral relations by 1965, especially given the level of general hostility and suspicion towards Japan in Australia that had existed immediately after the Pacific War, represented a remarkable shift in policy thinking in Canberra. Yet surprisingly little has been written about the political dimension of the relationship and the level of dialogue between Australia and Japan from 1952 to 1965 on regional matters. Developments in Indonesia and Indonesian foreign policies, in particular, were (and still remain) of immense strategic importance to both countries. These ad hoc meetings represented the beginnings of a new post-war relationship that has involved close cooperation and regular consultations on regional matters.

The aim of this chapter is to chart the views within the Department of External Affairs towards Japan in the period 1952 to 1965, and in particular the development of networks on regional security issues. The role of John McEwen (deputy prime minister 1958–71 and minister for trade 1949–71) and the Department of Trade as key actors in policy-making on matters concerning Japan is well documented.[1] Indeed the political dominance of McEwen (and his legendary ferocity when protecting his interests) led to the perception that External Affairs took a passive role in the post-war engagement with Japan. The fact, however, was that External Affairs officials were actively seeking to broaden relations with Japan in the political and security fields and, thereby, contributing to the gradual improvement in overall bilateral relations.

Shifts in Australian policy towards Japan

Japan's post-war foreign policy had significant implications for Australia. Tokyo's close alignment with the US and concentration on economic diplomacy and development in Southeast Asia affected the quality of bilateral relations. Indeed Japan's regional diplomacy touched on key aspects of the emerging post-war Australian regional diplomacy. The shift in attitude towards Japan within External Affairs, however, was initially slow and measured due to the tenuous early post-war bilateral relationship.

1952–7: lingering hostilities and the emergence of pragmatism

Formal diplomatic relations with Japan were resumed in February 1952, and by this time extensive trade relations had resumed. A coherent policy towards Japan, however, was not clearly articulated until August 1954. Earlier demands for a hard peace with Japan and lingering war memories and animosities ensured relations were tense. In the first few years after 1952 major issues still to be resolved included the pearl fisheries dispute; compensation for former prisoners of war of the Japanese; Japanese violation of Australian territorial waters; Japanese war criminals; and Japanese war dead in Australian territorial waters.[2] The most contentious and protracted issue was the pearl fishing dispute, which generated considerable acrimony and tension. According to Alan Watt, the dispute highlighted a fear of Japanese intentions and Japanese insensitivity to Australian concerns, and portrayed a lack of understanding by Australia of the Japanese need to reconstruct their shattered economy by any and every means.[3] However, the dispute lost its intensity in later part of 1957 due to a change in demand for pearl shell. During his 1957 visit to Australia, prime minister Kishi accepted the limits set by his hosts.[4]

By 1954, a more pragmatic approach towards Japan was evident within the Liberal-Country coalition government. Indicative of this change was a letter to Arthur Tange (secretary of external affairs) from then external affairs minister Richard Casey. The letter discussed a paper being written within the department on Australian policy towards Japan. Casey wrote '[we] have to live with Japan for the future and the tone of the paper should be that we give up our negative attitude towards the Japanese and be more forthcoming and civilised in our relationships with them'.[5] A few days later in a cabinet submission the external affairs minister gave a pragmatic reason for normalising relations:

> The concern of Japan forming an alliance with the Communist Bloc due to political and economic isolation; that Australia should aim to support a moderate government and to help to keep Japan in the Western camp; and that such policies accord with the views of the United States and the United Kingdom.[6]

The softening of Australian attitudes towards Japan therefore can be viewed as an unfolding process. The change in attitude reflected careful coordination with American and British foreign offices. As well, there was genuine concern within Canberra that an isolated Japan could rearm or join a communist bloc with mainland China and turn the Pacific into a 'communist lake'. Indeed, this appears to have been Casey's principal concern. In his cabinet submission, Casey noted that anti-Japanese sentiment in Australia could lead to Japan being denied access to food supplies and raw materials necessary for economic recovery, leading to increased trading ties with China.[7]

Understandably, these policy initiatives raised considerable debate within Australia. ALP leader Arthur Calwell's article in the *Truth* (February 1954) entitled 'We can't be soft on Jap butchers' is a reflection of these sensitivities. Calwell argued that the government's soft policy on Japan had already led to a long series of surrenders and humiliating betrayals of Australia's vital interests. He listed the following examples:

- A soft peace treaty with Japan which resulted in vigorous opposition;
- Supported admission of Japan to the United Nations in spite of the awful crimes committed against Australian and other prisoners of war from 1942 to 1945;
- Released Japanese war criminals from Manus Island to 'serve' the remainder of their sentence in Tokyo;
- Refusal to oppose Japanese admission to the GATT.[8]

Calwell's view did not prevail, however, and Canberra's new policy of normalisation was carried out bilaterally and multilaterally. By 1955, the Australian government was determined to normalise its relationship with Japan for reasons of national interest. Australia supported Japan's entry into the United Nations (UN) on 18 December 1956 and sponsored Japan's entry into the UN Security Council on 1 October 1957. The changes towards Japan were, nonetheless, incremental. A careful approach was adopted by the Department of External Affairs as a reflection of the awareness of public sensitivity on this issue. The level of caution is demonstrated in a letter written from Arthur Tange to Alan Watt (Australian ambassador to Japan) in April 1956. Tange wrote:

Public opinion here on Japan generally is less vocal and excitable now than it was two years ago. The more sensational of the local papers have adopted a more moderate line in their handling of news concerning Japan. . . . Various visits of Japanese to Australia over the past twelve months – [such as] the two Japanese cabinet ministers, Kawasaki and Miki – evoked little comment in the press and passed off completely without incident.

Tange confirmed:

It would be going too far to say that anti-Japanese feeling in Australia has evaporated. We must see that we do not get too far ahead of public opinion in our official dealings with Japan.[9]

Within these constraints, External Affairs officers were actively developing the relationship. Thomas Critchley, head of East Asian and Pacific and Americas Branch of External Affairs in 1955, for example, commented that any lingering animosities towards Japan had evaporated by 1954.[10] Disagreement, though, existed between key figures on how to deal with Japanese counterparts. In 1957, Alan Watt, who advocated a firmer stance towards Japan, was critical of Casey's approach towards Japanese officials after Peru and Iran, rather than Australia, co-sponsored Japan into the UN General Assembly. In a letter to Arthur Tange, Watt wrote:

> It will be remembered that I suggested that Mr Suzuki [Japanese ambassador in Canberra] should be given a 'touch' [by Casey] when Japan chose not to seek Australian sponsorship or co-sponsorship of a resolution in the Security Council regarding her membership of the United Nations. . . . So far as I am aware however, the only comment made to Mr Suzuki in Canberra on this matter was a statement that Australia had been glad to help in any way which Japan desired. I fear that such an attitude will merely encourage Japan to ignore Australian interests or Japanese obligations to Australia whenever she finds this convenient.[11]

The extent to which this debate affected policy is difficult to quantify. Casey was, no doubt, constrained in reproaching Japan on the sponsorship question in the United Nations. Australia was at the time supporting British and French policy in the Suez crisis, which received considerable criticism by the majority of nations in the General Assembly. Nonetheless, Watt's comments appeared to have influenced the prime minister's brief on Japan for the April 1957 visit. For example, the brief included a statement on the then Japanese prime minister Nobusuke Kishi's lack of awareness of Australia. The report stated that Kishi was apparently unaware of the Australian position on West New Guinea (WNG) and that this explained Japan's support for Indonesia in the United Nations General Assembly. Accordingly, the report recommended that a

> valuable consequence of the Prime Minister's visit to Japan could be a realisation by Kishi personally that Australia exists, that our friendship is worth having, and that our reactions and interests could have some consequence for Japan.[12]

Evidence of closer relations and enhanced interaction was the signing of the Agreement on Commerce (July) and the reciprocal visits by prime ministers Menzies (April) and Kishi (December) in 1957. These were tumultuous events in the history of bilateral relations, as they normalised relations and established the pattern for economic and political relations.[13] The reciprocal prime ministerial visits were also a watershed as they were the first visits in the history of the relationship. Moreover, Kishi's visit, which had the potential to be embarrassing for the Australian government, was largely incident-free.[14]

c.1958–62: broadening the base

The exchange of views continued in 1958. In that year there was a reciprocal exchange of parliamentary delegations. Watt, in a ministerial dispatch to Casey, noted that the Japanese were making a substantial effort to support this process. prime minister Kishi, for example, made the point of attending the farewell dinner for the Australian delegation despite the budget session in the Diet, problems within his faction, and President Sukarno's recent arrival.[15] The Japanese delegation to Australia included members of the Diet and House of Councillors. In a report of the visit to the House of Councillors, Masaru Nomizo (Japanese Socialist Party) stated:

> We noticed that the friendly feelings of the Prime Minister and those who had visited Japan had been an influence and that this genial atmosphere had penetrated into every nook and cranny of the country.[16]

Moreover, within External Affairs there was a growing appreciation of the importance of Japan as a regional actor. Evidence for this was considerable debate over the exclusion of the Tokyo mission from the 1958 Heads of Mission meeting. Gordon Jockel (head of the Americas and Pacific Branch) was particularly outspoken and managed to sway the departmental heads into including the Tokyo mission at the meeting. He argued that:

> Japan represents a non-Communist influence in competition with Communist China in Southeast Asia in many fields; Japan has made Southeast Asia an area of major Japanese interest for vital political and economic reasons; and Japanese reparations are an important element in the economy of certain Southeast Asian countries.[17]

Peter Heydon (Assistant Secretary, Division 1) commented on relations with Japan in October 1959 by raising concern at a recent parliamentary speech by the then immigration minister Alexander Downer snr, which rejected in principle Japanese migration to Australia. Implicit in Heydon's comments was a concern that the policy of fostering good relations with Japan was slipping due to a sense of complacency. Using rather strident language, Heydon wrote:

> Japan is one of six or seven countries in the world where our direct, practical interests are of some importance to us. As such, a continuing effort is required for the maintenance and development of the most advantageous relationship.[18]

Casey's 1959 visit to Tokyo and the exchange of political information

Foreign Minister Richard Casey's visit to Japan in March 1959 can be viewed as a turning point in terms of enhanced bilateral dialogue. Ministerial visits and a visit by prime minister Menzies had already assisted in improving overall relations. The External Affairs brief prepared for Casey indicated a strong desire to further expand the political relationship. The report stressed the need for more visits by government leaders and more liaison and consultations between officials. In particular, the report targeted increased consultations between Australia and Japan on issues related to the United Nations. As a result the report indicated a remarkably relaxed attitude towards Japan, which was not evident a few years beforehand. Even the previously sensitive area of defence policy was considered, subject to defence requirements, as an acceptable area to stimulate useful exchanges on a continuing basis.[19]

At the Ministry of Foreign Affairs, Casey and his counterpart Aiichiro Fujiyama discussed a number of topics including GATT, Taiwan, Berlin and Antarctica, but the WNG dispute and Indonesia's stance towards the dispute were key issues. Importantly the record of conversation of the meeting suggested that both foreign ministers were keen to discuss how they viewed issues and the need to exchange political information on regional developments at a broader level than Indonesia to include communist China and Taiwan.[20]

Casey's visit and the subsequent agreement to broaden political consultations between Australian and Japanese officials allowed for a wider range of issues to be discussed and was an early phase in the development of a more balanced and mature relationship. Consultations after Casey's visit, according to available material, tend to suggest the broadening of bilateral dialogue was beginning in earnest. Two weeks after the foreign minister's visit to Tokyo, for example, Japanese ambassador designate Katsushiro Narita told James Plimsoll (External Affairs officer) that he was keen to continue the practice of close and frequent discussion of a wide range of topics on international affairs – not only matters concerning Australia and Japan.[21]

In Canberra, Casey instructed External Affairs to examine ways to broaden cooperation with Japan. The process towards regular ad hoc exchange of political information raised considerable debate within the Department of External Affairs between 1959 and 1962. Much of the focus of the debate was on how to broaden the areas of cooperation. Senior officials expressed considerable concern over the question of security and the process involved in setting up the reciprocal arrangement. Gordon Jockel, head of the Americas and Pacific Branch, although supportive of enhancing relations with Japan, had reservations about exchanging information about Southeast Asia. He wrote:

> South East Asia may be a more delicate matter. Conceivably we could create resentment in some countries if it were known that we were taking

the Japanese into our confidence. Nor have we perhaps sufficient information on the quality of Japanese representation and degree of
influence in the area to enable us to decide how far to go.[22]

The principal issues, however, were where the information was to be vetted
and the need to ensure that Japan would not receive more information than
the United States and United Kingdom.[23]

By February 1962, there was a broad agreement for the regular exchange
of information among relevant section heads. Moreover, a formula for the
exchange of political information produced by David McNichol, First
Assistant Secretary, had received wide support within the department.[24] In
the draft McNichol wrote:

> We have been receiving from the Japanese frank and useful views and
> reports on developments, which in the case of China have been particu-
> larly valuable. We feel that this sort of exchange should be developed
> further and that this should be done on the basis of our provision of
> more Australian information to the Japanese in exchange for Japanese
> material. In practice they have shown much interest in obtaining
> Australian views and additional information about China, Korea and
> Southeast Asia.[25]

The support within External Affairs for a reciprocal exchange arrangement
with Japan was indicative of the level of interest in Japan. Initially these
exchanges were part of an overall strategy to align Japan more closely with
the West. However, Australian officials were becoming increasingly aware of
the advantages of receiving information from Japanese sources. A. J.
Eastman (Section Head of East and South East Asia), for example offered
support for the exchange of information in order to gain access to Japanese
information. He wrote:

> Such Japanese material as we have seen so far on South East Asia has
> added nothing of substance to our knowledge. Having regard, however,
> to what I understand to be the quite high standard of Japanese diplo-
> matic representation generally I would be prepared to believe that they
> have quite good holding of information on the area, and that we might
> obtain greater access to these if we showed a readiness to give some-
> thing substantial in return. . . . I therefore generally agree with your
> proposal to seek to promote such exchanges between the department
> and Japan on a reciprocal basis.[26]

The departmental debates on information sharing illustrated the level of
consultation already existing with Japan in early 1962, and the value
attached to further developing bilateral relations, including the sharing of
classified material up to confidential. Contact occurred at a variety of levels,

including the cultivation of personal ties with Japanese officials in Canberra, and at various locations such as international forums.

Garfield Barwick's ministerial visit to Japan in June 1962 was indicative of the expansion of regional dialogue. The visit was part of the foreign minister's tour of the region. During his stay in Japan, Barwick covered a wide range of issues with his Japanese counterpart Zentaro Kosaka. The detailed discussions that followed signalled the intent by both governments to cover regional issues as an integral part of bilateral meetings. Issues covered included most recent developments in Laos and Vietnam, the agreement to share information on Burma, the possibility of an Asian Common Market, bilateral trade issues, the European Economic Community, and developments in Korea and mainland China.[27]

By the end of 1962 bilateral relations had developed at a rate that would have been inconceivable ten years before. Moreover, the exchange of information and overall increased levels of dialogue and cooperation occurred at a rapid speed after 1959. This change was also reflected in the reports written by External Affairs officers on the bilateral relationship. In the 1962 report on bilateral relations, for example, negative attitudes towards Japan were no longer prominent. Indeed, the reports had a positive flavour. The bilateral relationship therefore, was broadening yet it remained within the narrow confines of the political and economic domain. At this stage there were no cultural or educational exchanges, and this continued to manifest misunderstanding within both countries. Both Alan Watt and Laurence MacIntyre, as Australian ambassadors to Japan, were aware of these limitations and strongly argued for greater emphasis on cultural relations and the need for a cultural attaché to be based in Tokyo.

1963–5: expanding regional dialogue – towards a broad and more balanced relationship

The period 1963–5 represented a serious upgrading of bilateral relations and the desire by External Affairs officers to develop closer political relations. By 1963, there appeared to be consensus within the department that Japan was of critical importance to Australian interests. It led to a series of initiatives by the department as part of an overall strategy to ensure closer alignment between Australian and Japanese policies.

Undoubtedly the political factors were affected by the expansion of trade ties. The 1963 amendment to the Commerce Agreement ended trade discrimination and began a rapid expansion of two-way trade. By 1965, trade was so rapid that Japan was overtaking the United Kingdom as Australia's principal trading partner.[28] The expansion in trade became a prime motivating force for enhanced bilateral relations, and had considerable impact on the domestic economic growth of both countries. What is not well known, though, are the discussions between Australia and Japan on regional developments in Indonesia and on *Konfrontasi* between Indonesia and Malaysia

(1963–6).[29] Japan had close contacts in Jakarta and an intimate knowledge of developments in Indonesia. Australian interests in receiving Japanese information on these issues of vital strategic importance to Australia, and Japanese efforts to mediate on the dispute, were motivating forces in the process towards closer cooperation. There was considerable concern within Canberra about the direction of Japanese initiatives, and External Affairs officers maintained a close watch on developments. Dialogue on these regional issues was based on fundamental disagreements on how to deal with Indonesian President Sukarno and on Indonesian policy. External Affairs officials were actively examining ways of influencing Japanese views.

1963 was a landmark year in the bilateral relationship. The Agreement on Commerce was amended and prime minister Hayato Ikeda visited Australia. Regional cooperation and, through this, the exchange of information, continued to expand.

The trade amendment (signed on 5 August 1963) was, in many respects, part of the final process towards total reconciliation in bilateral relations.[30] By 1963, trade had become a pressing issue and was an inhibiting factor in overall bilateral relations. The amendment, therefore, was an important watershed for both countries.

Moreover in 1963, senior officers within External Affairs were looking at ways in which to use the trade amendment as a catalyst for closer political relations. In June foreign minister Garfield Barwick wrote to Howard Beale (Australian ambassador in Washington) about ways in which to improve bilateral relations. Barwick expressed interest in the possibility for contacts with Japan on a broad range of issues.[31] By August the departmental position was clearly articulated:

> We consider Australian disinvocation of article 35 of GATT to be of political as well as economic significance; it is a dramatic indication of our intention to develop the closest possible rapport with Japan. . . . Her continuing friendship with the West is a matter of vital importance to Australia. What happens to Japan may determine Australian physical and economic security.[32]

Arthur Tange in his meeting with Japanese ambassador Ohta reiterated these sentiments. During the meeting Tange expressed hope that relations could develop from small steps such as exchange of information to a wider basis of cooperation. He offered examples of frequent discussions and the possibility of joint initiatives on foreign policy matters.[33] In a follow-up to this meeting Australian officials were buoyant about possibilities of long-term bilateral relations. Patrick Shaw in a letter to Laurence McIntyre (Australian ambassador to Japan) wrote about these developments:

> We regard the substance of the Tange/Ohta conversation as particularly important. The Ambassador was called in so that the Secretary could

inform him of the resolve at the governmental level that the closest possible relations with Japan should be developed as a matter of policy.

Shaw continued:

> We have in mind calling this in about a month's time to put forward our own views and to get the views of other departments about the way in which our future relations with Japan might be developed. Our ultimate objective is a new statement at the Cabinet level, of policy towards Japan, to replace the 1954 statement of policy.[34]

By early 1964, Tange was closely examining ways for the embassy in Tokyo to be more effective in the process of enhancing relations. In a letter to McIntyre, Tange believed Australia had to take the initiative and try to bring Japanese policy-makers to take more account of the Australian view. Tange also concurred with McIntyre about the need to use experienced officers, to make the most of Japanese language talent and the importance of junior officers learning the language.[35] Tange's views reflected the immense importance of Japan in departmental planning.

The Australian decision to encourage the exchange of confidential information was also given a fillip by the discovery that the British had pursued a similar policy. Comments on a confidential Anglo-Japanese relations paper provided to the Australian High Commission in London helped direct debate within Canberra. The British report (from Sir Oscar Moreland to Lord Home, dated 21 December 1962) argued the importance of developing a close and consultative relationship with Japan, including consultative machinery. In particular, Moreland's argument was based on the need to make Japan feel genuinely accepted as part of the 'free world' and draw her into world-wide responsibilities.[36]

The response within External Affairs to the British report was to express a heightened appreciation of closer relations with Japan. A senior officer made the following comment:

> I think we [External Affairs] are generally agreed that Japanese assessments particularly of Communist China are perceptive and of value to us. We not only want to make the Japanese feel they belong, we want to gain access to more of their serious thinking.[37]

Laurence McIntyre, moreover, made the comment that the British were only waking up to Japan over the past year or two. He fully agreed with the paper and supported the laying of a foundation for the habit of a relaxed and meaningful consultation.[38]

In part the establishment of a Research and Analysis Division (*Kokusai Shiryōbu*) within the Japanese Ministry of Foreign Affairs in 1962 further developed the exchange of information. McIntyre in a letter to Tange revealed a sense of importance placed in the establishment of the division and the potential to foster close links. In his report, McIntyre noted that the head of the division (Kinya Niiseki) had passed on eight documents on Sino-Soviet relations and asked for more information to exchange in return.[39] Within ten days Assistant Secretary Max Loveday was able to reply that the department agreed to supply a monthly report on mainland China.[40] The reports, carefully vetted, were condensed monthly summaries of China. The rapid response within the department suggested little resistance to expanding the process of exchange. It also reflected interest in the Japanese foreign ministry as a source for alternative information on China. Patrick Shaw raised this point in conversation with ambassador Ohta. He mentioned the paucity of direct information on mainland China and how the department valued extending sources of information.[41] Notably this sentiment appeared to be shared by Japanese counterparts. In a discussion with McIntyre, Mr Niiseki (head of the Research and Analysis Division) commented on the usefulness of Australian material, particularly for quick reference purposes.[42]

The range of information shared with Japan expanded significantly during 1963. In July, the exchange of information was extended to include the Soviet Union. External Affairs officer R. S. Laurie in recommending expanding the exchange of information noted that the Japanese had a large embassy in Moscow, staffed by both Russian- and Chinese-speaking officers. Moreover, Laurie suggested reports from Japan on Soviet affairs would diversify views received from Great Britain and United States.[43] By November 1963, discussions between Australian External affairs officials and representatives of the Japanese foreign ministry in Tokyo included the regular exchange of papers on China; special documents on the communist bloc; Sino-Soviet relations and oral discussions on Jakarta; as well as Rangoon and Moscow political summaries.[44]

The exchange of information at this level was a significant development. Perhaps the most important aspect, though, was the symbolic gesture that a new relationship was emerging between Australia and Japan. Moreover, the personal contacts and regular ad hoc discussions meant that Japanese and Australian officials could most likely get information beyond the level of confidential.[45]

Ikeda's visit of 1963 and discussion on Konfrontasi

In this context prime minister Hayato Ikeda's visit was seen to be of considerable importance. Originally it was to be an opportunity to cover a diverse range of topics affecting bilateral relations, including commercial issues and Japanese investment in Australia. Regional developments such as the Indonesian sacking of the British embassy in Jakarta and the escalating tensions between Indonesia and Malaysia changed the emphasis of the Japanese leader's visit. Ikeda had embarked on a mediation effort with Sukarno and Philippines president Macapagal prior to his arrival in

Australia. Accordingly the Ikeda visit (29 September–3 October 1963) was to be of immense interest to Australian officials. *Konfrontasi* dominated high level discussions. Ikeda and his accompanying officials provided Australian officials with in-depth oral reports.[46] In essence Ikeda, who expressed an understanding of, and empathy towards, Sukarno, wanted the parties principal in the dispute to resolve outstanding issues through frank discussions at a summit to be held in Tokyo.

During the next two years *Konfrontasi* was a focal point for discussion of regional matters. The Australian position, support for Malaysia and efforts to ensure that Japanese mediation did not disadvantage Malaysia, was clearly and firmly articulated. A chief concern within External Affairs was to balance measured support for Japanese attempts at active foreign policy with careful efforts to influence the direction of Japanese mediation initiatives. To do so, Australian officials continued to build personal relationships and became privy to intimate details of Japanese mediation efforts. Key officials were identified and cultivated. The most senior and most effective relationship was between ambassador McIntyre and Takio Oda (vice-minister at the Ministry of Foreign Affairs April 1964–October 1965). The relationship was based on shared postings (London and Jakarta) and an apparently genuine friendship. This offered McIntyre the opportunity to observe Japanese foreign policy developments at close range. Importantly, the relationship gave the Australian quick access to the head of the Japanese Ministry of Foreign Affairs. According to McIntyre, he was able to pick up the phone and get straight through to Oda and he would usually say 'Well come and see me in ten minutes time.'[47] Oda, moreover, had during his tenure as ambassador to Indonesia developed a close friendship with Sukarno and saw the Indonesian president when he visited Tokyo.[48] This connection also allowed McIntyre to gain insight into then current developments in Indonesia and Japan's policy towards that country.

In addition, there were several Japanese officials in influential positions who supported the Australian position on *Konfrontasi* and were also opposed to the aggressive and disruptive policies of the Sukarno regime. Prominent among these were Shinsaku Hogen (chief of the Bureau of European, Afro-Middle Eastern and Oceanic Affairs), Katsuo Okazaki (permanent Japanese representative at the United Nations) and Torao Ushiroku (director, Bureau of Asian Affairs). Hogen was particularly active and vocal in his views. He was seen as part of the Cold War camp that gave its support for the US alliance and Western connection. He was a keen supporter of enhanced bilateral ties with Australia and a part of a bloc within the ministry (which included his deputy Ki Nemoto and the Japanese ambassador to Australia Saburo Ota) seeking to develop a regular ministerial committee system with Australia in 1964–5.[49] According to a Canadian report, Hogen was identified as the most influential bureau chief whose influence extended into Asian matters. This was primarily due to the force of his personality and ability to sway fellow bureau chiefs at meetings.[50]

Okazaki, who was influential in post-war Japanese foreign policy, had worked closely with Ronald Walker (former Australian ambassador to Japan) and during this period with James Plimsoll at the United Nations. In confidential discussions reported by Plimsoll, Okazaki made it clear that he did not trust Sukarno – that he should be stopped, and expressed concern about the growing military strength of Indonesia.[51] Ushiroku was by 1964 clearly exasperated by Indonesian policy. His irritation with Indonesia and sympathy towards Malaysia were, according to McIntyre, very apparent. In discussion he had recommended that it was necessary to quickly mop up and evict all Indonesian infiltrators to strengthen Malaysia's position. He also supported Australia's policy of not seeking UN involvement that would buy time for Indonesia.[52]

By the middle of 1965, Australian officials were receiving detailed reports and general information on developments in Indonesia on a regular basis. Information was exchanged at various forums and during regular ad hoc bilateral discussions in Canberra, Tokyo and Jakarta, in which *Konfrontasi* often led the discussion agenda. As relations continued to develop and the exchange of information became more intimate, the information provided to Australia on domestic developments in Indonesia was more detailed. Japan was, by this stage, a crucial source of information. Japanese officials such as ambassador Shizuo Saito were viewed as a possible moderating influence and encouraged to work on these lines. By October, the aborted coup and rapid response by the military in Jakarta led to considerable confusion about who was in control of the country. Japanese information was particularly valuable. Australian efforts to engage with Japan had reaped some benefit, as detailed Japanese information was only shared with the US and Australia.[53]

The type of issues discussed between Australian and Japanese officials varied from regional and global developments to policy strategies on international organisations such as the UN Economic Commission for Asia and the Far East (ECAFE) and the Colombo Plan. As part of this process Australian policy, even if tentative, was provided through the Australian embassy in Tokyo. The importance of sharing information with Japan was illustrated by the speedy response within the Department of External Affairs when information was requested and by the types of strategies being developed to enhance collaboration. In a 'Review of the Year 1963–64', McIntyre had lamented the inability of the department to provide policy papers in sufficient time as to be useful. This brought a quick response from Tange, who wrote to McIntyre to re-assure him that the process would be expedited.[54] Moreover, D. J. Horne, in commenting on McIntyre's Post Review for 1963–4, discussed the need for closer departmental contacts especially before meetings of the UN General Assembly and Colombo Plan Consultative Committee. He noted that the two countries had, by 1963, regularly compared notes on agenda items for the General Assembly and put forward several interesting suggestions on how to encourage this process. In particular, Horne recommended that Australian delegates call at Tokyo en route to such meetings to enable discussion with the Japanese prior to UN meetings. The possibility of the two countries cooperating on certain small aid ventures in India and Cambodia was also raised.[55]

Horne's recommendations, although not acted upon immediately, were indicative of a trend within External Affairs to search for new means to broaden the base of bilateral relations. Senior officials within the Department of External Affairs were becoming considerably more relaxed and confident about Japan. There were a number of reasons for that. Perhaps the most important factors, from an External Affairs perspective, were that Japan was a firm ally of the US, had developed strong bilateral ties through trade and regional political dialogue with Australia, and was seen as a stabilising force in Indonesia. Key officers, such as McIntyre (now a deputy secretary in External Affairs), Max Loveday and Keith Shann (ambassador to Indonesia) were by the mid-1960s aware of and actively promoting the advantages of closer bilateral relations with Japan. In this context the Australian position was to encourage Japan to play a more active role in foreign policy.

Towards a new level of cooperation and the emergence of embryonic policy networks

The quality of cooperation and extent of exchange of information increased as bilateral interests overlapped. Early dialogue and exchanges of information had been limited in terms of the type of material being offered and the motivating forces behind such exchanges. Early Australian motives, as articulated in the minister's 1959 brief for Japan, were based primarily on ensuring that Japan remained within the Western alliance system. This in itself was not surprising, as it was a continuation of the 1954 cabinet policy on Japan. However, the approach changed by the early 1960s (as the growth in trade with Japan and ongoing developments in Indonesia altered Australian priorities) and this led to a fundamental shift in planning by 1963. Japan was undergoing extraordinary economic growth and was, along with Australia, a key ally of the US in the region. From an Australian perspective, these facts led to a strong interest in engaging in a wider range of dialogue. The rapport between officers, which had developed over the years due to regular contact, continued despite personnel changes. This was significant as it suggested that the bilateral relationship was relatively steady and not subject to sudden fluctuations. Clearly, the trade imperatives tended to dominate the agenda. The political focus of the bilateral relationship was emerging as an important area, though, and this resulted in a more balanced relationship.

The extent to which dialogue between Australia and Japan went beyond the US-led foreign policy imperatives is difficult to gauge. Clearly, both Australia and Japan had a close and unequal relationship with the US. Trade and shared concern over Indonesian foreign policy and its regional impact, however, offered both the disposition and the opportunity for dialogue to go beyond the limits of US interests. These issues were of national priority for both countries, and it led to active discussion and closer cooperation. However, the new relationship with Japan was not, in any sense, comparable to that of relations with the United Kingdom or the US. Indeed, Australian officials reacted sharply to an Ikeda press statement that suggested Japan was building such a relationship with Australia. Max Loveday (assistant secretary) in a file note to Patrick Shaw commented that relations with Japan were improving and would continue to develop, but were of a contractual nature between equals.[56] Despite this, it was clear that a new relationship had emerged with Japan. It was based on trade and political factors that had by 1965 diluted US imperatives with active Australian self-interest.

Accordingly, the regular ad hoc meetings and exchanges of information combined with a burgeoning trade relationship provided the scope for policy networks to emerge, initially at least, at the government level. This was not surprising as Australian and Japanese officials were essentially pro-US, anti-communist and committed to a stable Indonesia and Southeast Asia. Key individuals in both countries saw the importance of developing the bilateral relationship and ensuring that there was a closer alignment on mainstream policies. As such there already existed a framework for shared values. The sorts of bonds being developed included interaction between officers as they responded to each other both professionally and socially. Such interaction over time affected the world-view of policy-makers as well as their identities to each other and assisted in shaping policy networks.

In essence policy networks are the links between professionals and are designed to explain the role of information in policy formulation.[57] Embryonic policy networks, which were developing in the commercial ties as well as political/security matters, played an important role in the development of post-war bilateral relations.[58]

Examples of embryonic policy networks included the regular exchange of information and joint discussion of the agenda for UN General Assembly at the Australian embassy in Tokyo. In addition, from 1962, there was a regular exchange of intelligence information with the Ministry of Foreign Affairs' *Kokusai Shiryōbu*. The regular ad hoc meetings in Canberra and Tokyo, as well as a range of international forums, ensured senior officers within both ministries were involved in the consultation process. Importantly, regular meetings also offered a range of Australian officers the opportunity to gain some level of familiarity with their Japanese counterparts. Although difficult to quantify, the evidence would suggest that emerging networks were essential in helping establish the procedures and institutional structures on which the Australia-Japan relationship grew. If nothing else the networks ensured an easier atmosphere in which policy discussion could take place – an atmosphere that had not existed before in Australia's relations with Japan.[59]

The emerging networks up to 1965 were in the process of evolving. Nonetheless, the networks being established were already playing an important role in Australia's bilateral relationship with Japan and in the development of Australian regional diplomacy. Clearly, officials from both countries were using the regular meetings to enhance a joint understanding of the need for regional development and stability. Indeed, despite the lack of clear guidelines or rules of behaviour, policy networks were developing the knowledge base between governments and gradually changing and influencing the views of policy-makers.

The impact of policy networks: did they make a difference to the bilateral relationship between Australia and Japan?

Policy networks were being constructed in the areas of commerce, based on the rapidly developing volume of bilateral trade, and through regional security issues in Indonesia and the Southeast Asian region more generally. During the period under study, a knowledge base within External Affairs and the Japanese Ministry of Foreign Affairs was being built, albeit slowly, which was gradually changing and influencing the setting, standards and development of bilateral and regional policy. In particular, the construction of policy networks, and the subsequent personal bonds that were forged, assisted in settling disagreements and promoting cooperation between the two countries on regional matters. These efforts by key individuals assisted the development of regular ad hoc dialogue. Venues for discussion included Canberra and Tokyo, embassies in the region and multilateral forums such as the ECAFE and the UN General Assembly and Security Council. The subsequent regular dialogue, exchange of information and habit of association at international forums was a new and positive feature of the relationship. Increasingly the trend was to coordinate policies on matters of mutual interest prior to international meetings. The level of intimacy and frankness in dialogue and the practical usefulness of the exchange of intelligence information were factors in the overall improvement of post-war bilateral relations. Policy networks, as a consequence, were central to the climate of cooperation and confidence that led the beginnings of institutional links, such as preliminary discussions on regular ministerial meetings.

For Australia the policy networks, by 1965, had an impact on regional diplomacy. Japan was a significant trading partner and fellow junior partner in the US-led system. The growth in policy networks provided additional rich opportunities for consultation and dialogue. At the policy-making level Japanese material on Indonesia, mainland China and, by 1965, Vietnam, was giving alternative perspectives on issues of critical importance to Australian national interests. Consequently, the regular ad hoc consultations and exchange of intelligence information had an impact on Australian policy. Officials in External Affairs might have disagreed with the Japanese approach to the WNG and *Konfrontasi* disputes, but Japan could not be ignored. At the bilateral level, policy networks resulted in closer ties between Australian and Japanese officials. In this context, the networks were the vehicle for further engagement with Japan. Moreover, since the link with

Japan was Australia's first long-term bilateral relationship with an Asian country, the policy network model offered a framework for developing bilateral relations with other Asian countries. Finally at the regional level, embryonic networks resulted in early examples of regional coordination between Australia and Japan. A noticeable feature was a shift towards a more multidimensional relationship that included discussion of political and security matters in a regional context. Examples of early discussions on regional coordination included consultation on an Asian development bank, a Pacific economic community and a security forum involving Australia, Japan, New Zealand, the United States and Canada.

Importantly also, the dialogue with Japan had, by 1965, gone beyond the US framework into the building of stronger Australia-Japan bilateral relations. For both countries the region was vital to national interests and there was an appreciation of the importance of cooperation. Moreover, from an Australian perspective, Japan loomed large in foreign policy planning and came to be viewed as vital to Australian long-term interests. Individuals such as McIntyre and Shann supported initiatives to maintain and enhance the levels of engagement with Japan. In this context, a new relationship with Japan was emerging; a relationship that had an influence on overall Australian regional diplomacy.

Conclusion

This chapter demonstrated the importance of policy networks in the bilateral relationship. Evidence was provided that highlighted the intellectual and entrepreneurial leadership of those networks offered by Australian officials in External Affairs. Such leadership had a significant impact on overall bilateral relations with Japan. In particular the vision and innovative methods used by Australian officials in External Affairs to enhance, maintain and upgrade relations with Japan assisted in the development of strategic and diplomatic ties between the two countries.

It has also been demonstrated how regional politico-security issues and trends affected and indeed strengthened Australia-Japan bilateral ties and mutual policy formulation. A key focus throughout the period under study concerned political developments in Indonesia. A major factor behind the initial development of policy networks was the mutual desire of both Australia and Japan for a politically stable Indonesia. Accordingly, the rapid development of policy networks were, in part, a response to the politico-security trends in the region. Indeed, by the end of 1965 the level of cooperation was expanding beyond Indonesia-related matters and included a wide range of regional issues in the politico-strategic area.

Four aspects stand out in an assessment of policy networks. First, there were no established rules or guidelines on the formation of Australia-Japan bilateral policy networks. Indeed, initially it was a rather haphazard process. Nonetheless, key individuals in External Affairs and the Japanese Ministry of Foreign Affairs (MOFA) were actively involved in the gradual process of institutionalising the networks. For example, the 1962 agreement to exchange intelligence information up to the level of 'confidential' was an important development in this institutionalisation. The regular discussions that followed at international forums such as the UN General Assembly and in Canberra, Tokyo and Jakarta further cemented the habit of dialogue and exchange of information.

Second, the policy networks were a necessary feature. They allowed habits and patterns to develop. Given the future path of the relationship (very close personal links evident across many areas), this early association of close personal ties was crucial.

A third aspect is an assessment of the importance of policy networks for policy-making in Australia and Japan. Clearly, the policy networks were advantageous for the MOFA and Japan. The post-war relationship with Australia was an important factor in the economic take-off of the Japanese economy. Moreover, Australia was in the first band of countries to sponsor and support Japanese entry into global and regional forums. Appreciation for the bilateral relationship within Japan included the 'pro-Australia' lobby group within the MOFA articulating the importance of establishing a ministerial committee system with Australia.

Nonetheless, the policy networks did not benefit each country equally. In many respects Australia gained more advantage out of the process. As highlighted in discussions on *Konfrontasi*, Australian officials in Tokyo had quick access to MOFA senior officials and were able to develop detailed and informed views on developments in Japanese policy-making and on the Indonesian situation. Especially given the number of diplomatic missions in Tokyo (already more than 100) the access gained by McIntyre in particular was highly advantageous to External Affairs. Moreover, the ability of Australian officials to tap into Japanese thinking on Indonesian policies and leaders during *Konfrontasi* was useful as an alternative source of information.

Finally, the chapter has demonstrated that policy networks offer a new way of looking at the period under study. The political networks complemented the networks based on commercial ties, and were an essential part of the foundation of the post-war bilateral relationship. As demonstrated in the chapter, the networks formed the basis for closer ties and enhanced levels of familiarity that were, in many respects, the beginnings of close collaboration on regional issues. As well, the study of policy networks highlighted the willingness and commitment of senior officials in External Affairs to 'engage' with Japan in a new post-war bilateral relationship. This assists in our understanding of the construction of Australian regional diplomacy.

Notes

The bulk of research was conducted at the National Australian Archives of Australia, Canberra. Material is based on A1838 3103 series (external relations with Japan) and A5105 series (correspondence files of Australian embassy, Tokyo).

1 For a detailed account of the McEwen years see P. Golding, *McEwen: Political Gladiator*, Melbourne: Melbourne University Press, 1996; and the Sir John McEwen oral history interview, Australian National Library, TRC 311/4, Toorak Melbourne, 1974 and 1975. For a detailed account of post-war trade between Australia and Japan and the role of McEwen, see the numerous articles by Peter Drysdale and other scholars in the Pacific Economic Papers series, published through the Australia-Japan Research Centre, Australian National University, Canberra.
2 Cabinet submission no. 30, Australian Policy Towards Japan, 28 July 1954, item 1009,Commonwealth Record Service (hereafter CRS) A4940/1, National Archives of Australia, (hereafter NAA).
3 A. Watt, *The Evolution of Australian Foreign Policy*, Cambridge: Cambridge University Press, 1967, pp. 214–15.
4 T. B. Millar, *Australia in War and Peace*, Canberra: ANU Press, 1991, p. 230. For detailed accounts of the Pearling dispute see A. Rix, *The Australia-Japan Political Alignment: 1952 to the Present*, London: Routlege, 1999; and S. Scott, 'The inclusion of sedentary fisheries within the continental shelf doctrine', *The International and Comparative Law Quarterly*, vol. 41, October 1992, 788–807.
5 Letter to Secretary, Department of External Affairs (DEA) from Casey, 23 July 1954, file 3101/10/1 pt 2, CRS A1838/278, NAA.
6 Cabinet submission no. 30 'Policy towards Japan', 28 July 1954, file 3101/10/1 pt 2, CRS A1838/278, NAA.
7 Cabinet submission no. 30, 'Policy towards Japan', 28 July 1954, file 3101/10/1 pt 2, CRS A1838/278, NAA.
8 A. A. Caldwell, 'We can't be soft on Jap butchers', *Truth*, 14 February 1954, quoted in file 3103/10/1 pt 2, CRS A1838/278, NAA.
9 Letter to Alan Watt from Arthur Tange, 10 April 1956, file 3103/10/1 pt 4, CRS, A1838/278, NAA. Note that Miki was an influential LDP politician but not a cabinet minister at this time as indicated in the file note.
10 Interview with Thomas Critchley, 16 June 1998.
11 Confidential letter from Watt to Tange, 14 March 1957, file 223/1 pt 2, A5105/3, CRS, NAA.
12 Prime Minister's Brief on Japan for 1957 visit, April 1957, file 3103/10/11/2/1 pt 1, CRS, A1838/278, NAA. The report also highlighted the need for policy networks which emerge in the following years.
13 Renouf argues that the Agreement of Commerce, unlike the ANZUS treaty which was predictable, was an example of an imaginative and far-sighted initiative. A. Renouf, *The Frightened Country*, Melbourne: Macmillan, 1979, p. 64.
14 There were, however, two minor incidents during Kishi's visit. Twelve ALP parliamentarians boycotted a luncheon given by prime minister Menzies at Parliament House and a war veteran hurled copies of Australian charges against Japanese war criminals on the Remembrance Stone at the War Memorial after Kishi had laid a wreath. Kishi was some distance away and unaware of the incident. 'Coverage of Kishi's Visit', file no 3103/10/10/2 pt 4, CRS A1838/1, NAA. For a detailed account of the Kishi visit see Rix, *op. cit.*
15 Letter from ambassador Watt to foreign minister Casey, 30 January 1958, file 3103/10/10/2/1 pt 1, CRSA1838/283 NAA.
16 House of Councillors Steering Committee, Record of Discussions no. 4, 26 September 1958, cited in file 221/12/5/5/1, CRS A 3092/2 NAA. Nomizo raised

several interesting observations of his visit to Australia. An issue of contemporary relevance was his views on Australian independence:

> However independent a country Australia is, it is linked with politics of the British Commonwealth, which is centred on the English kings right down to Queen Elizabeth. There are two Houses of Parliament but the final signature is that of the Governor General and since he is appointed by England, to call a spade a spade takes on the appearance of a kind of Japanese Emperor. It is thus somewhat doubtful if it can be called an independent country.

17 Letter from Plimsoll to Jockel on Tokyo representation at Heads of Mission meeting, 10 February 1959, file 3103/10/6 pt 2, CRS A 1838/280 NAA.
18 Comments by Heydon on relations with Japan, 12 October 1959, file 3103/10/13 pt 1, CRS A 1838/1 NAA.
19 Foreign Ministers Brief on Japan, 1959. File no 303/10/11/2 pt 5, CRS, A 1838/1. NAA. The Department of Defence, however, had a very different view on this matter and was very slow in providing even basic information.
20 Record of conversation between Casey and foreign minister Fujiyama at the Gaimusho, Tokyo, 25 March 1959, file 3103, 10/11/1 pt1, CRS A1838/1 NAA.
21 Record of conversation between Narita (Japanese ambassador designate) and Plimsoll, 14 April 1959, file 3103/10/1 pt 7, CRS A1838/283 NAA.
22 Report prepared by Gordon Jockel on ministers' trip to Japan, 14 April 1959, file 3103/10/11/1 pt 1, CRS A1838 NAA.
23 Draft Savingram for comments on exchange of information, drafted by D. W. McNichol, 26 February 1962, file 3103/10/1 pt 9, CRS A1838/280 NAA.
24 Side comments on draft prepared by David McNichol, 26 February 1962, file 3103/10/1 pt 9, CRS A1838/280 NAA.
25 McNichol, 26 February 1962, file 3103/10/1 pt 9, CRS A1838/280 NAA.
26 Comment on McNichol's draft by A. J. Eastman, 2 March 1962, files 3103/10/1 CRS A1838/280 NAA.
27 Record of Conversation between Zentaro Kosaka and Sir Garfield Barwick on 12 June 1962, reported by H. D. Anderson 14 June 1962, file no. 3103/10/11/2 pt 5, CRS A1838/280 NAA.
28 D. Sissons, 'Australia and Japan, 1961–1965', in G. Greenwood and N. Harper (eds) *Australia in World Affairs*, Melbourne: F. W. Cheshire, 1967, p. 378.
29 The Philippines was also involved in the territorial dispute, but did not participate in the low-level military conflict.
30 It could be argued, however, that total reconciliation did not take place until the Basic Treaty of Friendship and Cooperation was signed in 1976. For a detailed account of the Basic Treaty, see A. Stockwin, 'Negotiating the Basic Treaty between Australia and Japan, 1973–1976', *Japanese Studies*, vol. 24, no. 2, September 2004, 201–15.
31 Barwick to Beale, 25 June 1963, file 3103/10/1 pt 9, CRS A 1838/280 NAA.
32 External Affairs paper, August 1963, file no 3103/10/1 pt 9, CRS A 1838/280 NAA.
33 Record of discussion between Arthur Tange and ambassador Ohta, 6 August, 1963, file no 3103/10/1 pt 9, CRS A 1838/280 NAA.
34 Letter from Shaw to McIntyre, 13 August 1963, file no 3103/10/1 pt 9, CRS A 1838/280 NAA.
35 Letter from Tange to McIntyre, file 3103/10/6 pt 2, CRS A1838/280 NAA.
36 Confidential Anglo-British relations paper, 1 March 1963, file 3103/10/1, CRS A1838/280 NAA.
37 Comments on confidential Anglo-British relations paper, 1 March 1963, file 3103/10/1, CRS A1838/280 NAA.
38 Ambassador McIntyre's comments on Anglo-Japanese relations paper, 23 May 1963, file 3103/10/1, CRS A1838/280 NAA.

39 Ambassador McIntyre to Tange, Memorandum no. 327, 16 April 1963, file 3103/10/1 pt 9, CRS A1838/280 NAA.

40 Comments by H. M. Loveday on request for exchange of information by McIntyre, 29 April 1963, file 3103/10/1 pt 9, CRS A1838/280 NAA.

41 Record of conversation between Shaw and Ohta, 5 June 1963, file 3103/10/1 pt 9, CRS A 1838/280 NAA.

42 McIntyre to Tange, 25 June 1963, memorandum no. 514, file 3103/10/1 pt 9, CRS A 1838/280 NAA

43 DEA report on information on Soviet affairs by R. S. M. Laurie, 4 July 1963, file 3103/10/1 pt 9, CRS A1838/280 NAA.

44 Love to Tange, 'Information given to Japan', 4 November 1963, file 3103/10/1 pt 9, CRS A 1838/280 NAA.

45 Based on comments made by former senior Australian diplomat Garry Woodard. Interview, 6 July 2000.

46 Cablegram to Australian Mission to United Nations, New York, 1 October 1963, cable no. 812, file 3103/10/10/5 pt 2, CRS A1838/280 NAA. The Australian position was to oppose a summit it on the grounds that it could exacerbate tension and disadvantage Malaysia if not handled carefully. The Ikeda visit is examined in detail in Chapter 5.

47 Uncorrected transcript of oral history interview. Sir Laurence McIntyre interviewed by Mel Pratt, Canberra, 9 September 1975, TRC 121/67, Oral History Unit, Australian National Library.

48 Sukarno made ten visits to Tokyo. Only one, however, was an official visit. M. Nishihara, *The Japanese and Sukarno's Indonesia*, Honolulu: University of Hawaii Press, 1976, p. 27.

49 Record of conversation between Nemoto, Booker (assistant secretary), Loveday and Takasugi (counsellor), 23 November 1964, file 221/12/5/5/1, CRS A3092/2 NAA.

50 P. D. Hill to External Affairs on enclosed report from Canadian Embassy in Tokyo, 3 June 1965, file 3103/3/1/1 pt 1, CRS A1838 280 NAA.

51 James Plimsoll to External Affairs, 28 January 1963, file 915/9 pt 35, CRS A5105/3 NAA.

52 McIntyre to External Affairs, cable no. 67, 21 July 1964, file 3103/11/108 pt 1, CRS A 1838/2 NAA and cable no. 716, 16 September 1964, file no 3103/11/108 pt 2, CRS A1838/2 NAA.

53 US ambassador to Indonesia Green made this comment in a cable sent to the State Department. Cable no. 1479 to State Department, 17 November 1965, file 3034/11/89 pt 6, A1838/321 NAA.

54 Letter from Tange to McIntyre, 4 June, file 3103/10/6 pt 2, A1838/280. NAA.

55 D. J. Horne to deputy secretary re. Japan Annual Review 1964, file 3103/10/21 pt 1, CRS A 1838/1 NAA.

56 File note Loveday to Shaw, 16 September 1963, file 3103/10/10/5 pt 1, CRS A 1838/280 NAA.

57 P. Hass, 'Introduction: Epistemic communities and international policy coordination', *International Organisation*, vol. 46, no. 1, winter 1992, p. 4.

58 Unlike the policy networks in the political and security area, which at this stage was restricted to government actors, policy networks in the commercial area also included a range of non-government actors, such as businessmen.

59 The contemporary bilateral relationship, with myriad networks and joint regional initiatives and an ever-expanding process to develop and enhance networks, including since 1994 an exchange program for junior officers to spend six months in Tokyo or Canberra, would certainly suggest this.

2 Japan, Australia and ASPAC

The rise and fall of an Asia-Pacific cooperative security framework

C. W. Braddick

Asia has no history of indigenous multilateral security cooperation.[1]

Introduction

Does the Asian-Pacific Council (ASPAC) represent a false start or a lost opportunity in the institutional history of Asia-Pacific regional security? Was it a stepping-stone towards an Australian-Japanese security partnership or a millstone weighing down their developing relationship? Now largely forgotten, when ASPAC is remembered, it is usually done so with distaste. Variously described by contemporary observers as a 'diehard anti-communist' and 'anti-Chinese' alliance, even a 'first step towards a Northeast Asian Treaty Organization', ASPAC was also disparaged for numerous other failings.[2] It was said to be 'rather somnolent', 'an exercise in collective soliciting', and 'little more than another regional body for discussion of economic problems [whose] scope was modest and . . . future unclear'.[3] In one post hoc assessment, an expert on Asia-Pacific regionalism noted that 'ASPAC never became an influential organisation . . . [since it] was not able to generate much regional cooperation'.[4] Australian scholars have been particularly scathing: 'ASPAC was used to denote a ministerial meeting suggesting a form and degree of organisation not supported by the factual situation. The purposes of ASPAC have been vague from the beginning', claimed one foreign policy expert.[5] It not only offered 'little evidence of any radical innovations in Pacific diplomacy', but 'ASPAC barely deserved serious discussion . . . since it seems doomed to a quiet and unlamented demise at an early date'.[6] Finally, and most recently, it has been criticised for exacerbating Japanese-Australian differences: '[ASPAC] highlighted . . . different Australian and Japanese outlooks on relations with China'.[7]

In addition to the very limited English and Japanese language secondary literature on ASPAC, this chapter draws mainly on the recently declassified files of the Australian and New Zealand governments for its information. This includes detailed records of all ASPAC meetings. Unfortunately, Japanese archives do not yet allow public access to similar materials.

The purpose of this chapter is to rescue ASPAC from an undeserved obscurity and to consider whether its overwhelmingly negative reputation is deserved. However, given the theme of this volume, in describing the evolution of this groundbreaking cooperative security organisation, the emphasis will be on analysing the role that Japan and Australia played in the development of ASPAC, as well as ASPAC's influence on Australia-Japan relations.

The life cycle of ASPAC can be divided into three phases: a long gestation period (from September 1964 to June 1966); followed by a steady growth in confidence and maturity (from June 1966 to July 1971); and finally, a period of crisis leading to its collapse in 1975.

Gestation

ASPAC grew out of a South Korean diplomatic initiative in September 1964. Having failed to interest Washington in a wider East Asian security organisation, the government of President Park Chung Hee invited foreign ministers from 'free nations in the Far East, Southeast Asia and Southwest Pacific region' to a conference in Seoul in April 1965. The stated objective was fourfold: to 'review and examine means and ways of strengthening a regional entity to defend ourselves against Communist subversion'; 'consolidating friendly bonds among free countries'; and 'promoting economic cooperation and cultural exchange among countries in the region'.[8] When this proposal met with a lukewarm response, South Korea dropped references to defence arrangements and downplayed the anti-communist rhetoric in favour of the last two goals. At Australian and others' prompting, it also added Japan to the list of invitees. However, although the United States came out in favour of the conference, fearing its impact on Indonesia and perhaps China, Tokyo decided to decline the invitation.[9]

Australia's position on the conference was somewhat ambiguous. Perhaps reflecting the attitude of his hosts, the ambassador in Tokyo was critical of its conception and timing and advocated a graceful withdrawal, but more senior members of the Department of External Affairs were actively engaged in a diplomatic campaign to persuade Japan to participate.[10] Their argument centred on a shared interest in regional stability and strengthened cooperation between like-minded countries, as well as the desirability of drawing South Korea 'out of its present position of semi-isolation'.[11]

Whether due to Canberra's persuasive skills or a desire to lay to rest its own reputation as the 'orphan of Asia', or even the fact that negotiations on normalising Japan-Korea diplomatic relations were at a delicate stage, Japan reluctantly agreed to attend a preliminary meeting of ambassadors in Bangkok in March 1965. In all nine countries were represented – Australia, the Republic of China (ROC, Taiwan), Japan, the Republic of Korea (ROK), Malaysia, New Zealand, the Philippines, Thailand, and the Republic of Vietnam (ROV) – and after a second preliminary meeting in April 1966, these were to become the founding members of ASPAC.

ASPAC was large: originally it comprised 8 per cent of the world's population, accounted for 10 per cent of world trade, and contributed more than 10 per cent of the United Nations' budget. From its inception, however, ASPAC had to accommodate many competing visions held by its disparate membership concerning the nature and functions of the organisation. Members presented great contrasts – politically, economically, culturally and geographically – and these resulted in conflicting priorities for the new organisation. The economically less developed members, including Thailand and the Philippines, hoped that ASPAC would offer substantial aid or even an economic union to help solve the economic and social problems of the region: a function opposed by the more developed Japan and Australia, who argued about duplication with other institutions and simple impracticality, but most of all feared the expense. For the same reasons, Australia and Japan also opposed the creation of a secretariat for the new grouping. The divided states – the ROK, ROC and ROV – as ASPAC's most insecure members, tended to favour a military role for the new grouping, or at least a strong ideological union. However, this idea was anathema to the more neutralist Japan and Malaysia, and unpopular in Australia and New Zealand. Instead, Canberra and Wellington promoted a free and open discussion of regional problems, including political and security issues, with the aim of creating a 'regional community of interest', as well as closer relations with Tokyo, in particular. Initially, at least, Japan was most reluctant to join in such discussions (as was Malaysia), preferring to leave such matters to bilateral fora.

Only Cold War logic could provide a thread to pull this disparate group of countries together: none was communist; all were allied to the US (except for Malaysia, an ally of Britain, Australia and New Zealand); most were contributing troops to the war in Vietnam (except for Japan, Malaysia and Taiwan); and to varying degrees all perceived the Peoples' Republic of China (PRC) as a threat. Nevertheless their differences seemed to outweigh any similarities.

Maturation

The atmosphere at the first full ministerial meeting of ASPAC, held in Seoul on 14–16 June 1966, was surprisingly friendly and cooperative. Laos attended as an observer, as it would all subsequent meetings. The group did not adopt any founding document, but instead issued a rather bland joint communiqué at the conclusion of the talks. This reaffirmed the ministers' 'dedication to the common cause of peace, freedom, and prosperity, and their determination to preserve their integrity and sovereignty in the face of external threats'.[12] It also opposed nuclear testing in the region, supported peaceful reunification of the Korean peninsula, and, more controversially, expressed sympathy for the plight of South Vietnam.[13] Japan was engaged in a holding operation and was pleased that it had avoided ASPAC becoming a 'narrow-minded anti-communist' grouping, but Tokyo remained unenthusiastic about the future.[14] Similarly, Australia's foreign minister had advised the conference to 'make haste slowly', but unlike his Japanese counterpart, Paul Hasluck left lauding the 'growing sense of an Asian community', happy to be a part of this project. Canberra also recognised that it shared a lot of common ground with Tokyo, although there were ongoing differences over the situation in Vietnam.[15]

During its first year, ASPAC added three extra dimensions to its activities. In addition to the annual meetings of foreign ministers, members agreed to hold regular standing committee meetings of ambassadors in the capital of the next host country. Second, it sponsored the creation of a series of small multilateral projects, beginning with a Registry of Scientific and Technical Services in Canberra – Australia's first international organisation – and a Social and Cultural Centre in Seoul, and later adding an Economic Cooperation Centre in Thailand and a Food and Fertiliser Technology Centre in Taiwan. Finally, at Australian initiative, the group began meeting as an informal caucus at international conferences, ranging from the UN and Red Cross to the International Atomic Energy Agency (IAEA) and Conference on Women. There were to be more than sixty such meetings held between mid-1967 and mid-1970.[16]

However, as the Australian participant in the standing committee meetings commented, 'The most sanguine optimist could not regard the first twelve months operation of ASPAC as a success.' He blamed the loss of impetus on Tokyo and Kuala Lumpur: 'much of the political and security substance of ASPAC had to be removed to meet objections by particularly Japan and Malaysia'. Nevertheless, he concluded optimistically that a 'reasonably sound basis had been laid' for the future.[17]

When the Japanese and Australian foreign ministers met in Tokyo in late March 1967, they agreed that ASPAC should be a high-level forum for multilateral consultation on global and regional political, economic and social issues.[18] Moreover, as Japanese diplomats subsequently conceded, 'in discussing political matters it was not always practicable to separate them from security and defence questions'. The Japanese Ministry of Foreign Affairs' (MOFA) main concern was to avoid association with political statements that would prove embarrassing if published.[19] However, despite having 'considerable sympathy with the Japanese view about the nature and functions of ASPAC', the Australians remained reluctant to openly support Japan in ASPAC lest they 'earn the disapproval of other Asian countries'.[20]

On the eve of the second ASPAC Ministerial Meeting, held in Bangkok from 5–7 July 1967, according to the head of its Asian Affairs Bureau, MOFA still regarded ASPAC as a 'hard-line anti-communist grouping' and foreign minister Miki Takeo 'did not want to "tarnish" . . . his Asia/Pacific Basin ideas . . . by too close an association with ASPAC'.[21] In Bangkok, however, Miki made a 'positive effort to impose his own conception of ASPAC on the other parties' and left feeling largely vindicated. In essence,

Miki's position comprised three principles, namely: no limits on subjects to be discussed; no binding resolutions; and no executive functions.[22]

Having offered Canberra as the venue for the next ministerial meeting, Australian foreign minister Paul Hasluck returned from Bangkok fired with enthusiasm and immediately instructed all Australian diplomatic posts to do 'everything possible . . . to support ASPAC'. His reasoning included the argument that membership 'associates Australia with Asian countries on a basis of equality and associates us with the region in a unique way'. Moreover, he felt that it enabled Australia 'to gain an insight into, and perhaps exert an influence on Japanese policies in the region'.[23] Hasluck was convinced that ASPAC was 'here to stay'.[24]

The success of the conference also attracted American attention, but since Australia valued ASPAC in part because the United States was not a member, Canberra tried to keep Washington at arm's length. It merely asked that the Americans acknowledge 'the value of self-reliant regionalism as a contribution to ensuring the long-term security and growth of Asia'.[25] Even a US proposal for a meeting with the ASPAC group at the UN was spurned by Canberra lest it 'give credence to the Communist charge that ASPAC is an American tool'.[26] Future president Richard M. Nixon went a lot further. In the October 1967 issue of the journal *Foreign Affairs*, he proposed that, given 'a solidifying awareness of China's threat', ASPAC should 'develop into an alliance actively dedicated to concerting whatever efforts might be necessary to maintain the security of the region'.[27]

To Australian eyes, Nixon's view appeared somewhat divorced from reality. Having earlier won over Japan to the idea of discussing political and security questions in ASPAC, Hasluck used his chairmanship of the first standing committee meeting in Canberra to encourage a dialogue on the situation in China, Vietnam, ASEAN and the British plan to withdraw from East of Suez. At the meeting, the Japanese ambassador agreed with his Korean counterpart that 'questions of security were critical to the region'; however, Tokyo immediately responded that such matters should be reserved for the ministerial meetings, or if discussed in the standing committee, that no record should be kept.[28] Miki was worried that given the existing serious divisions between member nations' perspectives, frequent discussion of polit-ical questions would result in immediate confrontations and the 'scaring off of the neutrals'.[29] Australia's Department of External Affairs (DEA) mean-while was concerned 'to avoid frightening Japan off'.[30]

When Prime Minister Satō Eisaku met with the Australian cabinet in October 1967, in a vague effort to push things forward, prime minister Harold Holt requested that 'Japan should play a leading and constructive role in . . . ASPAC'.[31] In Tokyo the following month, Australian diplomats explicitly requested Japanese support for political questions being discussed at ASPAC standing committee meetings, even if only on a basis of 'no recommendations, no consensus and no public statements'. They argued that such exchanges would help in 'building up a sense of regional community', in 'bringing about understanding of political realities', and in the 'education of some of the smaller less experienced members and the inculcation of a spirit of give and take'. The director of MOFA's Asian Affairs Bureau conceded that the ministry was divided on the future of ASPAC: he personally wished to minimise political discussions in the hope of broadening ASPAC's membership, but his counterpart from the European and Oceanic Affairs Bureau was happy to see Japan playing a more active role, if only to 'help to make Japanese policies better understood'. In a quite extraordinary turnabout, that afternoon Japanese officials concerned with ASPAC held a private meeting and agreed to accept Australia's position, although in practice Japan's ambassador rarely expressed views on political matters in subsequent meetings.[32]

During the first half of 1968, rumours were circulating that the Philippines, Thailand, South Korea and Taiwan were again considering proposing that ASPAC become a military alliance. Australia's position was subtle. Hasluck stated publicly that he thought Japan would play a greater role in the security of Southeast Asia and the Pacific in the future.[33] The Americans encouraged this view.[34] Moreover, as he told the ASPAC standing committee on 16 February 1968, Hasluck also believed that a new regional security organisation was required, although he did not think that ASPAC should take on that role.[35] Similarly, Australian defence policy predicted that 'Even in the longer term, it is extremely doubtful whether ASPAC members, and particularly Japan, will wish to involve the organisation directly in the security field.'[36] Nevertheless, the DEA continued to hope for a strengthened Japanese security role in the region:

> the Australian Government has not had occasion to consider the extent to which a Japanese military contribution should eventually be looked to as a contribution to the security of the region. The point is at present academic in the absence of any Japanese wish to become so involved. However, with the expansion of its diplomatic activity, Japan should progressively take on all the attributes of a Great Power.[37]

The Japanese response was predictably negative. The *Melbourne Age* quoted a MOFA spokesman rather ambiguously to the effect that 'Japan would favour any move which increases the stability of the region.'[38] However, the stories MOFA leaked to the Japanese press were more explicit, insisting that ASPAC should continue to focus on economic and cultural issues and that foreign minister Miki wanted to keep it as a 'place for the free exchange of views'.[39] Even so, June 1968 saw violent demonstrations by radical Japanese students target ASPAC, claiming that it was a front for the revival of Japanese imperialism in Asia.[40]

On the eve of the third ASPAC Ministerial Meeting, held in Canberra from 30 July–1 August 1968, the Philippines' foreign minister openly called for ASPAC to be converted into a military alliance. More significantly, the

ROK proposed the adoption of a seven-point ASPAC charter.[41] The latter contained several security-related clauses, most importantly: 'Mutual respect for national sovereignty, political independence and the preservation of territorial integrity'; 'Pursuit of peace, settlement of disputes by peaceful means, and reaffirmation of common consciousness of responsibility for the maintenance of peace in the region'; and 'Realization of a regional community where security, order and progress are ensured'.[42] The Australian and Japanese governments both dismissed these proposals. Both wished to preserve ASPAC's 'flexibility and informality', DEA arguing that the organisation would 'only progress if the "rules" are left unsaid as much as possible'.[43] While MOFA feared that it 'would tend to confirm suspicions ... that ASPAC was being converted into an anti-Communist security bloc'. Japan preferred the Commonwealth Prime Ministers' Conference to serve as the model for ASPAC, since this would allow it to continue functioning 'even if there were great differences and even conflicts between individual members'.[44]

Prime minister John Gorton opened the Ministerial Meeting with a speech bluntly declaring that 'ASPAC was in no sense a security organisation and in the view of the Australian government it should not attempt to become one': a view seconded by foreign minister Hasluck during the meeting.[45] Hasluck celebrated the growing 'sense of community', and the fact that there now appeared to be 'firm agreement that ASPAC is an organisation which enables a free exchange of views on political and even security problems, and on economic, cultural and social matters'.[46] In particular, he lauded the 'notable advance in Japan's attitude'. Yet Miki remained reluctant to discuss 'the concrete needs of the military side of security' or to take a public position on the communist states.[47] The Japanese and Korean delegations found themselves at opposite poles on most points, forcing the Australian hosts to play the role of mediator. The seven Korean principles were eventually adopted in the joint communiqué, but only after they had been stripped of security implications. On his return home Miki stated that Japan's position was 'to achieve security in the region through economic and social means and not a military build-up'.[48]

The US State Department continued to see 'considerable value in ASPAC as a focus for regional cooperation'. Moreover, it believed that Japanese attitudes to the organisation had changed, since they 'now see potential value for themselves in ASPAC'. The US was not prepared to enter into any new military commitments itself, but it would look kindly on the establishment of a new security organisation in the area.[49] Meanwhile president-elect Nixon revived his idea of converting ASPAC into an Asian collective security system. He may have regarded this as 'an obvious and sensible' move, but American officials remained cautious. They envisaged ASPAC playing a similar role to the Organization of American States in 'allaying suspicions and preventing border disputes'. They also thought that ASPAC was useful in helping Japan to 'develop a moderate and constructive role', but 'were sceptical about the prospects of getting Japan to take a lead in large-scale regional security arrangements and cautious about the desirability of this'.[50]

At the second round of Japanese-Australian officials' talks held in Tokyo in mid-November 1968, the Japanese deputy vice foreign minister dismissed Nixon's scheme on the grounds that there was 'no political identity or solidarity in Asia'. Participants agreed that 'the main threat was subversion and insurgency supported by outside forces'. Yet when the head of the Australian delegation offered his personal view that 'an adequate security system in the area could not be contemplated without Japan's participation', the head of the Asian Affairs Bureau fell back on Japan's 'constitutional limitations'. As current host of ASPAC, Japan was instead putting its energy into trying to persuade Singapore, Indonesia and Burma to join.[51] The Australians too remained sceptical, in part because they believed that it would be counterproductive to apply pressure on the Japanese to adopt a more active role, but also because they felt that without an American commitment the new organisation would be weaker than SEATO.[52] Hence, for the foreseeable future Canberra envisaged 'no possible external defence role for Japan wider than participation in a UN peace-keeping operation'.[53] Nevertheless, some members of DEA continued to hope that ASPAC would 'lead to the evolution of higher forms of cooperation, including discussion of common security interests'.[54]

Extensive political discussions were now taking place regularly at the ASPAC standing committee, but the organisation did not seek to actively resolve political differences. ASPAC avoided 'involvement in the internal affairs of member countries or in their bilateral disputes'. The Sabah dispute between the Philippines and Malaysia was kept off the agenda. Similarly, the ROC effort to get the ASPAC standing committee to express members' concern over Italian and Canadian moves towards recognition of the PRC met with firm resistance from Japan and Australia and was quietly dropped.[55]

During the first half of 1969, South Korea revived the idea of creating a new 'Organisation for Military Cooperation in the Asia and Pacific Area'. However, reflecting the fluidity in Nixon's thinking that would soon find expression in an eponymous doctrine which proclaimed that Asian nations should assume primary responsibility for their own defence, the US State Department made its opposition to a new Northeast Asian security treaty explicit.[56] Yet in an interesting role reversal, Australia's new foreign minister, Gordon Freeth – en route to the fourth ASPAC Ministerial Meeting – told the press that 'there might at some point of time in the future possibly or almost inevitably be some part for Japan to play as a guarantor of security in the area'.[57]

At the Ministerial Meeting, held in Kawana, Japan from 9–11 June 1969, Japan's new foreign minister Aichi Kiichi defined ASPAC as an 'organisation for cooperation for the self-determined development of Pacific Asian countries'. He outlined five indispensable (and familiar) principles for ASPAC: cooperation to promote peace and progress in the region; not becoming a military alliance; unanimity; practicability and flexibility; and an open door to new members. ASPAC was also of increasing value to Japan as an organisation that could strengthen the international influence of the area. An Australian proposal to include reference to the need for continuing support from outside of the region was accepted, although not without opposition, especially from Japan who feared that it might indicate opposition to Okinawa's return to Tokyo's control.[58] DEA thought that US support was still needed because of the 'weight and gravity of the threat to security in the region'. Nevertheless, Canberra welcomed 'efforts by countries of the region to assume a greater role in the promotion of the development and stability of the region'. For the Australians, ASPAC was 'a means to this end'.[59]

MOFA was satisfied with ASPAC's progress under its stewardship, believing that it was now generally accepted as a 'peaceful organisation' since there was 'no longer any serious likelihood of it becoming a militaristic or rabidly anti-Communist organ'. The head of the new Regional Policy Division of the Asian Affairs Bureau went so far as to describe the ASPAC council as the 'top of a pyramid', with the Japan-sponsored Ministerial Conference for Southeast Asian Development and the sub-regional ASEAN beneath.[60] However, while praising Japan's leadership of ASPAC for 'developing consultations in a relaxed and informal atmosphere on political and strategic problems common to the region as a whole', foreign minister Freeth continued to hanker for something more. As he told an audience in New York in mid-September 1969, 'Japan, with interests as large as, or greater than those of others at stake, must be expected to seek to assume some responsibility for the security and protection of those interests.'[61]

New Zealand's assumption of responsibility for ASPAC did not produce any dramatic changes. At the first standing committee meeting, long-serving prime minister and foreign minister Keith Holyoake suggested that the goal was not to develop agreed policies, but understanding each other's point of view and comparing assessments of major political developments. A lengthy discussion of the recent Soviet proposal for an Asian collective security system (excluding the PRC) followed, and members agreed to adopt a cautious attitude.[62]

Apparently, more rapid progress was being made in New York than in Wellington. In March 1970, the head of the Australian mission to the UN reported that 'the ASPAC Group is at the moment the most closely knit and effective informal consultative group within the UN, although its significance is not properly understood by the majority of the UN membership'. As well as the ASPAC nine, the gatherings attracted the active participation of the Laotian, Singaporean and Indonesian delegations. Its sense of unity was said to be based 'partly on personal relationships and partly on common acceptance of the fact that the rest of the UN knows and cares little about the realities of Asia'. DEA argued that the ASPAC group served Australia's 'real national interests' because most significantly 'Australians are regarded within this group not as Asian, but as independent people with an affinity for their neighbours in the region and a capacity to treat them as friends and equals.'[63] More generally, DEA recognised the interdependence of development and security and the need for the region to increasingly rely on its own efforts in both fields. It was true that ASPAC had 'explicitly rejected a security role and is not an aid organisation', but nonetheless DEA valued ASPAC because of its 'emphasis on mutual cooperation, self-reliance and the promotion of greater understanding'.[64]

In retrospect, the fifth Ministerial Meeting – held in Wellington, New Zealand from 17–19 June 1970 – represented the high-water mark for ASPAC. There were no surprises, but the atmosphere was amicable and the discussions frank. No-one raised the contentious question of converting ASPAC into a military alliance, and in return foreign minister Aichi promised that Japan would play a more positive role in contributing to peace and stability in the region. He also accepted the most explicitly anti-communist joint communiqué to date. Australia's new foreign minister, William McMahon, meanwhile emphasised the continuing communist Chinese threat, and was content to see ASPAC consolidate its achievements thus far.[65] ASPAC's declared purpose was now to:

uphold and strengthen the institutions of free societies in forms best suited to the needs and circumstances of their peoples; accelerate regional economic and social growth in a spirit of equal partnership, in order to strengthen the foundations for a prosperous community of Asian and Pacific nations; to preserve national integrity and independence against threats of any kind; to widen and deepen mutual understanding; and to cooperate closely with other nations and organisations pursuing similar objectives.[66]

At the fourth round of Australia-Japan official level consultations held at the end of October, the head of DEA's Pacific and Americas Branch expressed his belief that their respective positions on regional cooperation were 'almost identical'. Moreover, 'Australia regarded its relations with Japan in ASPAC as very important because it was the only regional organisation of which both were members, but which did not include any non-regional countries': a view endorsed by the assistant director-general of MOFA's Asian Affairs Bureau.[67] For Australia, although ASPAC was only 'a modest organisation', it was now considered an 'indispensable' one. ASPAC represented a 'pioneering venture in cooperation' since it provided 'a forum in which countries of the region can meet together to discuss their common problems in an atmosphere of trust and goodwill'. Furthermore, ASPAC was 'building up a sense of community, consciousness of common interests and common objectives in the Asian and Pacific region'. These were intangible, unspectacular developments, but nonetheless they were adjudged 'profoundly beneficial'.[68] ASPAC had finally settled into its stride, but already storm clouds were gathering on the horizon.

Crisis and collapse

By mid-1971, the strains were beginning to tell on ASPAC. It seems that as
soon as ASPAC stopped developing it started the slow process of decline
leading to collapse. According to the Policy Planning Group of Australia's
renamed Department of Foreign Affairs, 'total confusion . . . surrounds, but
has not yet descended upon, ASPAC'. The difficulties stemmed from the
Nixon Doctrine of 25 July 1969, and the current political climate in which
'few members are happy about the prospect of attending meetings convened
in Taipei'. It called for a reassessment of Australian policies towards ASPAC
with a view to siding with either the positive (Taiwan, South Vietnam, South
Korea and Thailand) or the negative camp (Malaysia and Indonesia).[69] The
Japanese could also have been added to the latter group since according to
Gordon Freeth, currently ambassador to Tokyo, they too 'did not regard
[ASPAC] very highly as an organisation'.[70]

The sixth ASPAC Ministerial Meeting, held in Manila from 14–16 July
1971, was the most confrontational in the history of the organisation.
Argument centred on references in the joint communiqué to 'sympathy' for
the ROC, suspicion of the PRC's newfound 'apparent amiability', and criticism of North Korea's 'provocative and aggressive acts'. Malaysia objected
vociferously to every 'anti-Communist' reference, ably supported by Japan.
The result was a 'hardening of ASPAC members into several groups': 'anti-
Communist hard-liners' (ROK, ROC and ROV); 'a moderate group'
(Australia, New Zealand, the Philippines and Thailand); and the most
dovish (Malaysia and Japan).[71] Members declined Taipei's offer to serve as
the next host of ASPAC and settled on Seoul instead.

The Ministerial Meeting coincided with two significant events that would
help to deepen the crisis. Having earlier declared his intention to recognise
the PRC government and break ties with Taiwan, Australian Labor Party
leader Gough Whitlam was visiting China and Japan. ASPAC was not
mentioned in Beijing, but in Tokyo Whitlam told his Japanese counterpart
that he thought ASPAC 'was largely ineffectual and would eventually fade
away'.[72] Whitlam's hostile attitude would prove decisive after he won the
December general election. However, Whitlam was not the only foreign
dignitary in Beijing at this time: US National Security Adviser Henry
Kissinger had arrived secretly via Pakistan. Shortly thereafter, on 15 July,
President Nixon announced to a stunned world that he would reverse
decades of hostility and personally visit China.

The Japanese and Australian governments were still reeling from the
'Nixon shock' when ten days later the fifth annual bilateral officials-level
consultations were held in Canberra. Australian attitudes towards ASPAC
were undergoing rapid change. The briefing for the meeting commented that
'ASPAC continues to play a useful if limited part within Australia's overall
arrangements for regional cooperation.' It assessed 'Japan's interest in
ASPAC [a]s probably greater than ours', since Australia 'would not wish to

invent ASPAC if it did not already exist'. Now, however, instead of being a means to strengthen ties with Tokyo, it argued that 'one reason to stay in is not to permit Japan to assume a dominant role'. Finally, it predicted accurately that 'Our original reasons for going into ASPAC are likely to become less relevant as we develop closer relations with China.'[73] At the meeting itself, ASPAC barely rated a mention.

In response to the earlier, overwhelmingly negative assessment of the Policy Planning Group came a remarkably penetrating analysis of ASPAC by J. M. Starey, a counsellor at the Australian embassy in Manila. He accepted that ASPAC suffered from 'structural weaknesses': the group lacked 'real geographical cohesion', 'a common ASPAC ideology', or an 'underlying economic rationale'. Nevertheless, Starey reported that most ambassadors had enthusiastically attended every standing committee meeting held during the past year, and the progress of the group's six developing members had engendered a 'sense of pride which it would be quite wrong to ignore or decry'. Looking back, he argued that 'Australia's interest in developing closer relations with South-east and East Asian countries, and promoting the growth of regional consciousness has to date been well served by ASPAC.' For Starey, the fundamental challenge now confronting ASPAC was to adapt to a radically changing regional environment: ASPAC members had shared a threat perception that focused on 'the existence, attitudes and actions of a militant Communist regime in Peking', but most were now 'exploring the possibility of a rapprochement with the PRC'. In a well balanced conclusion, Starey recommended that

> Australia should not be seen to be anxious to disassociate itself from ASPAC, and should indeed be prepared to play a full part in its activities. At the same time, however, Australia would not have anything to gain, or retain, by going out on a limb for the preservation of ASPAC.[74]

ASPAC struggled on for another four years. A quiet and uneventful seventh ASPAC Ministerial Meeting was held in Seoul in June 1972, but the eighth meeting, scheduled for Bangkok in mid-1973, was postponed indefinitely. A wide variety of diplomatic solutions were explored in the interim – increased membership, reduced membership, association with other regional institutions, creating a new institution, emphasising only the economic and cultural functions – without success, before the group formally disbanded following the fall of Saigon in May 1975.[75]

Concluding thoughts

In the words of its first chairman, the organisation was 'a high-level consultative forum . . . [that] enabled the countries in the Asia-Pacific region to foster the habit of constructive dialogue and consultation on political and security issues of common interest and concern'.[76] This sounds like a reasonable description of ASPAC, yet it dates from 1994, when after a twenty-year hiatus ASPAC re-emerged in the form of the ASEAN Regional Forum (ARF). This is not to argue that ARF is simply a replica of ASPAC – the differences are many – but they share certain distinctive features, which have been defined by an expert on post-Cold War Asian security practices as the 'Asian approach' to cooperative security. This approach is 'pre-eminently political, [being] focused on building trust and shared understandings'. It is also characterised by: 'non-interference in members' domestic affairs'; avoiding involvement 'in the containment and settlement of international conflicts'; a 'preference for bilateral negotiations and informal multilateral discussions'; and emphasis on 'long-range goals, diversity and equality, consensus-building and face-saving, informal networking and the fostering of interpersonal relations, unilateral and voluntary disclosures and conces-sions, incrementalism, negotiations, and . . . noncontroversial areas'.[77]

During its lifetime, ASPAC certainly sought to avoid discussing embar-rassing subjects, the internal affairs of member states, or their bilateral disputes. ASPAC's history also highlighted the importance of informality (it eschewed formal institutional trappings like a charter, permanent secretariat, or regular budget), flexibility, unanimity, equality, and personal chemistry – the loss of one of the group's 'founding fathers' often presaging a redefini-tion of the national interest.[78]

It is tempting to sum up Canberra's approach to ASPAC as keeping Japan in, the US out, and Australia in the middle. However, perhaps the most important feature of Australia's role in ASPAC was its whole-hearted endorse-ment of the 'Asian approach'. In the 1990s, Australia adopted a 'Western approach' to the ARF and APEC, emphasising 'concrete goals, immediate benefits, and binding agreements' in sharp contrast to that of the Asian members. In the 1960s, however, the Australian government was content to see ASPAC develop as an informal consultative political forum, allowing Canberra to discover what its neighbours in East Asia were thinking about the security and development problems confronting the region, and perhaps to influence them in some small way.

The Japanese government was never as enthusiastic about ASPAC as the Australian had been. MOFA's Sinophile Asian Affairs Bureau was particu-larly sceptical. On security questions MOFA displayed a distinct preference for bilateralism – including developing a parallel bilateral security dialogue with Australia – and its own 'comprehensive security' approach. The govern-ment felt it necessary to placate dissident opinion at home and to avoid provoking its communist neighbours in Asia. Hence, the repeated Japanese efforts to broaden ASPAC's membership to incorporate the Southeast Asian neutrals – though not those of South Asia, which it actively sought to exclude – to help weaken the grouping's perceived ideological bias.

Other members of ASPAC (and the US) repeatedly tried to turn ASPAC into a military alliance: a security relationship for which Japan and Australia were not prepared. Neither Tokyo nor Canberra was willing to give up its

American security blanket for the uncertainties of an untested multilateral regional security framework. Yet, these pressures helped Japan and Australia to define the kind of political and security relationship that they wanted.

ASPAC was a failure, but despite the tense divisions of the Cold War environment, it can point to some notable, albeit intangible, achievements. Not the least of these was the willingness of Japan and Australia to discuss political and security questions with their Asian neighbours and without the presence of their American protector. Moreover, ASPAC may be seen as a first step towards the development of an Asia-Pacific regional consciousness: an identity shared by Australia and Japan. Finally, the demise of ASPAC strengthened ASEAN and a narrower version of sub-regionalism, but this process has now gone full circle with the creation of ARF, and the December 2005 'East Asian Meeting', which included include both Australia and Japan.

Notes

1 M. Alagappa (ed.) *Asian Security Practice: Material and Ideational Influences*, Stanford CA: Stanford University Press, 1998, p. 640.
2 J. Halliday and G. McCormack, *Japanese Imperialism Today: Co-prosperity in Greater East Asia*, Harmondsworth: Penguin, 1973, p. 253n; J. A. C. Mackie (ed.) *Australia in the New World Order: Foreign Policy in the 1970s*, Melbourne: Nelson/Australian Institute of International Affairs, 1976, p. 88; Shibusawa; and unnamed Japanese intellectuals cited in L. Olson, *Japan in Postwar Asia*, London: Pall Mall Press/Council on Foreign Relations, 1970, p. 157.
3 H. Hinton, *Three and a Half Powers: The New Balance in Asia*, Bloomington: Indiana University Press, 1975, p.128; an unnamed Southeast Asian prime minister cited in D. Wilson, *Asia Awakes*, Harmondsworth: Penguin, 1972, p. 413 n22; and Olson, *op. cit.*, p.157.
4 P. Korhonen, *Japan and the Pacific Free Trade Area*, London: Routledge, 1994, p.153; and *Japan and Asia Pacific Integration: Pacific Romances 1968–1996*, London: Routledge, 1998, p. 45.
5 T. B. Millar, *Australia's Foreign Policy*, Sydney: Angus and Robertson, 1968, p.110.
6 J. A. Camilleri, *An Introduction to Australian Foreign Policy*, 2nd edn, Milton QLD: Jacaranda Press, 1975, p. 62; Mackie, *op. cit.*, p. 88.
7 A. Rix, *The Australia-Japan Political Alignment: 1952 to the Present*, London: Routledge, 1999, p. 157.
8 'Communist Attitudes to ASPAC', draft, no date (hereafter n.d.), A1838, 541/1/7, National Archives of Australia, Canberra (hereafter NAA).
9 McIntyre (Tokyo) to Secretary of External Affairs (Canberra) (hereafter SEA), 11 November 1964, A1838, 3103/10/1 part 10, NAA.
10 McIntyre to SEA, 7 January 1965, A1838, 541/6/1 part 1, NAA.
11 Record of Conversation, K. Takasugi and A. Tange, 30 Dec. 1964, A1838, 541/6/1 part 1, NAA. See also, Record of Conversation, Ki Nemoto and M. R. Booker, 23 November 1964, A1838, 3103/10/1 part 10, NAA.
12 Australian embassy (Seoul) to Department of External Affairs (hereafter DEA), 16 June 1966, A1838, 3103/7/1 part 5, NAA.
13 Brief for prime minister's interview with U. Nyuw, 22 September 1966, A1838, 541/1/4, NAA.
14 DEA (Canberra) to Australian embassy Tokyo, 10 June 1966, A1838, 3103/7/1 part 5, NAA.

15 Record of Conversation, Takasugi and Booker, 13 July 1966, A1838, 3103/10/1 part 12, NAA.
16 DEA to All Posts, 8 May 1970, A1838, 541/1/1 part 3, NAA.
17 A. H. Loomes (Bangkok) to SEA, 15 June 1967, A1838, 541/1/1 part 1, NAA.
18 Japan-Australia ministerial level talks, Tokyo, 29–30 March 1967, A1838, 3103/10/1 part 13, NAA.
19 Record of Conversation, Suzuki Takeo and Booker, 6 June 1967, A1838, 541/6/1 part 1, NAA.
20 F. C. Pryor (Treasury) to SEA, 9 June 1967, A1838, 541/1/1 part 1; Record of inter-departmental meeting at External Affairs, 31 May 1967, A1838, 740/4/18 part 1, NAA.
21 New Zealand embassy (Tokyo) to DEA (Wellington), 28 June 1967, A1838, 541/6/1 part 1, NAA.
22 Canadian embassy (Tokyo) to DEA (Ottawa), 13 July 1967, A9564/1, 221/4/15 part 2, NAA.
23 DEA to All Posts, 14 July 1967, A9564/1, 221/4/15 part 2, NAA.
24 Draft submission to cabinet on second Ministerial Meeting by Hasluck, 21 July 1967, A1838, 541/1/1 part 1, NAA.
25 Booker to Hasluck, n.d.; Hasluck to Edward Clark, 17 July 1967, A1838, 541/1/2 part 2, NAA.
26 J. C. Ingram to Australian mission to UN, 21 September 1967, A1838, 541/1/2 part 1, NAA.
27 To be fair, he did not underestimate the difficulties, especially in Japan where 'public opinion still lags behind official awareness of military needs'. R. M. Nixon, 'Asia after Vietnam', *Foreign Affairs*, October 1967, pp. 111–25.
28 Percival (Tokyo) to DEA, 3 August 1967; Record of Conversation, Suzuki and Ingram, 5 September 1967; Booker to Hasluck, n.d., A1838, 541/6/1 part 1, NAA.
29 Australian embassy (Washington) to DEA, 19 September 1967, A1838, 3103/11/161, part 14, NAA.
30 Booker for the minister, 8 September 1967, A1838, 541/6/1 part 1, NAA.
31 McIntyre record of prime minister of Japan meeting with Australian cabinet, 12 October 1967, A4940/1, C4682, NAA.
32 Record of Discussion at Japanese Ministry of Foreign Affairs, 7 November 1967; Record of Conversation, Fumihiko Kai and Sir Lawrence McIntyre, 8 December 1967, A1838, 541/6/1 part 2; brief for third Ministerial Meeting of ASPAC, 26 July 1968, A1838, 541/1/13 part 1, NAA.
33 Press conference in Wellington by Hasluck, 13 February 1968, A1838, 541/1/1 part 1, NAA.
34 'Japan now realized that she had to take an interest in internal security situations in Asian countries . . . and she might be coaxed into giving assistance in this field through some indirect channel'. Australian embassy (Washington) to DEA, 12 February 1968, A1838, 541/6/1 part 2, NAA.
35 Record of Conversation, C. M. Shen and Booker, 28 February 1968, A1838, 541/1/1 part 1, NAA.
36 Strategic Basis [of Australian Defence Policy], alternative draft, JSR 62/1968, 5 July 1968, A1838, TS677/3 part 13, NAA.
37 Japan for prime minister's brief, 13 May 1968, A1838, 3103/7/1 part 6, NAA.
38 M. Suich, *Melbourne Age*, 12 March 1968.
39 See, for example, *Mainichi Shimbun*, 10 March 1968; *Yomiuri Shimbun*, 18 June 1968.
40 *UPI Tokyo*, 22 June 1968.
41 *The Australian*, 29 July 1968.
42 ROK embassy (Canberra) to DEA, 23 July 1968, A1838, 541/1/13 part 1, NAA.

43 A. D. G. White (Legal and Treaties Branch) to Ingram, 24 July 1968, A1838, 541/1/13 part 1, NAA.
44 Record of Conversation, Kai and Booker, 26 July 1968, A1838, 541/6/1 part 2, NAA.
45 'The Australian delegation certainly does not suggest for a moment that ASPAC should be turned into a military alliance'. Draft All Posts Savingram on ASPAC as a regional security organisation, 8 January 1969, A1838, 541/1/13 part 2, NAA.
46 Hasluck to Waller (Washington), enclosed in J. Plimsoll to Hasluck, 2 August 1968, A1838, 541/1/1 part 2, NAA.
47 ASPAC third Ministerial Meeting report by Hasluck, 30 July – 1 August 1968, A5882/2, CO310, NAA.
48 Draft All Posts Savingram on ASPAC as a regional security organisation, 8 January 1969, A1838, 541/1/13 part 2, NAA.
49 Australian embassy (Tokyo) to DEA, 2 October 1968, A1838, 827/3/10 part 3; Australian embassy (Washington) to DEA, 26 September 1968, A1838, 3103/11/161 part 14, NAA.
50 US paper prepared for November 1968 ANZUS officials' discussions, A1838, 541/1/13 part 2; Australian embassy (Washington) to DEA, 21 November 1968, A1838, 3103/1/1 part 3, NAA. However, the head of the State Department's Japan desk felt that the change in the Japanese attitude towards ASPAC was something that should be built on, perhaps in a Pacific Council, including other developed nations. Australian embassy (Washington) to DEA, 25 November 1968, A1838, 919/12/13 part 2, NAA.
51 Australian embassy (Tokyo) to DEA, 14 November 1968, A1838, 541/1/13 part 1; Summary Record of talks between Japanese and Australian officials, 14 – 15 November 1968, A1838, 3103/10/1 part 14, NAA.
52 Australian embassy (Taipei) to DEA, 19 November 1968, A1838, 541/1/13 part 1, NAA.
53 Commonwealth Prime Ministers' Meeting in London, January 1969, Japan Brief, A1838, 3103/10/1 part 14, NAA.
54 Commonwealth Prime Ministers' Meeting in London, January 1969, Regionalism in Asia and the Pacific Brief, A1838, 541/1/13 part 2, NAA.
55 Brief for prime minister's visit to USA, March/April 1969, 13 March 1969, A1838, 541/1/13 part 2, NAA.
56 Jockel (Djakarta) to DEA, 28 March 1969; New Zealand embassy (Washington) to SEA (Wellington), 10 and 11 April 1969; Record of Conversation Prasong Buncheon and Sir James Plimsoll, 23 April 1969, A1838, 541/1/13 part 2, NAA.
57 Press conference given by minister, 5 June 1969, A1838, 3103/10/1 part 14, NAA.
58 ASPAC – fourth Ministerial Meeting, report by minister for external affairs, June 1969, A1838, 541/2/4 part 3; ASPAC brief for Japan-Australia talks, October 1970, A1838, 541/1/1 part 4, NAA.
59 ASPAC, n.d., DEA paper mid-July 1969, A1838, 541/1/13 part 2, NAA.
60 New Zealand embassy (Tokyo) to SEA (Wellington), 10 July 1969, ABHS950, W4627, 268/3/10 part 1, New Zealand Archives, Wellington.
61 Extract from minister's address to American-Australian Association, New York, 18 September 1969, A1838, 3103/7/1 part 6, NAA.
62 Australian High Commission (Wellington) to DEA, 1 August 1969, A1838, 541/4/8 part 1, NAA. Most innovative was the sixth meeting, where New Zealand's introduction of the issue of regional trade sparked enthusiastic discussion amongst most members except for Australia and Japan. DEA to All Posts, 8 May 1970, A1838, 541/1/1 part 3, NAA.
63 Shaw (New York) to DEA, 20 March 1970; position of UN groups from PIB, 1 May 1970, A1838, 541/1/1 part 3, NAA.
64 DEA to All Posts, 8 May 1970, A1838, 541/1/1 part 3, NAA.

65 ASPAC – fifth Ministerial Meeting – report by William McMahon, 17 – 19 June 1970, A5882/2, CO310, NAA.
66 Australia's views on ASPAC, Department of Foreign Affairs (hereafter DFA) paper, 9 June 1971, A1838, 541/1/1 part 4, NAA.
67 Record of fourth round of Australia-Japan official level consultations, Tokyo, 29–30 October 1970, A1838, 3103/10/1/9 part 4, NAA.
68 Australia's views on ASPAC, DFA paper, 9 June 1971, A1838, 541/1/1 part 4, NAA.
69 Policy planning paper LP 8/71, 30 June 1971, A1838, 3006/9/1; J. M. Stacey (Manila) to SFA, 30 July 1971, A1838, 541/1/13 part 2, NAA.
70 Heads of Mission Meeting, Singapore 1971, A9564/2, 251/4/1 part 1, NAA.
71 ASPAC report on sixth Ministerial Meeting, A1838, 541/2/6 part 3, NAA.
72 Record of Conversation, Narita and Whitlam, 16 July 1971, A1838, 3103/10/11/11, NAA.
73 1971 briefing on regional political cooperation: ASPAC, n.d., A1838, 541/6/1 part 3, NAA.
74 J. M. Stacey (Manila) to SFA, 30 July 1971, A1838, 541/1/13 part 2, NAA.
75 Gaimushō Gaikōshiryōkan, 'Ajia Taiheiyō Kyōgikai', *Nihon Gaikōshi Jiten*, Tokyo: Yamakawa Shuppansha, 1992, pp. 8–9.
76 First ASEAN Regional Forum, 'Chairman's statement', 25 July 1994, http://www.aseansec.org/3621.htm (accessed 19 April 2005).
77 Alagappa, *op. cit.*, p. 643.
78 Examples include the replacement of Paul Hasluck as Australia's minister for external affairs by the more ambitious Gordon Freeth, and the substitution of Aichi Kiichi by Fukuda Takeo. In the latter case, Aichi continued to attend the Ministerial Meetings when Fukuda developed a 'diplomatic illness'.

3 Japanese security perceptions of Australia

Naoko Sajima

Introduction

This chapter mainly focuses on Japanese security perceptions of Australia. Through a critical survey of the Japan's geo-strategic positions throughout history, it describes the evolution of how Japan has looked at Australia from the 1850s onwards. Both realistically and psychologically it examines the origins and developments of Japan's views of the outside world. Viewing the emerging security agendas, the chapter also highlights the security roles Japan expects of Australia. On the basis of these analyses, it concludes that a reliable security partnership between Japan and Australia in the twenty-first century is plausible.

Japan as a frontrunner in Asia: the 1850s onwards

In the traditional balance of power context, Japan viewed Australia as a natural partner of the Western powers. When the European colonial powers appeared in China, the Chinese rulers perceived them as neighbouring ethnics and permitted them to have certain protected interests, which it had given members of the Chinese-civilisation order. However, several of Japan's elites, who led the Meiji Restoration, observed that the European colonial powers had destroyed Chinese autonomy, and learnt important lessons from China's experiences. Tokyo preferred therefore to open the country on a more equal footing.[1] This was a turning point. Japan became a frontrunner of modernisation and Western-style industrialisation in Asia.

After opening up the country in the 1850s, Japan started to engage mainland China. For the Japanese, China was not a country that threatened Japan, but was rather a cultural and social master. During this time, most Japanese were surprised and disappointed to see the Europeans take control of China and felt sympathy for the Chinese people. However, the problem was that such sympathy gradually developed into a feeling of superiority towards the Chinese. Japan wanted to re-civilise the other Asian countries in accordance with Japanese manners and customs, and assume China's hitherto dominant position in Asia.[2]

The Japanese sought recognition from the European powers as a respected Asian leader. Such ambitions were encouraged by victories in the Sino-Japanese War (1894–5) and the Russo-Japanese War (1904–5). The signing of the Anglo-Japanese Alliance in 1902 advanced this desire. Accordingly, in the early twentieth century, Japan considered Australia to be an indirect ally through the pax-Britannica bond. During the First World War, the UK requested that the Japanese naval vessel *Ibuki* escort Australian and New Zealand forces to Egypt as a mission of the Anglo-Japanese alliance.[3]

Japan was very proud to be an ally of the British Empire and saw Australia and New Zealand as natural partners. Though Japan sometimes wanted to take on a paternalistic view of the Anglo-Japanese alliance, looking down on Australia – not a few Japanese referred to Australia's origins as a penal colony of the United Kingdom – Japan's contributions as an ally were offered without any hesitation.

However, even during the period of the Anglo-Japanese Alliance, Australia's attitude was one of reluctance, in comparison with that of the United Kingdom or even New Zealand.[4] Australia's traditional threat perceptions derived from its distance from Europe, cultural isolation and overwhelming fear of cultural invasion.[5] The idea of the 'Yellow Peril' did not refer to a military threat, but rather expressed a fear of Asian immigrants who might disrupt the Australian way of life. These 'xenophobic images were powerful evocations which fuelled and reinforced the nation's security neurosis'.[6]

Australia's mistrust of Japan was deeply rooted, and Australia questioned Japanese control over the Pacific. Australia had a different view of Japan from the United Kingdom, which sparked the 'Japanese problem' in Australia. This view was embedded in the Immigration Act of 1901, the 1905 National Defence League and other aspects of the White Australia policy, which impeded the realisation of the Japanese dream of equal status with the European powers.

During this period, obstacles to cooperation came mainly from Australia. Australia felt a psychological repugnance of Japan, which it loathed. However,

> the fear, hostility and suspicion that characterised Australian attitudes towards Japan in the 1920s were based on racial prejudice and ignorance rather than objective strategic analysis or any prescience of the events which were to unfold into the war in the Pacific in 1941.[7]

Feelings of profound isolation: the 1920s onwards

After the First World War, the humiliation of the White Australia policy and the 'Yellow Peril' view prevented the development of an indirect alliance between Australia and Japan. Tokyo felt that Australia got in Japan's way and subsequently felt antipathy towards Australia. Indeed, Japan's modernisation, linked with disengagement from Asia and association with Europe (*datsua'nyuo*) resulted in more harm than good, because it invited jealousy and suspicion from the West, as well as fear and hatred from Asia. Japan's primary aim of modernisation as a basis for acceptance as an international power in the Western alliance was fulfilled when the country ranked amongst the Big Five at the Versailles peace conference at the end of the First World War. But thereafter, the Japanese were inflicted with a sense of deep-felt isolation in the world, whilst failing to be respected by fellow Asians.[8] Edward Olsen has speculated:

> If the world had been ready to accord Japan the equality and fair treatment Japanese liberals sought in the post-World War I years, it would not have driven Japan into an economic and strategic corner where military fascists were able to seize control.[9]

The Japanese desire for international recognition manifested itself in a hegemonic strategy and militant approach, leading eventually to the 'Great East Asia Doctrine', which espoused a pan-Asian liberation ideology.[10] Though it was beyond Japan's capacity, most of the Japanese public believed in the idea of liberation by Asian hands and dreamt of a 'Greater East Asia Co-prosperity Sphere'.

This mission was rejected by Indochinese people who wanted self-determination, rather than control by puppet governments. However, no one can deny that 'Japan was (at least) an indirect liberator'.[11] Moreover, thousands of Japanese soldiers remained in Southeast Asia after the end of the Second World War and continued fighting against the European colonial powers.[12] Vietnam's famous General Vo Nguyen Giap, who led the resistance to Japan and defeated France and the United States, said: 'I remember, however, that some Japanese troops lost their lives when they joined our fight against France after the end of the Second World War.' He added that 'this is important to be noted in our history'.[13]

Accordingly, during the Second World War, Japan and Australia confronted each other. Japan's objective was to thwart the US–Australia line and Tokyo conducted the so-called *Hokugo-sakusen* (North Australia Operation).[14] This aimed at cutting US logistical support to Australia and targeted the huge air and sea gap of the Western Pacific. Australia was seen as a real enemy of Japan. In the Second World War Japan and Australia fought bitterly, and Australia experienced the first attack upon its soil in the history of European settlement.

Japan as a 'northern anchor' of the Western alliance: 1945 onwards

After the Second World War, security agreements with the United States were contained within the context of the Western alliance. Throughout the

Cold War period, Japan was in an alliance relationship with the United States together with Australia. This rigid bond, the so-called 'hub and spokes' links in the Asia-Pacific,[15] largely defined their strategic positions. Tokyo viewed Australia as one of the members of the West and a shareholder of the Free World.

After the war, Australia wanted reassurances against a possible resurgence of Japanese military power and ambitions. Australia's defence and security agreement with the United States, the ANZUS treaty, was bound up with such needs. When Japan was given, and accepted, the role of an ally, Australia adjusted itself to this new reality. However, 'Australia's association with Japan was not simply a matter of Australia following the United States' directions.'[16] Nonetheless, 'Japan and Australia were often referred to as the northern and southern anchors of the free world or at least the Western Pacific.'[17] This analogy clearly represented the Pentagon's view of Australia and Japan's place in the Cold War era. Japan and Australia were parallel 'anchors'. The United States treated Japan and Australia as a 'knife and fork'. Whatever they considered themselves respectively, they were 'a pair' in the United States' global strategy.

Such US assurances allowed them to develop remarkable economic linkages and deepened their relationship. Profits in the economic field were well divided between Japan and Australia. As members of the Western alliance, they shared in the economic prosperity of the 'free world'.

For Japan, Australia has one of its most reliable providers of natural resources. Without Australia's willingness to export raw materials, especially iron ore, to its former enemy, the Japanese economic recovery after the Second World War would have been delayed. The cultivation of economic relations with Australia has obviously been to the benefit of Japan.

Meanwhile, in terms of their respective roles in supporting the United States' defence posture in the Asia-Pacific, however, Japan and Australia were very different. For much of the period since the Korean War, Japan's role as a 'northern anchor' has seen it provide a major base for US forces and steadily build its defence capability in order to avoid creating a power vacuum in the Northeast Asia, where the major powers confronted each other.

However, due to constitutional limitations and domestic political constraints, Japan's defence policy was very restrained. The defence budget was limited to around 1 per cent of GNP for more than twenty years.[18] The Japanese defence budget per capita has been mostly half that of Australia.[19] In reality, the Japanese defence establishment is relatively small compared to other major countries.[20]

Australia had a more intimate alliance relationship with the United States in the fight against the threat of communism, providing forces for participation in the Korean and Vietnam wars. The hosting of important US facilities by Australia since the 1960s, at Northwest Cape, Pine Gap and Nurrungar, also confirmed Australia's status as a close ally of the United States.

In the Cold War era, each country fulfilled its security role for the US deterrence strategy in a different way as a member of the Western alliance. Though the origins of the alliances and their security perceptions throughout the Cold War period were not the same, the roles Australia and Japan played were welcomed by the United States.

Despite such links between the two countries and Australia's export dependency *vis-à-vis* Northeast Asia, it was difficult for Australia to share Japan's imminent threat perceptions. Their threat perceptions were apparently different. Therefore, as described above, they contributed to the alliance but did not jointly work for it.

Nonetheless, Japanese public perceptions of Australia were highly favourable. No doubt they reflected the relatively long, complementary trade relationship, cultural exchanges and tourism.[21]

At the same time, most Japanese, even academics, did not know the origin of the ANZUS treaty, nor did they any have an understanding of Australia's historical threat perceptions or its sensitivities.[22] Most of the younger generation in Japan were unaware that Japan and Australia had once fought each other. The only image of Australia they had was that of a place to visit on a honeymoon.

Searching for new roles: 1989 onwards

When the Cold War ended and the possibilities of a global war receded, Japan was forced to create not only new security roles as an ally but also new approaches as a regional/global contributor. Tokyo gradually came to see Australia as a co-player in regional security.

However, in spite of its enormous economic contribution, including official development assistance (ODA), Japan continued to be cautious about sharing security responsibilities in the region.[23] Japan was restrained in deals relating to regional security concerns outside the Japan–United States security relationship. The end of the Cold War brought about radical changes in the security environment but Japan could not immediately reformulate its security policies.

The first panic occurred at the time of the Gulf crisis. Japan could not respond as did other international members by participating in the multinational task force. As a result, although Japan provided US$12 billion to the cost of the war, Japan was not amongst the countries thanked by the Kuwaiti government after the crisis in a *New York Times* advertisement. This left Japan feeling more isolated in the international community than it had felt for seventy years.[24] According to Ichiro Ozawa, 'Japan suffered a serious defeat in the Gulf War period.'[25] Japanese policy-makers suddenly realised that the ideas behind its security policies, which had been firmly maintained in the 'long peace' of the Cold War, were out of date. Japan therefore began a journey in search of its own security posture and role in the post-Cold War world.

However, past Japanese behaviour has constrained Japan's attitude towards regional political engagement. Tokyo has been very hesitant to participate in the new regional framework because of the fear that its intentions might be misunderstood by its neighbours. Actually, as long as the Japanese defence build-up occurred within the context of the US alliance, it did not stimulate a regional arms race. Because the US Seventh Fleet has guaranteed Japan's trade routes through the South China Sea for almost fifty years, Japan's restrained defence build-up over this lengthy period has eased the region's suspicions of it. These views are not pleasant for the Japanese, but cannot be ignored. As Singapore's elder statesman Lee Kuan Yew noted, as long as the United States–Japan security relationship remains viable, Asian states need not fear a major Japanese naval or air build-up to protect Japan's maritime trade routes and access to Persian Gulf oil. They believe that for this Japan has foregone the development of its own power-projection capacity, specifically aircraft carriers and long-range bombers.[26] As long as Japan does not develop an independent long-range force-projection capacity, Korea and China will be less tempted to strike out with their own forces.[27] Therefore, the Japanese security aim must be a part of the global strategy of the United States. When Japan has restricted its own defence posture, and at least as long as Tokyo's security intentions have been within the framework of alliance activities, Japan's neighbours have accepted it.[28]

It is difficult for Japan to undertake security initiatives unilaterally. However, in order to avoid such biased views on the part of its neighbours and to normalise relations with them, Japan's security activities are to be rationally regulated within the regional framework and supported by other partners in the region. Japan needs alternative comrades-in-arms.

By chance, the Cambodian peace process, which was encouraged by the change in the international climate, forced Japan to take drastic measures to improve the situation. Both Japan and Australia, as regional major actors, need to not only show political leadership but also make peacekeeping efforts.[29]

Though Japanese academic attitudes were very hesitant and public opinion was divided, in 1992, the government finally enunciated the 'Basic Guidelines for Japan's Participation in Peacekeeping Forces' (the so-called Five Principles) and dispatched the Self Defence Forces to the United Nations Transitional Authority in Cambodia (UNTAC). It was the first time that Japan had participated in international peacekeeping activities. Through the Cambodian peace initiative, Australia and Japan demonstrated that their cooperation could help to establish peace and stability in the region.

However, under the Guidelines, the Self Defense Force's (SDF) involvement in UN peacekeeping operations conducted under the International Peace Cooperation Law may never entail the use of force or the dispatch of armed forces to foreign countries for the purpose of using force, this being prohibited by Article 9 of the Constitution.

Meanwhile, Australia had made the more explicit and visible moves from the Cold War scenario to set up new and complementary arrangements. Australia, during the early to mid-1990s, desired to build further on its growing economic links with Asia. In fact, Australia started a post-Cold War reorientation of its defence posture earlier than any other country in the region.

Prior to the early 1970s, Australia's operational force deployments were carried out in support of the United States. However, such policies of forward defence and dependence upon the United States were abandoned soon after the announcement of the 'Nixon Doctrine' in February 1970, and were replaced by a policy of self-reliance.[30] Thereafter, Australia began a shift from Cold War strategic thinking to focusing primarily on the defence of Australia.[31] In the 1987 White Paper, *The Defence of Australia*, the core of Australia's defence policy was the concept of self-reliant defence for credible contingencies. Concurrently, Australian defence policy became more closely integrated with constructive engagement with Asia.[32]

In addition, since the Cold War concept of a Western strategic community receded, Australia tried to take more independent initiatives and became more influential in the region. Gareth Evans, the Minister for Foreign Affairs and Trade (1988–96), consistently suggested developing a new pattern of security cooperation amongst various countries in the region.[33] Subsequently, Australia has sought to go beyond bilateral linkages to develop an interlocking web of contacts, dialogue arrangements and cooperative strategies in Southeast Asia. Moreover, in July 1990, Senator Evans proposed a conference on security and cooperation in Asia, which became the Council for Security Cooperation in the Asia-Pacific (CSCAP) – analogous to the European CSCE – and developed proposals for the reduction of US naval forces in the Pacific. Though these CSCAP proposals did not eventuate, Australia had encouraged a multilateral framework for security dialogue in the region, not only by utilising the existing framework of economic cooperation such as the Asia-Pacific Economic Cooperation (APEC) for that purpose, but also by enthusiastically assisting the foundation of the ASEAN Regional Forum (ARF) in 1994. Consequently, *Strategic Review 1993* set the process of adapting Australia's strategic and defence policies to the post-Cold War world and *Defending Australia: Defence White Paper 1994* emphasised further close multilateral and bilateral engagement with the region.[34] One area in the defence White Paper clearly influenced by the government's emphasis on regional engagement was defence cooperation with Indonesia.[35] This policy reached a climax when the Australia-Indonesia Agreement on Maintaining Security was signed in December 1995.[36]

Australia looked like the only country in the region with enough capacity to cope with readjustment to the new environment. Australia was already experienced in the field of international security, which Japan sought to emulate. Being restricted in a military sense, Japan's comprehensive diplomatic approach looked significant domestically and yet internationally hesitant. Japan's insufficient military knowledge and experience made it naive, whilst Australia was confident.

Moreover, as Japan needed to pay considerable attention to its neighbours, building security relations with them became very delicate work. On the contrary, from Tokyo's perspective, it did not need to be as cautious in its dealings with Australia. Tokyo thought that Australia might be in a similar position in the Asia-Pacific region. Because of Australia's status as a descendant of a colonial power, Japan could develop relations without the need to exercise as much caution as it did in its relations with its Asian neighbours. These ideas were very common amongst academics who were familiar with Australia. A distinguished Japanese academic, Watanabe, once stated:

> A more challenging problem before us is how to overcome the tyranny of not geographical but cultural distance, because if the clash of civilisations, particularly that between the East and the West (or a New Cultural Cold War) is permitted to develop, the future will be very gloomy indeed for all mankind but especially for such nations as Japan and Australia. However difficult it may be, we have to work out a formula of peaceful and creative coexistence between the East and the West. Australia and Japan can be ideal colleagues in pursuing that important goal.[37]

In reality, Australia was concerned with the legacies of the past more than the Japanese and did not welcome such suggestions.[38]

Especially for Japanese defence and security officials, strategic linkages which had been unconsciously established between Japan and Australia, gradually became valuable remnants of the Cold War. These ties not only benefited Australia and Japan but also produced a sense of security for both countries' Asian neighbours. Tokyo assumed that within the framework of 'indirect alliances', neighbours might not misinterpret Japan's security intentions.[39] In that sense, Australia's acknowledgement of Japan seemed very important, not only for Japan but also for the region as a whole.

Above all, though Japan and Australia did not fight together against common enemies during the Cold War period, the strategic relationship between the two countries was clear and still well managed in the global context. With the end of the Cold War, the principal common threat against Japan and Australia disappeared. However, this did not mean the disappearance of common ground for Japan and Australia in maintaining their own peace. There was already a close economic relationship and common interests had been cultivated in various fields. There were also several firm reasons for Japan to believe that strategic cooperation with Australia might favourably work in the post-Cold War world.

In the post-Cold War era, from the Japanese perspective, there existed common security ground where Japan and Australia were able to work together in order to maintain their common interests in a new strategic environment. However, despite this mutual interest, until the mid-1990s there was still a significant difference in each country's approach to regional security.[40] In 1995, the author published a monograph entitled *Japan and Australia: A New Security Partnership?* from the Strategic and Defence Studies Centre at the Australian National University. Many Australian colleagues were sceptical of the working paper's conclusions. Only a few showed interest in such a 'unique approach' but cited various obstacles, particularly 'historical legacies'.[41]

In this context, the Australian Labor government was very keen to take initiatives, while a new multilateral regime, which Australia idealistically pursued, was never established. On the contrary, Asia-Pacific regionalism corrupted the idea before it materialised. From the early 1990s, Japan and Australia have individually searched for ways to cope with the uncertainties and uneasiness of the post-Cold War world.

Japan as a responsible player: 1996 onwards

Unlike Europe and even other parts of the Asia-Pacific, tensions were still high in Northeast Asia in the 1990s. Russian forces in the Far East still possessed tremendous military capabilities. These included weapons Russia transferred from west of the Urals and others relocated from Eastern Europe after the Conventional Armed Forces in Europe (CFE) treaty took effect.[42] Russia's armed forces have undergone reform, but both the Japanese Defense Agency and the Pentagon observed that future military trends might be uncertain. On the Korean peninsula too, tension had heightened over North Korea's suspected development of nuclear weapons and its research and development on extending the range of a surface-to-surface missile, the *Nodong*.[43] Such developments could be destabilising not only in Northeast Asia, but also in the Asia-Pacific region.

Therefore, after a long period of debate, the United States declared in early 1995 that the presence of US forces in the region, comprising approximately 100,000 personnel, would be maintained through the beginning of the twenty-first century.[44] Having accepted this, the Japanese government decided to continue shouldering expenses for the stationing of US forces to increase the reliability of the Japan-United States Security Treaty.[45]

Then, in April 1996, the Japan-US Joint Declaration on Security, which showed the direction of bilateral cooperation for the twenty-first century, was signed at the Japan-US summit meeting in Tokyo. Thus, affirmation of the role of the alliance in the post-Cold War era was settled. As Article VI of the Japan-United States Security Treaty stated, the treaty's second objective was to contribute to the maintenance of international peace.[46] Observers recognised that the treaty was not only a military alliance but aimed at broader mutual cooperation between Japan and the United States.

Moreover, following the reaffirmation by the Joint Declaration of the role played by the Japan-US partnership in the maintenance of peace and stability in the Asia-Pacific region, the two countries formulated the new 'Guidelines for Japan-US Defence Cooperation' in 1997. In order to ensure the effectiveness of the guidelines, Japan enacted the 'Law Concerning Measures to Ensure the Peace and Security of Japan in Situations in Areas Surrounding Japan'. Through these agreements, the two countries have studied joint defence planning for armed attacks against Japan and cooperative planning for situations in areas surrounding Japan. Furthermore, Japan established the Coordination Mechanism which aimed to coordinate the respective activities of the two countries in emergencies.[47]

At the same time, the conservative Australian Liberal government, which came to power in 1996, started to redefine its position as an ally of the US. It publicly supported American naval intervention in the showdown between China and Taiwan during the latter's presidential election in March, and it offered to pre-position American military weapons and supplies on Australian soil. In December, the 'Sydney Declaration', which reaffirmed the Australia–US security relationship, was announced.[48] Indeed, a majority of 'ordinary Australians' who supported the conservatives in the election, including prime minister John Howard, thought that the Labor government's use of regional multilateral forums during the early to mid-1990s did not produce the expected outcomes, namely both regional integration and acceptance as a regional power.

Former prime minister Paul Keating (1991–6) wanted Australia to be considered an Asian country in regional multilateral forums. However, Labor's idea of finding a path towards security 'with Asia not against Asia'[49] has not eventuated to the degree that it could have during the early to mid-1990s. In late 1995 when Senator Evans was asked if 'Asia' might include Australia, he definitely said 'I believe, yes'. In March 1996, regrettably, when the first Asia-Europe Meeting (ASEM) was held, Australia was excluded, despite its enthusiastic efforts to be included. Up to 2005, Australia has been an outsider of ASEM.[50]

The Howard government published its first defence White Paper, *Australia's Strategic Policy*, in 1997 and showed a strong willingness to revive traditional security approaches, namely to place a great deal of weight on the bilateral US alliance.[51] Importantly, the Asian economic crisis of 1997 devastated many regional economies, causing political and economic instability throughout the region. Consequently, there was a feeling of drift in Australia's past Asian diplomacy. This was reflected in a number of the prime minister's foreign policy pronouncements, including the observation that Australia acted as America's 'deputy sheriff' following its successful leadership of the International Force East Timor (INTERFET) mission in 1999.[52] However, spearheading East Timor's liberation from Indonesia damaged official relations with Indonesia.

There was a steady diminution of regional multilateralism after 1997. This, combined with increased regional instability, meant that it was important to be able to act as facilitators for US military diplomacy, in order to maintain and enhance East Asia's geopolitical *status quo ante*. This sentiment was shared by both Japan and Australia in the late 1990s.

Therefore, to step up policy cooperation and coordination, bilateral security links between Japan and Australia were urgently needed. The first Japan–Australia politico-military talks were officially started in 1996, after several unofficial meetings. Various defence exchange programs, including 'high-level defence officials', 'regular consultations between defence officials' and 'unit to unit defence exchange' have also been promoted to date.[53]

In sum, Australia expected to be a regional initiator but suffered from isolation. During this period, Japan cautiously converted itself from a hesitant (doubtful) flatterer to a responsible player and saw Australia in a similar light. Japan's irresolute attitudes and Australia's rough-and-ready methods finally came together. The so-called 'historical legacies' or remnants of the past did not prevent bilateral rapprochement.

Fighting together: 2001 onwards

Following the major terrorist strikes against the United States on 11 September 2001, Japan, led by Prime Minister Junichiro Koizumi, deployed the Maritime Self Defense Force (MSDF) to the Indian Ocean in support of US and British operations in Afghanistan.[54] Koizumi, who came to office in March 2001, supported the United States' war on terrorism. Though Japan could not participate in the war against Iraq in 2003 due to constitutional reasons, after the war, in early 2004, Koizumi showed strong leadership and dispatched around 600 troops to Iraq. Their mission was humanitarian assistance but it was the first time the Ground Self Defense Force (GSDF) had operated in a combat zone. Similarly, Australia aggressively assisted President George W. Bush and his war on terror. Australia deployed special forces troops to Afghanistan (2001) and Iraq (2003). In addition, the horrific attacks of October 2002 in Bali, in which many Australian tourists lost their lives, accelerated Canberra's enthusiasm for a defence restructuring process in order to tackle the new threat of terrorism.[55]

Now, both Japan and Australia are most significant participants in 'a coalition of the willing', led by the United States. In Iraq, the humanitarian activities of SDF troops are protected by Australian and British forces, which are committed to the internal security of Iraq.[56] This collaboration reminds one of the glory years of the Anglo-Japanese Alliance.

Meanwhile, Japan and Australia worked together and contributed not only to the alliance but also to the region. In the case of the East Timor crisis in 1999, Japan was unable to participate in INTERFET activities because of constitutional restrictions, but from February 2002, in response to a request to participate in peacekeeping operations (PKO) by the United Nations Transitional Administration in East Timor (UNTAET), Tokyo dispatched its largest SDF unit. In December 2001, Japan amended the 'International Peace Cooperation Law' to lift the suspension on the SDF's participation in the core operations of peacekeeping forces.

Furthermore, given their strong concerns regarding WMD and missile proliferation, both Japan and Australia participate in the Proliferation Security Initiative (PSI), which President Bush announced in Poland in May 2003. Additionally, both governments have approved participation in the US ballistic missile defence plan, though no decision has yet been made on the specific details regarding their participation. In 1998, Japan decided to begin joint Japan–US technical research on a sea-based upper-tier missile defence system, and the Howard government signed up to participate on 4 December 2003.[57]

In the post-September 11 world, Japanese and Australian security activities, both as allies of the United States and as regional actors, have become closer than ever. Both Japan and Australia are great contributors to the 'coalition of the willing' and their security linkages are direct and close. Their defence cooperation works so well that Japanese security perspectives of Australia in total have become very positive. However, though they are called 'little NATO', their security roles are independently organised. Indeed, despite the considerable security links between two, to date, the arrangements are irregular.

Beyond anchors

Australia's positive attributes

From a Japanese perspective, Australia's geopolitical environment has several positive features compared with Japan. Indeed, Australia has the time and margin to plan new external policies[58] and can be supported by a defence-in-depth strategy,[59] while Japan has little depth in defence strategy and its diplomatic options are limited. Japan does not have the same time and margin to afford it a generous view as does Australia. Japan's external policy must be pragmatic, given the continuing pressure to maintain standards of living.

From Tokyo's viewpoint, Australia's possesses the following geopolitical advantages.[60] First, the Australian Defence Force doctrine is very flexible in adapting to the emerging environment. As there are not any legal restrictions on its activities, defence decisions are made through controversial yet open debates. Conversely, Japan has various political constraints on the activities of the SDF, which will be described later.

Second, because of its long history of deploying troops abroad, the Australian public is very supportive and has confidence in the military. In June 2000, when the Howard government pursued a new defence build-up and tried expanding the Australian Defence Force's roles, the government's nationwide campaign was largely welcomed and accepted by the public.[61] Simultaneously, Japan started reviewing its strategic outlook from the mid-1990s. The government endorsed the New Defence Outline in 1995 and revised it in 2004. However, Japanese public attitudes are very dull, the media's reaction is sceptical and only few academics are interested in it. It will take some time to develop the New Defence Outline and attract nation-wide support.[62]

Third, Australia's regional approach in the security field did not refer to a critical threat but instead aimed to promote an environment which sustains a stable pattern of strategic relationships and avoids destabilising competition.[63] The 'results [of this defence diplomacy] have undoubtedly been quite positive in terms of increasing trust, reducing the likelihood of misperceptions and misunderstandings, promoting constructive security discourses and modalities, and improving the regional security environment', though this entails performance costs. For example, even during and after the East Timor crisis, defence relations between Australia and Indonesia were well managed and contributed to a stable nation-to-nation relationship.[64] Whilst Japan has hesitantly started dialogue with some regional countries from the mid-1990s,[65] with certain exceptions, the achievements of these programs are not clearly appreciated.[66]

Fourth, in the context of the relationship with the United States, Australia's defence alliance looks very stable. At least, they appear to be getting along better than Japan and the United States. As the stationing of US forces in Japan (USFJ) has continued since the defeat of Japan in the Second World War, the negative images of the occupying forces and the accompanying sense of resentment have remained amongst the Japanese public. As the Japan-United States Security Treaty's military aim is primarily limited to defending Japanese territory,[67] Japan is providing exclusive use of its land to the US in order to meet its reciprocal obligations to defend the United States. However, Japanese sovereignty does not fully extend to the personnel of USFJ, thus it is difficult for the local police to investigate crimes committed by US soldiers. These crimes are annually in excess of 1,000 cases and frequently cast a shadow over the Japan-US relationship. In addition to the evident complexity of this alliance, the cultural gap and linguistic misinterpretations sometimes heighten tensions. On the other hand, while Australia-US security relations are codified by the ANZUS treaty,[68] there is no threat of cultural difference or linguistic misinterpretation.[69]

Fifth, in the global context, Australia's substantial alliance and peace-keeping experience in the framework of the United Nations has brought operational credibility to its forces. Though the Japanese Self-Defense Forces have achieved excellent results through their recent activities abroad, their means are restricted. Even as Japan gradually broadens the geographic scope of its participation in peacekeeping efforts, the 'International Peace Cooperation Law', which was passed in 1992, permits only very small numbers of armed forces to be dispatched abroad and their range of activities is extremely limited, including an outright prohibition on a direct combat role. Moreover, as the SDF has never been in battle, its real combat capabilities are still unknown.

Sixth, Australia has a unique historical relationship as a result of the Five Power Defence Arrangements (FPDA). Though the FPDA is a more limited arrangement than an alliance, it makes Australia's potential military capabilities more versatile. Australia has access to the forces of several other nations to bolster its deterrence. Japan does not have this option. For Japan, the United States is the first and only partner in the security field. In short, Australia has various security means and is well prepared to contribute to peace and stability in the region. In this context, it has advantages over Japan.

Australia's constructive roles

Accordingly, Australia has four major constructive security roles to play, which may encourage Japanese security reforms in the twenty-first century. First, Australia's response to the US military presence and to Japan's security situation is of greater importance than for Australia's own defence. Though the US military presence does not directly contribute towards the defence of Australia, as long as the ANZUS treaty is based on the presence of US forces in the Pacific,[70] and as long as Australia's primary interest in the alliance lies in continuing to engage US military interests in the Asia-Pacific region, the security relationship between Australia and the United States should be balanced to reinforce the Japan-United States security relationship. With regard to security issues, during the Cold War period, Japan could ask the countries of NATO to take on a similar role to a Western ally. However, since the end of Cold War, NATO countries no longer play the same roles. 'The ANZUS [treaty's] most compelling rationale, taken in conjunction with the preservation of the Japan-US connection, yielded a deep trough of regional reassurances.'[71] Japan would prefer to adjust to the anticipated US military 'transformation' in cooperation with Australia. Japan would be grateful if Australia could shoulder some of the burden of providing bases for US forces, particularly from Okinawa. In a sense, it is only Australia that can help mediate the dispute between Japan and the United States if it arises because Australia still has the status of an ANZUS partner. Given its close relationship with both countries and the capacity to deal with both, Australia can devise policies which may blunt the friction between Washington and Tokyo. If the importance of the Japan-United States security relationship in the broader Asia-Pacific context is continuously upheld by a power like Australia, it surely has more credence. But if Australia should assess the necessity of the US presence in the region in terms of its own defence and try to replace the United States in playing the role of a stabiliser, this assessment would dangerously extend it beyond its capacity.

Second, Australia can assist and hasten Japan's process of determining a new defence posture. Under the post-September 11 circumstances, Japan has just started the process of defence re-orientation. The *2004 Outline* will recast the role of the SDF from a force dedicated to defending Japanese territory to a force equally capable of performing various missions, such as UN PKO and internal security functions, dealing with large-scale natural

disasters and terrorism.[72] Japan's defence objective has long been to maintain a capacity sufficient to deal with 'limited and small-scale aggression'. As
a result of constitutional constraints and political considerations amongst
the major countries, Japan's capacity has always been limited, even during
the Cold War period. This concept, the so-called 'basic and standard
defence capability as an independent state', was mentioned in the 1996
Outline. However, the *2004 Outline* pays more attention to various kinds of
risks or dangers that lurk in an unstable and unpredictable situation. This
could mean new missions, new modernisation priorities and new ways of
thinking about defence and national security. The Japanese SDF is now
staking a claim to a range of non-traditional military missions that include
low-intensity conflict operations. However, these new missions are similar to
those being developed by Australia.[73] Japan may face difficulties similar
to those Australia has faced or may face in its transition. These include
budgetary pressures and heavy expenditure on new capital equipment. There
will be demographic difficulties in attracting recruits,[74] in maintaining the
morale of military forces in an uncertain security environment and in
providing capable reserve forces for less credible, but possible contingencies.
These requirements will compete with a popular demand for military reduc-
tions, which means that the SDF will have to seek new ways of maintaining
military effectiveness with smaller forces. In this context, there are possibilities that the Australian Defence Force management process may provide a
model for Japan. Japan can learn much from Australia's defence restructuring experiences through strengthening links in the security field.
Australia, with its broad experience in military activities, including UN
PKO, needs to appreciate Japan's inexperience in some areas. As new
projects for missile defence systems highlight commonalities, there might be
other possibilities for cooperation.

Third, Australia's national security policy of constructive engagement
envisages not only a traditional military role but also incorporates diplomatic relations, economic cooperation and development assistance,
measures against non-military threats (drugs, refugees, etc.) and reciprocal
exchanges of military personnel. Australia's military links, such as cooperative air and maritime exercises with ASEAN countries and, more recently,
the hosting of combined military exercises in Australia for regional nations,
is instructive for Northeast Asia. The development of security relations
between Indonesia and Australia is an appropriate example, which Japan
and South Korea could pursue in order to overcome obstacles to future
cooperation. Australia does not advocate a wider military role for Japan, but
a process in which Japan's strategic posture is blended more with that of
other regional players. There is a wide range of reassuring measures that
Japan and Australia could take as regional leaders promoting regional security. This cooperation could begin as a phased approach to longer-term
goals, but in the shorter term would include continuing, perhaps with more
frequency, existing measures such as joint training, personnel exchanges,

joint research and joint UN PKO studies. This cooperation would not be with a view to combined operations, but rather it would provide an example to other countries in the region of confidence-building in action.

Fourth, Japan expects that it could share both regional and global intelligence, as well as cooperating in information-gathering operations with Australia. Australia has an advantage in that it possesses intelligence links with the UK and other international organisations and may contribute to enhancing anti-terrorism measures in the region.

In sum, both countries could work more effectively and reliably by balancing with the United States and the region. In this context, as stated, the US military transformation would not need to be respectively arranged but jointly coordinated by Japan and Australia. As South Korea's reliance on the United States has lessened, because of its anti-American/anti-Japanese sentiments, the partnerships of Japan and Australia with the United States have become more important than before. Because the complex domestic political situation makes it difficult for South Korean policy-makers to focus solely on the US alliance,[75] the Japan–US and ANZUS alliances may be well placed to take regional initiatives. Australia could evolve from a dependent ally to a self-reliant regional initiator. Japan could evolve from an obedient ally – a free rider – to a regional security player. For that purpose, both need to become more interoperable not only through the United States but also directly with each other. However, as Japan could not cope with non-traditional threats by traditional means, various approaches might be welcomed. Not only traditional collective defence approaches, which have been prohibited by Japan's Constitution, but some case-by-case arrangements of coalition activities, such as those evaluated within FPDA, seem applicable to Japan-Australia security relations.[76]

Conclusion: beyond anchors

The *Defense of Japan 2004* stated:

> Australia, which shares the same fundamental democratic values such as respect for freedom and human rights with Japan, is an important partner for Japan in the Asia-Pacific region. On the security front, both countries being allies of the United States, share their same strategic interest, and there are many issues of mutual concern in the area of defense. In this context, it is important for Japan to promote defense exchanges with Australia, deepen mutual understanding and mutual confidence, and step up policy cooperation and coordination, in order to secure peace and stability in the Asia-Pacific region.

This is the first time that the *Defense of Japan,* the Japanese annual defence White Paper, which has been published since the 1970s, has devoted a section to Australia and described the importance of its security links.[77]

Indeed, 'Japan and Australia have had an indirect alliance for more than seventy years'.[78] This indirect alliance is not only a product of the Cold War but also the result of geopolitical strategies. In the early twentieth century, Australia was a similar indirect ally of Japan through the pax-Britannica bond. Regrettably, the changing strategic environment after the First World War led to the breakup of this relationship. However, Japan has maintained a common ground with Australia in the post-Cold War world and is now trying to strengthen bilateral ties.

As long as international order exists, as long as it involves the Asia-Pacific nations and as long as it provides security assurance to the region, Japan, the front runner of Asian economic modernisation, could take on greater regional responsibilities with Australia.

In the decade following the end of the Cold War, Japan has eagerly evaluated its role as an ally of the US and is now developing bilateral security relations with Australia. Furthermore, international security trends after the September 11 terrorist attacks have encouraged these developments. Now, two bilateral alliances, namely the Japan-US security arrangement and ANZUS, are contributing to the creation of a trilateral security relationship. Security collaboration between Japan, Australia and the United States has been variously described by commentators as a relationship of 'anchoring triliteralism',[79] a 'little NATO' or 'shadow alliance'[80] in the region. Consequently, security relations between Japan and Australia are very important factors for the future strategic climate of the Asia-Pacific region.

In reality, from a Japanese security perspective, Australia can play several constructive roles. Though Japan is the most modernised, democratised and developed country in the region, despite its enormous economic power, Japan lacks security experience and is hesitant to pursue such initiatives alone. Japan needs to understand better the merit of closer security relations to offset its lack of military experience in the security environment and in the international community. Conversely, in spite of its relatively small economy, Australia has various security means. Australia is well prepared to contribute to peace and stability in the post-September 11 world. If Australia does not limit its strategic involvement to the military context but adopts a comprehensive security approach, there are many opportunities to contribute to Japan's new security dimensions. Should Australia realise the importance of Japan, Australia can support the Japanese in their challenge to emulate Australia's global and regional experiences.

Without Australia's understanding and cooperation, Japan will have difficulty shouldering greater responsibility. In the post-September 11 world, there appears to be some need for Japan to establish more direct security relations with Australia, although there are still various limits on its going beyond the *status quo ante*. In addition, there are indications of a few perception gaps between the two, such as that pertaining to China's intentions.[81]

However, Japan has already shared some security experiences with Australia such as in Cambodia, East Timor and Iraq. These achievements were all short-term but promoted mutual cooperation. Therefore, their links may be enhanced not only within a traditional alliance context but also within the framework of various arrangements on an individual basis. In other words, just as NATO is undergoing transition from a Cold War-era organisation to a useful military mechanism for both global and regional purposes, Japan and Australia might also shift away from being 'northern and southern anchors' to important security partners of a democratic community in the Asia-Pacific region. In building this new 'Pacific Pact', the author appreciates that Japan, instead of being considered a threat, will emerge as one of the region's credible partners. The community of JANZUS (Japan and ANZUS) might be a first step in this direction. Through these processes, Japan and Australia will consequently establish a more reliable security partnership. In order to sustain their existing bonds, at the Australia-Japan summit meeting in April 2005, both prime ministers emphasised that they must strengthen relations in order to contribute to establishing global peace as well as stability in the region.[82] Now in 2005, Australia looks to be a highly appropriate partner for Japan, and relations between the two countries might pave the way for a wider Japanese security role in the region.

Notes

1 See details in N. Sajima, 'Japan: Strategic culture at a crossroads', in K. Booth and R. Trood (eds) *Strategic Cultures in the Asia-Pacific Region*, London: Macmillan, 1999, pp. 69–91.
2 M. Uchiyama, 'The Sino-Japanese War (1894–95): A re-evaluation after 100 years', issue on 'Japan's Wartime Diplomacy and the Post-war Visions', *International Relations*, vol. 109, May 1995, 141–9.
3 Ever since, a scale model of the *Ibuki* has been on exhibition in the Wellington Maritime Museum, with the inscription: 'Thank you for your friendship'. The Wellington Maritime Museum is located at Queen's Wharf, Wellington, New Zealand.
4 See A. Dupont, *Australia's Threat Perceptions: A Search for Security*, Canberra Papers on Strategy and Defence no. 82, Canberra: Strategic and Defence Studies Centre, Australian National University, 1991, pp. 10–11.
5 See G. Blainey, *The Tyranny of Distance: How Distance Shaped Australia's History*, Melbourne: Sun Books, 1967.
6 Dupont, *op. cit.*, p.92.
7 D. Ball, 'Australia's strategy for Asia-Pacific security', paper prepared for an international conference entitled 'Asia-Pacific Collective Security in the Post-Cold War Era', co-sponsored by ISODARCO and the Institute for National Policy Research (INPR), Taipei, held in Taipei, Republic of China, on 12–14 April 1995, p. 4.
8 See A. Watanabe, 'Japan and Australia: A comparison of their strategies for coexistence with Asia and America', in P. King and Y. Kibata (eds) *Peace Building in Asia-Pacific Region*, St Leonards NSW: Allen and Unwin, 1996, pp. 6–15; B. D. Porter, *War and the Rise of the State: The Military Foundations of Modern Politics*, New York: Macmillan, 1994, pp. 146–7.
9 E. A. Olsen, 'The evolution of Japan's security policy options', in Y. W. Kihl and L. E. Grinter (eds) *Security, Strategy, and Policy Responses in the Pacific Rim*, Boulder CO: Lynne Rienner, 1989, p. 126.

10 Regarding the concept of Great East Asian Doctrine, see A. Irie, *Power and Culture: The Japanese-American War 1941–1945*, Cambridge MA: Harvard University Press, 1979, pp.120–1; J. C. Lebra (ed.) *Japan's Greater East Asia Co-prosperity Sphere in World War II: Selected Readings and Documents*, New York: Oxford University Press, 1975; S. Hatano, 'Foreign Minister Shigemitsu Mamoru and the Greater East Asian Declaration of 1943', *International Relations*, vol. 109, May 1995, 38–53; T. Sakai, 'The political economy of the new East Asian Declaration of 1943', *International Relations*, vol. 97, May 1991, 51–66.

11 This view was presented by Henry Frei at the History Conference, '1945: War and Peace in the Pacific', at the Australian National University on 28 September 1995.

12 For example, more than 3,000 Japanese troops joined the Viet Minh and lost their lives fighting for the Vietnamese at the battle of Dien Bien Phu in 1954. One of those Japanese officers was promoted to a major-general in the Vietnamese army. This view was presented by Ikuhiko Hata at the history conference, '1945: War and Peace in the Pacific' at the Australian National University on 28 September 1995.

13 *Asahi Evening News*, 10–11 December 1994.

14 See details in *Senshi Sosho*, the War History series, which is a series of 102 volumes, and was compiled by the Military History Department on the History of World War II. The compilation was conducted from 1966 through 1980. Although the *Senshi Sosho* has already gone out of print, it is available for public reading at the Military Archival Library at the National Institute for Defense Studies, Japan.

15 In this monograph, the Asia-Pacific is mostly defined in the same way as the Western Pacific, including Northeast Asia, Southeast Asia, Australia and New Zealand.

16 R. Dalrymple, 'Japan and Australia as anchors: Do the chains still bind?', in King and Kibata, *op. cit.*, p. 41.

17 Ibid., pp. 38–52.

18 Ibid., pp. 122–3.

19 See, annually published by the International Institute for Strategic Studies, *The Military Balance*, London: Oxford University Press.

20 Japanese governments since 1954 – when the SDF was established – have interpreted the framework of Article 9 as follows:

> As long as Japan is a sovereign state, it is recognised that the provisions of Article 9 do not deny Japan's inherent right of self-defence. Since this right is not denied, Japan maintains the armed strength necessary to exercise self-defence. In accordance with an exclusively defence-oriented policy, Japan can maintain self-defence strength as an armed organisation, and take steps to improve self-defence capabilities and to ensure their efficient operation.

With such constitutional restrictions, Japan has secured civilian control over the military; resolved the Ban on Military Dispatch Abroad in 1954; adhered to the three Non-Nuclear Principles in 1967 (not possessing nuclear weapons, not producing them and not permitting their introduction in Japan); and maintained an exclusive defence-oriented policy. 'Not to become a military power' has come to be a fixed line of national policy.

21 R. Garnaut, *Australia and the Northeast Asian Ascendancy*, Canberra: Australian Government Publishing Service, 1990, pp. 324–6.

22 It was in 1981 that the first comprehensive literature of Australia-Japan relations was published in Japan. See 'The Historical Evolution of Australia-Japan Relations', in The Japan Association of International Relations (ed.) *International Relations No. 68*, Tokyo: Yuhikaku, 1981.

23 See 'Japanese hesitancies and struggles over its international contributions during the Gulf crisis', in P. Polomka, *Japan as Peacekeeper: Samurai State, or New Civilian Power?*, Canberra Papers on Strategy and Defence no. 97, Canberra: Strategic and Defence Studies Centre, Australian National University, 1991; J. S. Maswood, 'The regional context of Japanese security', in V. Selochan (ed.) *Security in the Asia-Pacific Region: The Challenge of a Changing Environment*, Canberra: Australian Defence Studies Centre, Australian Defence Force Academy, 1993, pp.151–67.

24 Some scholars suggest that an overly self-conscious attitude towards the international community stems from the traditional Japanese attitude to the village, which required the harmonious behaviour of each member.

25 A. Milner (ed.) *Perceiving 'National Security'*, Australian-Asian Perceptions Project Working Paper no. 5, Academy of the Social Sciences in Australia, Canberra, 1994, pp. 15–16.

26 S. W. Simon, 'East Asian security: The playing field has changed', *Asian Survey*, vol. XXXIV, no. 12, December 1994, 1052.

27 Cited in ibid.

28 These situations were exactly the same as those of Italy and Germany. Both countries have self-restricted their military capacities and must limit their activities within those of an alliance, namely the North Atlantic Treaty Organization (NATO). However, after the end of Cold War, in the European theatre, together with the so-called European process, the NATO has demographically and geographically expanded. In fact, these expansions of NATO have caused a number of controversies in Italy and Germany. Nonetheless, they could have collaborated with other NATO counties to cope with these agendas. Conversely, Japan has been alone.

29 See the process and the result of UNTAC in H. Smith (ed.) *International Peacekeeping: Asian and Regional Perspectives*, Canberra: Australian Defence Studies Centre, Australian Defence Force Academy, 1993.

30 Ball, *op. cit.*, pp. 4–5.

31 *The 1975 Strategic Basis Paper* asserted the concept of the 'core force' (to be 'a force able to undertake peacetime tasks, a force sufficiently versatile to deter or cope with the range of low-level contingencies which have sufficient credibility, and a force with relevant skills and equipment capable of timely expansion to deter or meet a developing situation'), and the 'core force' concept soon proved to be an insufficient basis for effective defence planning. The *1976 Defence White Paper* clearly recognised that simply to defend Australia required forces able to be deployed over long distances and to operate in areas with limited infrastructure. See S. Woodman, 'Australian security planning at the crossroads: The challenge of the nineties', Working Paper no. 271, Canberra: Strategic and Defence Studies Centre, Australian National University, 1993, pp. 4–6.

32 Department of Defence, *The Defence of Australia 1987*, Canberra: Australian Government Publishing Service, 1987, p. 1.

33 G. Evans, *Australia's Regional Security*, Ministerial Statement, Canberra: Department of Foreign Affairs and Trade, 1989. See also G. Evans, *Managing Australia's Asian Future*, Third Asia Lecture, Asia-Australia Institute, University of New South Wales, 2 October 1991; G. Evans and B. Grant, *Australia's Foreign Relations*, Melbourne: Melbourne University Press, 2nd edn, 1995, pp. 348–52; G. Evans, 'Australia in East Asia and the Asia-Pacific: Beyond the looking glass', *Australian Journal of International Affairs*, vol. 49, no. 1, May 1995, 102–4.

34 See Department of Defence, *Strategic Review 1993*, Canberra: Defence Centre, 1993; and Department of Defence, *Defending Australia: Defence White Paper 1994*, Canberra: Defence Centre, 1994.

35 P. Jennings and J. Bonnor, 'Australia's Regional Diplomacy', paper prepared for the Asia-Australia Survey 1995, Canberra: Centre for the Study of Asia Australia Relations/Macmillan, 1995, pp. 8–9.
36 See the details of its process in N. Sajima, 'Naze kyōtei wa musubaretaka?' (Why was the agreement signed?), *Gaikō Jihō*, no. 1333, 1996, 50–78.
37 Watanabe, *op. cit.* p. 16.
38 See such perception gaps in King and Kibata, *op. cit.*
39 In 1990, the Japanese minister for defence, Yozo Ishikawa, visited Australia for the first time, a visit which had little policy content. However, it was extremely reassuring to those who wanted a strategic dialogue and the opening of defence contacts between the two countries.
40 See details in N. Sajima, 'Japan and Australia: A new security partnership?', Working Paper no. 292, Canberra: Strategic and Defence Studies Centre, Australian National University, 1996.
41 Ibid.
42 Japan Defense Agency, *Defense of Japan 1994*, Tokyo: Inter Group, 1994, p. 43.
43 Ibid., pp. 34–57.
44 US Department of Defense, Office of International Security Affairs, *United States Security Strategy for the East Asia-Pacific Region*, Washington DC: US Government Printing Office, February 1995, p. 32.
45 The cost of hosting US troops in Japan has been continuing over US$5 billion, which equates to an average of 11 per cent of Japan's total self-defence budget.
46 'For the purpose of contribution to the security of Japan and the maintenance of international peace and security in the Far East, the United States of America is granted the use by its land, air and naval forces of facilities and areas in Japan' (Article VI, Japan-United States Security Treaty).
47 Japan Defense Agency, *Defense of Japan 2004*, Tokyo: Inter Group, 2004, pp. 131–48.
48 The comparative studies between the new US-Japan security arrangements and ANZUS redefinition are in N. Sajima, 'Changing ANZUS: The future of northern and southern anchors', *International Affairs*, no. 446, May 1996, 22–39.
49 See Department of Defence, 1994, *op. cit.*
50 See J. Cotton and J. Ravenhill (eds) *Seeking Asian Engagement: Australia in World Affairs, 1991–1995*, Melbourne: Oxford University Press, 1997.
51 Department of Defence, *Australia's Strategic Policy*, Canberra: Directorate of Publishing and Visual Communications, 1997.
52 This provoked strong antipathy amongst the Southeast Asian countries.
53 Japan Defense Agency, *Defense of Japan 2004*, Tokyo: Inter Group, 2004, p.301.
54 The missions of MSDF fuelling ships expanded to other coalitions including Australia and New Zealand.
55 Department of Defence, *Australia's National Security: A Defence Update 2003*.
56 After the withdrawal of Dutch forces in March 2005, the internal security of Samawa, where the SDF is dispatched to, is being maintained by the forces of U.K. and Australia.
57 Senator the Hon. Robert Hill, 'Australia to participate in US missile defence program', press release, 3 December 2004.
58 If uranium was the only natural resource Australia could export, would Australia have taken anti-nuclear initiatives as it did in past? If the centre of the Australian continent were not the desert but sea, would Australia maintain the same rate of self-sufficiency in defence?
59 Department of Defence, 1987, *op. cit.*, p. vii. See the details of the process and idea of Australia's defence planning in P. Dibb, *The Conceptual Basis of Australia's Defence Planning and Force Structure Development*, Canberra Papers on Strategy and Defence no. 88, Canberra: Strategic and Defence Studies Centre, Australian National University, 1992.

60 Sajima, *op. cit.*, 1996, pp. 8–10.
61 The government released *Public Discussion Paper* and a Community Consultation Team visited capital cities and some regional centres listening to community feedback.
62 In 2002, only 15.8 per cent agreed to enhance the SDF, though this rate was the highest in history. Japan Defense Agency, *Defense of Japan 2004*, p. 535.
63 Department of Defence, 1994, *op. cit.*, p. 85.
64 See evidence in J. Cotton, *Australia's East Timor Experience: Military Lessons and Security Dilemmas*, Canberra: University of New South Wales/ Australian Defence Force Academy, 2002.
65 Japan Defense Agency, *Defense of Japan 1994*, Tokyo: Inter Group Corp., 2004, pp. 296–321.
66 Susumu Yamakage, *Higashi Ajia no Chiikishugi to Nihon Gaikō (Regionalism in the East Asia and Japan's Diplomacy)*, Tokyo: Japan Institute of International Affairs, 2003, pp. 67–103.
67 'consult together . . . at the request of either Party, whenever the security of Japan of international peace and security in the Far East is threatened' (Article IV);

> Each Party recognises that an armed attack against either Party in the territories under the administration of Japan would be dangerous to its own peace and safety and declares that it would act to meet the common danger in accordance with its constitutional provisions and processes.
>
> (Article V, *Treaty of Mutual Cooperation and Security between Japan and the United States of America*, 23 June 1960 [Treaty no. 6]).

68 'The Parties will consult together whenever *in the opinion of any of them the territorial integrity, political independence or security of any of the Parties is threatened in the Pacific*' (Article HI); 'Each Party recognises that an armed *attack in the Pacific Area on any of the Parties would be dangerous to its own peace and safety* and declares that it would act to *meet the common danger* in accordance with its constitutional processes' (Article IV, emphasis added), *Security Treaty between Australia, New Zealand, and the United States of America*, 29 April 1952. 'Australia can contribute to the alliance that has suited its purposes so well for the last 40 years on a much more equal basis.' P. Dibb, *The Future of Australia's Defence Relationship with the United States*, Sydney: Australian Centre for American Studies, 1993, p. 71.
69 See related arguments about the Australian-US security alliance in H. Albinski (ed.) *Australia and the United States*, Canberra: Australian Defence Studies Centre, Australian Defence Force Academy, 1993.
70   Noting that the United States already has arrangements pursuant to which its armed forces are stationed in the Philippines, and has armed forces and administrative responsibilities in the Ryukyu, and upon the coming into force of the Japanese Peace Treaty may also station armed forces in and about Japan to assist in the preservation of peace and security in the Japan Area.

> (Preamble of *the Security Treaty between Australia, New Zealand, and the United States of America*.)

71 See W. T. Tow, 'Reshaping Asia-Pacific security', *Journal of East Asian Affairs*, vol. 8, no. 1, winter/spring 1994, 95–6.
72 *National Defense Program Guideline for FY 2005 and after* (approved by the Security Council and the Cabinet on 10 December 2004).
73 Department of Defence, *Australia's National Security: Australia Defence Update 2003*, Canberra: Defence Centre, 2003.

74 The Japanese male population of recruitment age (18–27) peaked at about 9 million in 1994 and has been decreasing rapidly thereafter.

75 Winston Lord urged that the US partners to help pressure North Korea and said that South Korea's approaches endanger alliance. See his interview by Bernard Gwertzman, Council on Foreign Relations, 23 February 2003, http://www.cfr. org/bio.php?meety = &id = 414&puby = 2003#p (accessed 11 January 2003).

76 N. Sajima, 'FPDA no konnichiteki igi' (New dimension of FPDA), *Gaiko Jiho,* no. 1322, October 1995, 4–31.

77 See details of the recent defence exchanges between Japan and Australia in Japan Defense Agency, *Defense of Japan 2004,* Tokyo: Inter Group Corporation, 2004, pp. 301–2.

78 H. P. Frei (trans. Toshiki Gomi), 'In direct alliance in the Pacific Rim: Japan-Australia relationship under the Pax Britannica and Pax Americana', *International Relations,* vol. 68, no. 2, 1981.

79 A. Searle and I. Kamae, 'Anchoring trilateralism: Can Australia-Japan-US security relations work?', *Australian Journal of International Affairs,* vol. 58, no. 4, December 2004, 465–78.

80 P. Jain and J. Bruni, 'Japan, Australia and the United States: Little NATO or shadow alliance?', *International Relations of the Asia-Pacific,* vol. 4, no. 2, 2004, 265–85.

81 These views are indicated in the speech of the Hon. Alexander Downer, MP to the Japan Institute for International Affairs, 'The Australia–Japan partnership: Growing stronger together', 22 March 2005.

82 Shushō Kantei, 'Nichi-Gō shunō kaidango no kyōdō kisha kaiken', joint press conference following the Japan–Australia leaders' summit, 20 April 2005, http://www.kantei.go.jp/jp/koizumispeech/2005/04/20press.html (accessed 3 May 2005).

4   The 'anchors'

Collaborative security, substance or
smokescreen?

William T. Tow and Russell Trood

Introduction

The idea of Australia and Japan strengthening their postwar security cooperation is hardly new. Both countries were stalwart allies of the United
States during the Cold War which shared Washington's antipathy toward
the growth of Soviet military power and were key players in the US
strategy to contain it. As maritime states and US allies on the near
extremes of the East Asian littoral, Australia and Japan have frequently
been viewed by critics of US strategy in the region as the 'northern and
southern anchors' of the American regional alliance system in East Asia.
The two countries remain resource-dependent on fossil fuels and economically reliant on stable trade routes for their own national prosperity. Both
sustain cultures and identities that often lead regional elites from Chinese,
Korean and Malay constituencies to declare that their 'Western' underpin-
nings isolate them from the 'core' of East Asia. Though somewhat
ironically perhaps given its European culture, Australia with its membership of the Five Power Defence Arrangement (FPDA) and its former
participation in the South East Asia Treaty Organisation (SEATO) has
considerably more experience of regional defence partnerships in East
Asian than Japan. Adopting the reasoning of difference, Samuel
Huntington has labelled Australia as a 'torn country' and Japan as a
country that possesses its own 'civilisation' apart from other key regional
actors.[1]

While such a view may be too deterministic, there can be little doubt that
Australia and Japan have both confronted what the constructivist faction in
international relations theory would label images of 'otherness' within Asia.
At the start of the twenty-first century, however, more interesting and
central questions about the Australia-Japan security dyad are now emerging:
(1) to what extent are their respective alliances with the United States
allowing them to compensate effectively for their traditional feelings of
regional vulnerability and isolation; and (2) how are evolving strategic
dynamics in the region affecting Australian and Japanese attitudes towards
each other as possible *strategic* collaborators?

The broad argument of this chapter is that there are increasing imperatives for Australia-Japan strategic cooperation in the East Asia. In the face of Washington's current challenge to more coherently integrate its regional (Asia-Pacific) and global strategies, especially the global war on terror, and in the context of China's growing self-confidence and diplomatic accomplishments in regional security politics, Canberra and Tokyo are likely to discover increasing opportunities for collaboration. This will likely reinforce the 'north/south anchor component' of Australian-Japanese security relations, both with Washington and independently of their bilateral alliances with the US.

The first section of the chapter will provide a short background to early thinking about Australian–Japanese security from the latter stages of the Cold War to the signing of a key bilateral memorandum of understanding (MOU) between Australian and Japanese defence officials in September 2003. During the late 1970s and early 1980s, analysis by independent observers considered the hypothetical advantages a JANZUS alliance might provide within the context of the San Francisco system of bilateral alliances managed by Washington. Arguments for strengthening the Australian-Japanese component of the 'hub and spokes' architecture underlying the US security treaty network in the Asia-Pacific included the Carter administration's alleged tendencies toward strategic retrenchment from East Asia, Japanese prime minister Nakasone's drive in the early 1980s to intensify Japan's 'burden-sharing' capacity within the US–Japan alliance and the perceived growth of Soviet offshore power throughout the Pacific and Indian Oceans during the same time. Many of the propositions underlying these initiatives proved to be misguided or premature. Even so, those who have traditionally felt targeted by what they view as a perpetual American containment strategy in the region (i.e. China and North Korea) have closely tracked indications of closer defence relations among US regional allies. They have been inclined to interpret developments as signs that closer Australian-Japanese coordination in security policy areas spells trouble for them and for overall regional stability.

The second part of the chapter will focus on more contemporary developments. It deals with the contention that the Australian-Japanese security collaboration that has occurred is as much a 'smokescreen' in response to ambiguous US global strategy as it is a genuine effort to cultivate collaboration for its own sake. The July 2003 Australian-Japan Joint Statement on Cooperation To Combat International Terrorism (labelled the 'Action Plan') will be examined, as will Australia's and Japan's recent mutual participation in the Proliferation Security Initiative (PSI), and their multilateral peacekeeping initiatives in East Timor, Iraq and elsewhere. Of particular interest here is the way in which these developments are serving to shape security cooperation between Australia and Japan and the impact they are likely to have on the United States' ongoing transformation strategy for reconstituting and redeploying its military power in the East Asian region. There may be an emerging framework of long-term strategic collaboration in recent Australia-Japan policy. If so, it is a very different pattern from that which has traditionally been of most concern to China and other Asian observers.

The final part of the chapter will offer some policy recommendations on the way emerging Australia-Japan security relations might be pursued over the next few years. These prescriptions are hardly intended to provide a 'grand strategy' for future relations. Rather, they are intended to provide policy-makers in both Canberra and Tokyo with some different perspectives from those currently dominating the modest literature on the subject. They will emphasise what might be termed a 'neo-functionalist' approach to developing and operationalising cooperation over the next few years and beyond.[2] They include observations on how Australia and Japan might coordinate and target joint policy initiatives in regional multilateral forums, and on how regional and global components of strategy supported by the world's developed powers might be facilitated or impaired by a more active or robust Australian-Japanese security dyad. They will also touch briefly upon Australian and Japanese coordination of policy on the North Korean nuclear crisis and initiatives that might be explored to strengthen such coordination.

Our basic argument is that the 'jury is still out' as to whether Australia-Japan security relations can ever move beyond the 'smokescreen' status of much rhetoric, but little real strategic collaboration that currently characterises relations. The key to such an evolution will be the evolution of America's own regional strategy, as the key 'independent variable' driving the context and rationales of the Australia-Japan security collaboration over the remainder of this decade and beyond. Notwithstanding the 'American factor', however, there may well be separate and sound policy rationales for cultivating stronger strategic collaboration between Australia and Japan. This chapter is intended to be a contribution to the growing debate on the prospects and ramifications of such a prospect.

Australia and Japan: a strategic legacy?

A substantial literature exists on post-war Australian-Japan politico-diplomatic relations.[3] However, interest in the development of those two countries' security ties has been far less extensive, as both Tokyo and Canberra have been largely content to relate to each other strategically via their own bilateral alliances with the United States. Until recently, proposals for closer Australia-Japan defence cooperation have surfaced only when concerns have intensified that the United States' strategic presence in the Asia-Pacific region might decline or the Asia-Pacific region's balance of power was under threat. This was the case during the late 1970s and early 1980s when expanding Soviet naval power in the Pacific and Indian oceans, combined with a perceived reduction of US power projection capabilities under the Carter administration, led to calls for greater allied (and particularly

Japanese) defence burden-sharing. A JANZUS arrangement was raised as one possible means for complementing the existing ANZUS and US–Japan alliance, and for pursuing multilateral collective defence strategy more effectively against a Soviet maritime challenge in the Asia-Pacific to supplement NATO strategy against a Soviet land threat in Europe.[4] In 1984, one conservative Japanese scholar proposed a West Pacific Treaty Organisation (WEPTO) to interact more closely with NATO. Already maintaining extensive bilateral or multilateral security ties in the Asia-Pacific through force deployments and/or various military exercises, the US, Britain, France and Canada – all NATO members – were logical candidates to work with Japan and Australia to achieve such coordination. Japan began sending Diet members to the NATO Assembly in late 1980, and this too could be viewed as a foundation for greater US-European-Japanese-Australian collective defence collaboration.[5]

These ambitious proposals, however, proved to be ill timed and hardly suited to the strict constructionist interpretation of 'self-defence' observed by successive Japanese governments during the Cold War. Tokyo favoured the continuation of US extended deterrence guarantees embedded within its own bilateral security treaty with Washington – a sentiment that proved to be visionary when the ANZUS dispute erupted a few short years later and Australia walked a tightrope between its quarrelling American and New Zealand allies. Nor was there strong Australian interest in the proposal. The Japanese posture of voluntary strategic restraint was reconstituted in 1978 with the formulation of the Guidelines for US–Japan Defense Cooperation. The guidelines were a 'reaffirmation of the Yoshida [Doctrine's early postwar] commitment to a minimal defence establishment and the continued reliance upon the United States' for Japan's own security.[6]

Speculation about closer Australia-Japan security relations intensified once more during the late 1990s. Although the Cold War had dissipated with the Soviet Union's passing, the San Francisco system had remained intact as a hedging or balancing mechanism against the trend of rising Chinese power, a deterrent against a new Korean War and an instrument of American strategic presence and power in a region experiencing the world's most dynamic economic growth. Japan revised its National Defense Program Outline in 1995 and highlighted the critical relevance of the US defence tie in the aftermath of the 1994 Korean nuclear crisis. Australia's new coalition government led by John Howard crafted the 'Sydney Declaration' with its American counterpart in July 1996 that underscored the ANZUS alliance's orientation as a predominantly regional security pact rather than a component of US global extended deterrence strategy. Both of these initiatives were consistent with the Clinton administration's East Asia Strategy Report (EASR or 'Nye Report'), released in February 1995 and written primarily by Joseph Nye, Clinton's Assistant Secretary of Defense for International Security Affairs. The 'Nye Report' endorsed the United States sustaining a major forward deployment of US military forces throughout the Asia-Pacific region as an instrument of strategic reassurance for those apprehensive about new and potentially hostile power configurations that may arise there.[7]

Sensitive to criticism from his critics that his foreign policy was inconsistent, oscillating between engagement and containment with China while largely ignoring the United States' traditional allies, President Clinton travelled throughout the region in 1996 determined to show his enthusiasm and competency for orchestrating alliance relations. This translated into American support for Asia-Pacific allies broadening their own interaction in the security arena, both bilaterally and multilaterally. One could view this process as a delayed implementation of the 1969 Nixon Doctrine nearly three decades after its formulation. In the context of changing domestic perceptions of the role, value and importance of traditional security links to the US, regional allies were now more prepared to take the initiative for managing critical aspects of their regional security politics. But such a process was still underwritten by American security guarantees as embodied in their bilateral security treaties with the United States.

In the context of Australia–Japan relations, the momentum for more comprehensive security relations was well under way even prior to the Nye Report's release. Bilateral security dialogues between Australian and Japanese political and defence officials had already commenced in 1990, and these were subsequently formalised into annual Political-Military ('Pol-Mil') and Military-Military ('Mil-Mil') consultations by early 1996. In August 1997, an Australia-Japan Partnership Agenda was concluded. This built upon a Joint Declaration issued two years before which had proclaimed that Japan welcomed Australia as an 'indispensable partner in regional affairs'.[8] The August 1997 document covered a wide array of security-related cooperative ventures, but the most critical point was that both countries pledged to 'contribute to the promotion of regional security' by increasing 'the coordination of their policies on key international issues, both in the Asia-Pacific region and globally'.[9] This has been put into practice by the convening of annual prime ministerial summits (from April 1997 onward), Japanese support for Australian membership in key regional organisations, mutual participation in various international peace building and peacekeeping operations and enhanced intelligence collaboration.

Momentum continued to build for shaping a more distinct Australia-Japan 'security dyad' shortly before and immediately following the September 11 terrorist attacks in New York and Washington. In April 2001, the Sydney Declaration for Australia–Japan Creative Partnership formalised what was clearly becoming a more conspicuous bilateral politico-security relationship between those two countries. In May 2002, Prime Minister Koizumi visited Australia and issued a joint statement with his Australian counterpart that emphasised their two countries' determination to strengthen their bilateral ties, including in security policy-related sectors. In September 2003, Australia's defence minister, Senator Robert Hill, visited

Tokyo and signed a 'Memorandum of Understanding [MOU] on Defence Exchanges between the Japan Defence Agency and the Australian Department of Defence'. The document addressed both regional and international security imperatives and called for increased cooperation in such areas as counter-terrorism and counter-proliferation. Australian defence ministers and defence force chiefs would meet regularly to communicate and, where appropriate, coordinate their respective countries' security postures with their Japanese counterparts. Bilateral military exercises between Australian and Japanese defence forces would be regularised. Australian-Japanese consultations on each other's security collaboration with the United States, especially in such areas as missile defence technology and intelligence, would be upgraded.[10]

As the momentum for more direct security collaboration between Australia and Japan intensified, the 'JANZUS debate' was resurrected. It was launched by Robert D. Blackwill, a professor in international security at Harvard University and a close adviser to George W. Bush's presidential campaign, in an edited volume prepared by respected Australian and American analysts. Setting forth his 'action agenda' for strengthening the San Francisco System, Blackwill proposed that America's 'three primary alliances in Asia' – those with Japan, South Korea and Australia – should be integrated more effectively to engage in collective strategic dialogue, harmonise their relations toward China, coordinate their diplomacy with respect to North Korea and work together towards creating more effective multilateral security mechanisms in the Asia-Pacific region.[11] Other contributors to the volume dissented, insisting that policy priorities should be assigned to strengthening the existing bilateral components of US alliances in the region in response to a stronger China, to geographic disparities in threat identification and to intermittent changes in US global strategy that would require creative and judicious responses from its bilateral allies.[12]

Due to Blackwill's high visibility in the US policy community and to the Howard government's commitment to 'reinvigorate' Australian-American security ties, the 'alliance agenda' he proposed captured the interest of Australian and at least some US journalists and policy analysts. US-South Korean security relations became increasingly uncertain in the early days of President George W. Bush's administration as it philosophically opposed Seoul's 'Sunshine Policy' of reconciliation directed at North Korea. Accordingly, the trilateralisation of the US-Japan and US-Australia bilateral alliances commanded increased attention.

While South Korea's participation in some form of the San Francisco System's multilateralisation seemed increasingly problematic, proponents of closer trilateral ties between Australia, Japan and the US pointed to the already strong 'historical links' between the US–Japan Mutual Security Treaty, the Australia-US defence relationship, and the fact that 'Australia and Japan are natural trans-Pacific friends and allies' holding similar values and pursuing similar economic and diplomatic objectives.

> Trilateralising the military relationship would anchor the US more firmly in the region, formalise their security and trade interests across and up and down the Pacific, and provide ballast to the fledgling ARF [ASEAN Regional Forum] as the preeminent [Asia-Pacific] security dialogue forum.

This process was viewed by its advocates as a seamless and highly rationalist approach for guiding Japan into an era of strategic transition from a self-contained defence actor to a more 'normal' strategic associate.[13]

Sceptics of the trilateral vision asserted that no real geopolitical logic existed for the US to sponsor any such expansion in collective defence.

> It was one thing to carry such a global burden during the Cold War, when the Soviet Union and its many surrogates threatened friendly nations that had been wrecked or weakened by World War II. But the threats have dissipated and the Western states are far stronger than their potential antagonists.[14]

Other critics insisted that the San Francisco System should not be fixed by such initiatives because it was hardly broken. As one noted, the extent of interoperability already existing between US and allied forces in the region, both bilaterally and in broader settings, provided the core for any relevant coalition of the willing to be established in a future regional crisis.[15] While more regular dialogues could be pursued on issues such as Indonesian stability, international peacekeeping and China, this was hardly the stuff of alliance formalisation.

In July 2001, the 'second JANZUS debate' reached something of a climax at the Australian-United States Ministerial Meeting (AUSMIN) convened in Canberra and attended by both the American and Australian foreign and defence secretaries/ministers. At a 'round table' press conference both US secretary of state Colin Powell and Australian foreign minister Alexander Downer disclosed that an 'idea' of trilateral US-Japan-Australian defence consultations had been discussed during the meeting, but that no 'Asian NATO' of the type envisioned by Blackwill and others was contemplated.[16] As Ralph Cossa subsequently observed, Downer's insertion of the 'N' word actually fuelled the debate rather than mitigating it because it played into China's long-held suspicion that any such trilateral initiative would be part of a new American containment posture directed against itself.[17] Perhaps not surprisingly, the Australian shadow opposition foreign minister, Laurie Brereton, endeavoured to make political capital out of the issue the following week in an ABC television interview:

QUESTION: And what about these proposed defence linkages between Australia, South Korea, Japan, United States – is that aimed at China?
BRERETON: Well I thought that was a pretty oddball arrangement, especially

the way in which it was made public. At the press conference following the Ausmin talks, it was as if it slipped out and the government spent the next day in damage control saying there wasn't much to it. But it shows the sensitivity and we ought to be very mindful of all of these actions in the context of how they are seen in our neighbourhood and Australia's role should be to take an independent view of our strategic circumstances and to then be a forceful voice speaking out in support of non-proliferation and nuclear disarmament, being gung-ho as we've seen from our Government in the last twelve months.

QUESTION: So what about the reaction from China and how harmful is that to Australia?

BRERETON: Well I think Australia has an important role to play, we're a good friend of China, we are a friend and an ally of the United States, and we should be attempting to be a bridge between them in encouraging greater understanding.[18]

The notion of a formal JANZUS died a quiet death within weeks of the AUSMIN meeting because it was the wrong initiative floated at the wrong time. It risked alienating China just when Sino-American relations appeared to be on the upswing after the Hainan EP-3 crisis had been defused earlier in the year. It also complicated Japanese security politics at a time when Japanese nationalism and Okinawa's resentment against the US basing operations there was intensifying. Having just won a mandate for instituting painful and long overdue domestic economic reforms, the Koizumi government would have had little political capital left to expend on revising the US-Japan bilateral alliance in any substantial way. The whole messy affair made clear to Washington that maximum sensitivity needed to be exercised in shoring up political support for the existing US-Japan security treaty rather than radically revising that arrangement to something that looked more like an Asian NATO in search of a threat.[19] Finally, it was bad for Australia's image in Southeast Asia, coming on the heels of accusations that Australia was a 'deputy sheriff' for US (and, by extension, Japanese) interests in Southeast Asia and was insensitive to both Chinese and ASEAN prerogatives for managing regional security outside the confines of formal alliance politics.[20]

What did emerge from this episode, however, was a new formula for pursuing informal 'trilateralism' through what Ralph Cossa has termed a 'virtual alliance' strategy.[21] While Cossa applied this concept to US-Japan-South Korea defence consultations, it is equally applicable to explaining the evolution of the US-Japan-Australia security triangle during 2002 and 2003. Cossa's concept can be usefully extended by applying some theoretical guidelines to explain virtual alliance as an element of strategic triangularity and as a driver for a 'virtual JANZUS'. A virtual alliance posture, Cossa argues, is characterised by three basic traits: (1) the formation of security consultative mechanisms reflecting common interests and values; (2) the lack of formal treaty or legislative obligations underwriting the parties who are collaborating; and (3) the tendency for such collaborators to diversify their avenues of security cooperation into different regional and global institutions or forums so as to mitigate suspicions by other states that an alliance containment posture is being formulated against themselves.

The US–Japan–Australia Trilateral Security Dialogue (also known in US quarters as the 'Trilateral Strategic Dialogue') was initially announced in August 2002 when Japanese prime minister Koizumi visited Canberra. Five Dialogue 'sessions' had convened by February 2004, usually as 'add-ons' to the already well established US–Japan Strategic Dialogue and normally lasting one half to one full day. These talks are conducted at the vice-ministerial level and are deliberately kept low-key to reassure China that the Japanese and Australian 'anchors' are not consorting with Washington to contain Chinese power. While the content of specific discussions at these sessions has not been disclosed, such issues as North Korea, the Iraq war and counter-terrorism were almost certainly raised.[22] In response to a question about the Dialogue's purpose, Prime Minister Howard sought to differentiate the meaning and intent of 'dialogue' as opposed to 'forum':

> it's not . . . a forum is too formal a word, it's not that it's just a dialogue at an officials level, a senior officials level, in the way that I would envisage [a] resumed dialogue with China. So it should not be seen in any way as being against China. We are happy to have a similar dialogue . . . [with] China.[23]

This representation conforms to the third criterion for a virtual alliance.

Common values and interests (the first criterion) have been linked to the core rationales of the Dialogue in public statements offered by both the Australian and Japanese foreign ministers and by the US Department of State. In an address to the National Conference of Australia–Japan Societies in September 2003, Alexander Downer described the Trilateral Security Dialogue as developing into strategic cooperation as Australia and Japan worked with the US to transform 'common perspectives' into tangible strategic cooperation.[24] In a subsequent press release (late January 2004), Downer appeared to override his prime minister's earlier denial that the Dialogue had not reached 'forum' or institutional status, characterising that entity as providing 'a forum for high-level strategic discussion, reflecting our shared interests in international security and an appreciation of the contribution made by each country in the Asia-Pacific region'.[25] At the same time, a spokesperson for the Japan's Ministry of Foreign Affairs (MOFA) relayed that both global and regional issues were considered in Dialogue discussions, with particular emphasis on nuclear non-proliferation as it relates to North Korea and the Iraq War and its reconstruction, and US State Department public dispatches confirmed this agenda.[26]

This consultative process has developed along *ad hoc* or informal lines, thereby evading the need for its legislative ratification by the domestic legislatures or polities of the three countries concerned (and fulfilling the second criterion of virtual alliance). If it were to be subjected to such review and approval, the process would almost certainly expire for the lack of such approval. While debate in Japan over that country making various adjustments to its no-war constitution is gradually increasing, any such change can for now only occur within the context of the formal US–Japan Defence Guidelines. Any effort to expand the bilateral context of the Mutual Security Treaty in a formal way would be politically infeasible without the cultivation of long-term precedents in prescribed Australian-Japanese or trilateral defence cooperation. Nor would the US Senate be likely to ratify new regional security treaty commitments at a time when informal 'coalitions of the willing' will most likely involve both Australian and Japanese defence personnel supporting American forces in counter-terrorist operations or in international peacekeeping ventures. After nearly a decade of Australian efforts to strengthen the depth and scope of ANZUS, the future of this policy may now be in the balance depending on the outcome of the Australian election likely to be held by the end of 2004. Should a Labor government come to office, it is unlikely to be as prone as its predecessor to bandwagon with US global strategy. The US alliance is more likely to be balanced against a renewed Australian effort to repair its problematic image with its Asian neighbours in the aftermath of East Timor and Iraq.

If caution toward trilateral security collaboration is progressively more evident in the policy orientations of all three Dialogue partners, can the probability for such cooperation be measured usefully? As noted above, how US regional and global strategic postures develop over the remainder of this decade and beyond, constitutes the key intervening variable in determining trilateralism's relevance to the three security dyads (US-Japan; Japan-Australia; Australia-US) under review. In this context, the following part of the paper will examine three specific dimensions of the 'American factor' as it may affect strategic collaboration between Washington and its Australian and Japanese 'anchors' in Asia-Pacific alliance politics: (1) the ability of Australia and Japan to reconcile their primarily 'region-centric' security concerns with American global strategy that is increasingly focusing on counter-terrorism and anti-proliferation of weapons of mass destruction (WMD); (2) the identification of specific 'functional' defence missions and capabilities that can best be defined and operationalised along trilateral lines as opposed to remaining predominantly in the bilateral domain; and (3) the degree of success that the US, Japan and Australia experience in integrating the purpose and products of the Trilateral Security Dialogue into other existing regional institutions without undermining those institutions' viability.

Reconciling globalism and regionalism

Japan and Australia comprise two of the foremost maritime powers in the Asia-Pacific region and thus are integral to the United States' overall global strategy. During the Cold War, American access to bases in Japan was critical for US global strategy because, as Robyn Lim has recently observed, 'American maritime power and nuclear weapons were essential in countering the Soviet bid for hegemony over Eurasia made on the basis of proximity.'[27] US bases in Japan allowed American commanders to target the USSR on multiple fronts and exploit its strategic vulnerability east of the Ural Mountains and to apply substantial surge capabilities against a technologically deficient Chinese military infrastructure. Following the Soviet Union's demise, Japanese bases have played a key role in underscoring US air and maritime projection capabilities into Northeast Asia and the East China Sea, although some analysts argue that these functions will be less important over time as US surge capabilities develop a truly global reach over very short periods of time.[28] Along with Japan and perhaps Singapore, Australia is the only country in the region with enough sophisticated military technology to engage the demands of the Revolution in Military Affairs. Its joint facility at Pine Gap constitutes an integral contribution to the United States' global intelligence capabilities. In summary, both the US-Japan and US-Australia alliances through their respective mission statements (the 1997 Defence Guidelines and the Sydney Statement) emphasise dimensions of both regional and global security.[29]

With the end of the Cold War and the United States assuming unipolar status in the contemporary international security environment, American policy-planners have moved to review and adjust US global strategy. In June 2004, US national security officials provided an update on this ongoing evaluation process and emphasised five key dimensions of what has become known as the 'US Global Posture Review': (1) strengthening relationships with allies and building new partnerships; (2) achieving maximum flexibility and agility; (3) including a regional, as well as a global, focus; (4) emphasising speed by projecting and deploying force assets as rapidly as possible; and (5) focusing primarily on force capabilities, rather than on numbers. Considered overall, American global force posture calculations go well beyond military basing readjustments and entail gaining more surge capability and realising greater force interoperability with allies and friends around the world.[30]

One of the more important dimensions of the new global posture in terms of its applicability to Trilateral Security Dialogue relates to integrating the 'global' and 'regional' aspects of American strategic planning and force presence. South Korea's designation of 3,000 troops towards reconstruction efforts in Iraq, and Japan's dispatch of several hundred SDF personnel to support the US-led 'coalition of the willing' both underscore the significance of this issue. These allied commitments were announced just a few months before the United States formally disclosed the reduction and relocation of its own forces on the Korean peninsula (from 37,000 to around 25,000 by 2008) and its intention to consolidate its force structure in Japan. Yet this was hardly an 'asymmetrical' trade-off. The Bush administration had already announced in 2003 a $US11 billion package for strengthening its overall deterrence posture in Korea, Japan and throughout Northeast Asia. US long-range airpower in the region was reinforced by the deployment of additional B-52 bombers in Guam. The US began discussions with Japan for relocating an army brigade from Washington State to Camp Zama in the Kanagawa Prefecture and for Japan to relocate its Air Defense Command and Air Support Command from Fuchu to Yokota to achieve greater command and control integration with US force components already stationed there. A second US carrier task force to be stationed in Guam or Hawaii in support of the USS *Kitty Hawk* at Yokosuka was also being planned.[31] It does not require too much imagination to come up with scenarios on how such developments could be incorporated into a virtual JANZUS strategy. The tracking and interception of Chinese submarines by US and Japanese oceanographic vessels, the interception of North Korean vessels carrying WMD-related materials, or crisis management using intelligence data provided to American and Japanese satellites by the Pine Gap joint installation, offer some examples.[32] Australian force commitments, perhaps in the form of special forces, air and naval elements, to any new conflict breaking out on the Korean peninsula offers another dimension of trilateralism. These might well be coordinated with Japanese logistical support.[33]

American strategic superiority in the post-Cold War era has raised doubts over the continued importance of alliances relative to 'coalitions of the willing' and other mechanisms designed for responding to international terrorism, humanitarian crises and asymmetrical threat. But US unipolarity has not fundamentally transformed the nature and purpose of either the US-Japan Mutual Security Treaty or ANZUS. Both Tokyo and Canberra remain among the most loyal allies the United States has in the Asia-Pacific. Both of these allies have offered consistent and loyal support to America's strategic postures at both the regional and global level. Australia supported US intervention in the 1996 Taiwan Strait crisis, sought and received US logistical and intelligence support for the International Force East Timor (INTERFET) operation in East Timor, stabilised the Solomon Islands, advanced a 'Pacific Doctrine' for neutralising future crises in the South Pacific, and coordinated its own series of regional bilateral security dialogues that complement the role of strategic reassurance that America's own bilateral alliances in the region are designed to promote. Japan has participated in the Six-Party Talks intended to stabilise nuclear politics on the Korean peninsula, sustained substantial economic assistance programs to Southeast Asia and hosted the most extensive basing system for US forces in the entire region. Globally, both Australia and Japan have committed forces to American-led coalition operations in Iraq and Afghanistan, geared intelligence capabilities and earmarked military resources for joint counter-terrorism and counter-proliferation operations such as the Proliferation Security Initiative, intensified military participation for a variety of extra-regional peacekeeping and crisis management missions (i.e. Japan in the Indian Ocean and Australia in the Persian Gulf) and bought into various aspects of US missile defence (MD) technology development. Japan and Australia are also core contributors to maintaining the United States' access to key sea and air lines of communication (SLOCs) in the region. These are needed to sustain trade and commerce at the levels required for preserving Washington's overall global power and influence.

'Functional' security cooperation

In the absence of an overriding charter of strategic purpose such as the North Atlantic Treaty's underwriting of NATO in Europe, the logic of a virtual JANZUS reverts by default to the definition and fulfilment of specific tactical functions that may be better accomplished in this context rather than within existing bilateral or multilateral security arrangements. We are unconvinced that Japanese intelligence capabilities can be developed rapidly enough to justify forming even a JANZUS command and control to complement – much less supplement – the US Pacific Command's dominance of current intelligence capabilities. We are also sceptical that the United States will find basing options in Australia to be centrally relevant to likely or unpredicted contingencies that may arise in the Asia-Pacific security environment over the short-to-mid-term (up to the year 2020). There are, however, at least three tangible tasks where JANZUS consultations and coordination could directly relate and contribute to regional stability and to US global strategy in ways that Australia and Japan could both benefit from.

First, specific tasks could be demarcated more consistently and systematically between Japan and Australia in the event that the United States is compelled to go to war against North Korea. There are several ways in which a Trilateral Security Dialogue could enhance planning among groups of high-ranking military officers from the three countries in relation to specific Mil-Mil sessions. One obvious opportunity would be to explore the extent to which existing US-Japan Defence Guidelines could be extended to include Australian military deployments and personnel (i.e. Australian special forces dispatched to locate and destroy North Korean missile sites) in support of a US or UN defence of South Korea where this might require access to or transit across Japanese territory. Another is theatre missile defence coordination involving both Japanese and Australian maritime elements operating either independently or under de facto US command. A third planning task might look to the ways Australia might participate with Japanese and American personnel in responding to North Korean refugee flows or to Japanese casualties resulting from North Korean missile strikes or naval/ special forces attacks against Japanese military bases or selected urban areas.

A second policy task is to calibrate a unified and enduring JANZUS approach to China strategy. This presents several challenges emanating from each leg of the JANZUS triangle. Japan is now confronted with a very different China from the one that contested its alliance with the United States for most of the post-war era. China is now downplaying its resistance to the Mutual Security Treaty in favour of cultivating Tokyo for greater politico-economic cooperation in the ASEAN Plus 3 and other regional fora. Nevertheless, Sino-Japanese tensions remain over sovereignty issues (the Dyaotai/Senkaku Islands dispute), historical legacies (Japanese officials continuing to visit the Yakusuni war shrine), Japanese participation in the US missile defence program, and over Chinese apprehensions about Japan's 'real' position concerning Taiwan. Australia is less burdened than is Japan by a negative historical legacy towards China but, like the Japanese, is subject to intermittent Chinese criticism over its close security ties with Washington. The most probable testing ground for JANZUS cohesion on China would be a Sino-American confrontation over Taiwan if that island moved towards independence from the PRC thus instigating a military response by Beijing. In this event, Japan could resort to a strict constructionist interpretation of its 'peace constitution', but Australia lacks such a rationale and would be under immense pressure from the United States to at least side with Washington in any such confrontation if not formally contribute to Taiwan's defence.[34] If Taiwan were to be incorporated into the PRC by force or other means, Japan's strategic calculations regarding SLOC access through the East China Sea into the ASEAN straits area and to points west (the Indian Ocean and Persian Gulf) would be affected substantially. Such geopolitical considerations would appear to provide an ample basis for geopolitical discussion and policy formulation with the Trilateral Security Dialogue and any subsidiary groupings that may eventually flow from it.

A third JANZUS task would be to forge a more consensual US-Japan-Australia approach to the ASEAN region. All three powers have image problems with various ASEAN states even while sustaining important economic and security ties with the Southeast Asian region. Reflecting a worldwide trend, American counter-terrorism postures directed towards parts of the Philippines, Thailand and Indonesia appear as often to play into the hands of Islamic factions opposing the United States as to facilitate those who support the West in those countries. Australia has incurred guilt by association with the United States in the global war on terror, either being accused of insensitivity (by the Philippines and to a lesser extent by Indonesia) to Southeast Asian countries' unique national interests that lead them to approach terrorism issues in different ways from the US and its coalition partners or of serving as Washington's 'deputy sheriff' in the region.[35] As is the case with China, Japan still suffers from its wartime legacy throughout much of Southeast Asia – a factor that plays into China's hands and strengthens its influence at Japan's expense, notwithstanding Japan's far greater levels of investment and trade in the ASEAN region.

Despite such problems, there is potential for a more coordinated JANZUS policy-planning approach towards Southeast Asia. Australia has recently moved to strengthen (and perhaps expand) its FPDA with Malaysia, Singapore, New Zealand and the United Kingdom by shifting its mission orientation more towards counter-terrorism.[36] This initiative coincides with US negotiations to reach a comprehensive strategic framework agreement with the Singaporeans to expand cooperation in areas such as counter-terrorism, counter-proliferation of weapons of mass destruction, joint military exercises, training, policy dialogues and defence technology.[37] Instability in Indonesia since 1999 has forced Japan to engage in contingency planning for the evacuation of its citizens living and working there if future crises were to endanger them. It is also working to negotiate with Singapore for the use of that city-state's air and naval facilities during future emergency operations.[38] The 'Singapore connection' could be further developed to gradually form a 'spider web' of informal JANZUS coordination of anti-piracy capabilities and to link up US and Australian military planners and operations more systematically with Malay, Filipino and other counter-terrorism operations. But any such cultivation would have to be done gradually and with sufficiently high levels of sensitivity and transparency to avoid Chinese accusations of JANZUS containment of its own interests by stealth – accusations that could readily garner the sympathy of various ASEAN factions already inclined to assail one or more of the JANZUS powers.

Trilateralism and institutionalism

Planning for regional security contingencies and quietly negotiating for more integrated regional security arrangements at appropriate intervals leads into a third potential dimension of upgraded JANZUS security collaboration: coordination and, if possible, harmonisation of trilateral security diplomacy with other existing regional and global organisations to realise greater Asia-Pacific and international stability. Indeed, precedents for this type of collaboration already exist. Australia and Japan supplied the largest number of forces to the United Nations Transitional Administration in East Timor (UNTAET) and the United Nations Mission of Support in East Timor (UNMISET), respectively. Indonesia's tacit acceptance of Australian and Japanese co-leadership during East Timor's period of political transition was a notable development. So too has been the SDF's participation with Australia, the US and other founding states in the PSI and its requisite maritime interception exercise during September 2003 and Japan's training of Southeast Asian customs personnel to intercept illicit trade of WMD components.[39] In February 2005, moreover, in response to a request from Prime Minister Koizumi, Australia announced it would deploy 450 troops to protect SDF engineering personnel involved with reconstruction projects in southern Iraq. Replacing departing Dutch forces, the Australian contingent represented an opportunity to develop further Australia's strategic relationship with Japan. This rationale was specifically earmarked by Prime Minister Howard during his announcement of his government's decision to send Australian forces to support the SDF.[40]

JANZUS might do well to explore at least two other key areas of institutional collaboration over the near-term. One is to shape a common approach to the Asia-Pacific Economic Cooperation (APEC) grouping's Secure Trade in the APEC Region (STAR) initiative launched by Chile's defence minister, Michelle Bachelet Jeria, in March 2004. STAR envisions closer cooperation between APEC, the Group of 8, the ASEAN Regional Forum and other institutions in implementing more effective measures to safeguard air transportation, the security of maritime traffic lanes, refugee safety and monitoring and international finance.[41] It would appear that an American-Australian-Japanese subcommittee would be very well placed to derive and implement specific policy measures to transform STAR from concept into reality.

A second area of policy coordination would be to identify a common trilateral policy towards China's New Security Concept (NSC) diplomacy. As Beijing becomes more adept in transposing its unique brand of *realpolitik* into multilateral settings, the Trilateral Security Dialogue will be challenged to respond with innovative and cooperative proposals and programs to encourage the modification of competitiveness ingrained within the NSC and that reflects China's desire to eventually neutralise the San Francisco System. Closer coordination between the Trilateral Security Dialogue and a regularised three-way summit or 'Trialogue' involving Chinese, Japanese and American officials at the ministerial or vice-ministerial level could also be established. To date, China has resisted entering into a 'Trialogue' due to its fear that it might signal an implicit recognition of the US-Japan MST and could allow Washington and Tokyo to apply increased pressure on China on various policy issues (China believes it is much better served by positioning itself in a 'pivot' or broker position on regional security issues such as has been the case with the Six Power Talks on Korea). Yet, as Ralph Cossa has observed:

> China, Japan and the United States all have 'a common interest in promoting peace and stability regionally and globally; seeing an end to ethnic, religious, or territorial disputes; halting the proliferation of weapons of mass destruction on the Korean Peninsula and elsewhere; maintaining a generally benign Northeast Asian security environment; and continued economic progress and reform. All three also want to see the China-Taiwan issue settled by peaceful means.' All also have a vested interest in ensuring freedom of navigation and the security of the vital Asia-Pacific sea lanes upon which their respective economies rely.[42]

Establishing a Sino–Japan–US 'Trialogue' to complement the Australia-Japan–US Dialogue would help minimise Chinese tendencies to characterise JANZUS consultation and collaboration as containment directed against itself, strengthen transparency in overall regional security relations and consolidate the common interests shared by both 'minilateral' configurations.

Notes

1 In a footnote documenting his now seminal article on the 'Clash of Civilizations', Huntington cites Australian analyst Owen Harries as the source for his designation of Australia as a 'torn state'. See S. Huntington, 'The clash of civilizations', *Foreign Affairs*, vol. 72, no. 3, summer 1993, 50.

2 Ernst B. Haas was the forefather of the neo-functionalist perspective. See his two key writings, *Beyond the Nation State*, Stanford CA: Stanford University Press, 1971; and *The Obsolescence of Regional Integration Theory*, Research Studies 25, Berkeley CA: Institute of International Studies, 1975.

3 Two of the more comprehensive studies are A. Rix, *The Australia-Japan Political Alignment: 1952 to the Present*, London: Routledge, 1998; and D. Walton, 'Regional dialogue in Australia-Japan relations: 1952–1965: The beginnings of a political relationship in regional affairs', Ph.D. Thesis, St Lucia QLD: University of Queensland, 2001.

4 See, for example, W. T. Tow, 'The Janzus option: A key to Asian/Pacific security', *Asian Survey*, vol. 2, no. 4, March 1981, 1221–34; and E. Olsen, 'Adding a J to ANZUS', *The New York Times*, 13 May 1981.

5 Y. Nakagawa, 'The WEPTO option', *Asian Survey*, vol. 24, no. 8, August 1984, 828–39.

6 T. U. Berger, 'Alliance politics and Japan's postwar culture of antimilitarism', in M. J. Green and P. M. Cronin (eds) *The US-Japan Alliance: Past, Present, and Future*, New York: Council on Foreign Relations Press, 1999, p. 198.

7 United States Department of Defense, Office of International Security Affairs, *United States Security Strategy for the East Asia-Pacific Region*, Washington DC: USGPO, February 1995.

8 See Australia Department of Foreign Affairs and Trade, 'Japan country brief – May 2004: Bilateral relations overview', http://www.dfat.gov.au/geo/japan/japan _ brief _ bilateral.html (accessed 15 July 2004).

9 A copy of the text can be found at http://www.dfat.gov.au/geo/japan/ pertnership _ agenda.html (accessed 20 July 2004).

10 Perhaps the best and most comprehensive account of the recent evolution in Australian-Japanese security ties is by D. Ball, '"Hard" security cooperation between Japan and Australia: current elements and future prospects', see chap 8.

11 R. Blackwill, 'An action agenda to strengthen America's alliances in the Asia-Pacific region', in R. Blackwill and Paul Dibb (eds) *America's Asian Alliances*, Cambridge MA: MIT Press, 2000, pp. 126–34.

12 See especially the dissenting comments on Blackwill's proposal by Paul Dibb, the volume's Australian co-editor. Dibb argued that 'the first priority must be to attend to the current fraying of U.S. alliance relationships at the bilateral level'. 'Comments', ibid., p. 135.

13 R. Thakur, 'Japan, Australia define regional responsibility', *Asahi Shimbun*, 29 May 2000.

14 D. Bandow, 'Canberra's quaint naiveté', *Jewish World Review*, 21 August 2001, http://www.jewishworldreview.com/cols/bandlow082101.asp (accessed 15 November 2004).

15 R. Cossa, 'US Asia policy: Does an alliance based policy still make sense?', *Issues and Insights*, no. 3–01, September 2001, p. 21, http://www.csis.org/pacfor/issues _ usasia _ report.pdf. (accessed 15 November 2004).

16 Press conference by Secretary of State Colin L. Powell, Secretary of Defense Donald H. Rumsfeld, Admiral Dennis C. Blair, Foreign Minister Alexander Downer, Minister of Defense Peter Reith, and Admiral Chris Barrie, Parliament House, Canberra, Australia, 30 July 2001, http://usembassy-australia.state. gov/ausmin/jointpc.html (accessed 16 November 2004).

17 Cossa, *op. cit.*, p. 21.

18 Interview with Chris Masters, *Four Corners* ABC documentary program, 6 August 2001, http://abc.net.au/4corners/roguestate/interviews/brereton.htm (accessed 16 November 2004).

19 See W. Tow and R. Lyon, 'Everyone loses in ill-timed "JANZUS" talks', *The Age*, 2 August 2001.

20 As observed by Alan Dupont in an interview with ABC's *The World Today* radio broadcast, 31 July 2001, and reprinted at http://www.abc.net.au/worldtoday/ s338096.htm (accessed 16 November 2004). See also Dupont's seminal chapter on 'The Australian-Japan security relationship' in his *Unsheathing the Samurai Sword: Japan Changing Security Policy*, Sydney: Lowy Institute for International Policy, 2004, pp. 45–52.

21 Cossa, *op. cit.*, pp. 13–14.

22 Two Australian-based analysts have projected concern about these dialogues' evident lack of transparency, noting that 'due to the "shadowy" nature of these meetings it is not yet possible to get a detailed understanding of their content, or a sense of their ultimate purpose in terms of developing a bilaterally networked multilateral agenda'. This process has taken shape by stealth in spite of their mutual sensitivity to the need for avoiding an undermining of nascent multilateral regional security initiatives. See P. Jain and J. Bruni, 'Japan, Australia and the United States: Little NATO or shadow alliance?', *International Relations of the Asia-Pacific*, vol. 4, no. 2, 2004, 281–2.

23 'Transcript of the Prime Minister, The Hon. John Howard MP, briefing for Chinese media', Canberra, Parliament House, 16 May 2002, http://www.pm.gov.au/news/interviews/2002/interview1649.htm (accessed 15 November 2004).

24 The Hon. Alexander Downer MP, Minister for Foreign Affairs, Australia, 'Australia and Japan: Shared interests, a mature understanding', speech to the National Conference of Australia-Japan Societies, Adelaide, 20 September 2003, http://www.foreignminister.gov.au/speeches/2003/030920 _ australia _ japan.html (accessed 16 November 2004).

25 The Hon. Alexander Downer MP, Minister for Foreign Affairs, Australia, 'Australia, Japan and the US to hold security talks', media release, 23 January 2004, http://www.foreignminister.gov.au/releases/2004/fa008 _ 04.html (accessed 15 November 2004).

26 The Ministry of Foreign Affairs of Japan, 'Press conference 27 January 2004', http://www.mofa.go.jp/announce/press/2004/1/0127.html (accessed 20 July 2004); and US Department of State, International Information Programs, 'Text: US-Japan-Australia strategic dialogue discussions set', *Washington File*, 4 June 2003.

27 R. Lim, 'Japan as the "New South Korea?"', ICAS Special Contribution no. 2003-0305-RxL, March 2003, http://www.icasinc.org/2003l/lim _ rob1.html#fn4 (accessed 15 November 2004).

28 Ibid.

29 As noted by T. Inoguchi, 'A North-east Asian perspective', *Australian Journal of International Affairs*, special issue: 'ANZUS Turns 50', vol. 55, no. 2, July 2001, 202.

30 Embassy of the United States, Japan, 'US global posture strategy getting thorough review', http://japan.usembassy.gov/e/p/tp-20040614-60.html (accessed 15 November 2004); and Jim Garamone, 'Officials discuss global posture process', American Forces Press Service, 9 June 2004, http://www.defenselink.mil/ news/Jun2004/n06092004 _ 200406097.html (accessed 15 November 2004).

31 'US plans second flattop in Pacific', *Asahi Shimbun*, 17 July 2004. The *Kitty Hawk* would be replaced after its decommissioning in 2008.

32 See Ball, *op. cit.*, and T. Okano, 'Analysis: Military presence growing in East

Asia', *Asahi Shimbun*, 17 July 2004.

33 W. Tow and R. Trood, *Power Shift: Challenges for Australia in Northeast Asia*, Canberra: Australian Strategic Policy Institute, June 2004, pp. 28, 30.

34 W. T. Tow and L. Hay, 'Australia, the United States and a "China growing strong": Managing conflict avoidance', *Australian Journal of International Affairs*, vol. 55, no. 1, April 2001, 37–54.

35 W. T. Tow, 'Deputy sheriff or independent ally? Evolving Australian-American ties in an ambiguous world order', *The Pacific Review*, vol. 17, no. 2, June 2004, 271–90.

36 'Hill Floats Revised Asia Security Pact', *Sydney Morning Herald*, 5 June 2004.

37 See 'Singapore–US strategic framework agreement on track', exclusive interview with Ambassador Frank Lavin by Augustine Anthuvan, Asst. Programme Director, Radio Singapore International, MediaCorp Radio, 8 May 2004, http://singapore.usembassy.gov/speeches/2004/May_8.shtml (accessed 15 November 2004).

38 See Stratfor analysis reprinted on the Singaporean business and current affairs website 'Little Speck', 'Japan's defense: Getting involved in Southeast Asia', 30 November 2002, http://www.littlespeck.com/region/CForeign-Jp-021130.htm (accessed 15 November 2004).

39 On the Japanese WMD interception training program, see *Asahi Shimbun*, 3 July 2004, www.asahi.com/business/update/0703/007.html (accessed 16 November 2004).

40 J. Kremmer, 'Politics of Iraqi security draw Australia, Japan closer', *Christian Science Monitor*, 2 March 2005.

41 See 'Chile Defense Minister calls for closer APEC security cooperation with international organizations', APEC news release, Vina del Mar, Chile, 5 March 2004, http://www.apecsec.org.sg/apec/news-media/media_releases/060304_chile defencemin.html (accessed 17 November 2004).

42 R. Cossa, 'U.S.–Japan–China relations: Can three part harmony be sustained?', *The Brown Journal of World Affairs*, vol. 6, no. 2, summer/fall 1999, 86.

5 American acolytes

Tokyo, Canberra and Washington's emerging 'Pacific Axis'[1]

Purnendra Jain and John Bruni

Introduction

American international relations scholar Joseph S. Nye Jr contends that the contemporary period of history is marked by the fact that the United States has reached the zenith of its international power and influence. No power, except for that of ancient Rome, has so dominated the international landscape, inspiring a mixture of awe, fear, envy and suspicion from the world community of nations.[2] Importantly, senior policy-makers in the US State Department and the Pentagon have for some time been engaged in a hotly contested debate over how American power should be exercised. Should US power and influence attempt to enmesh and blend its policy agendas within the broader international community through a consensus approach based on multilateral forums?[3] Or, should the United States, more controversially, project its power and influence without the support of multilateral forums which by their very nature, would seek to check and balance US power and could ultimately thwart US national interests? While this critical debate is far from over, it seems from America's current situation with Iraq, that those who favour a more unilateralist approach are winning the policy debate in Washington. But in spite of unilateralism being an ascendant policy position, America still needs the support of other countries, especially its close allies, in order for it to legitimise its aims and objectives internationally, no matter how single-mindedly 'US-orientated' they may seem.

The objective of this chapter is to analyse the trilateral security dialogue process put forward by Australian foreign minister Alexander Downer and endorsed by then US secretary of state Colin Powell and then Foreign Minister of Japan Tanaka Makiko , in July 2001.[4] The proposal was put forward in light of the weakening of the multilateral processes such as the Asia-Pacific Economic Cooperation (APEC) and ASEAN Regional Forum (ARF) in economic and security spheres, and growing concerns by these three nations over nuclear-capable communist North Korea and China's intentions in relation to Taiwan and that country's ever growing defence capabilities. These and other security-related concerns led conservative governments in Australia and Japan to link themselves strongly with the US and between each other. This chapter attempts to analyse how this concept, proposed prior to 9/11, may or may not work in the new international environment, especially in light of some defining moments such as the terrorist attacks on the US, the war on Iraq and the continuing nuclear brinkmanship of North Korea – all of which have dramatically altered the course of international relations in the Asia-Pacific and globally.

Multilateralism in the region

During the Clinton years (1992–2000), the United States steadily furthered the importance of long-standing, post-World War II alliances with countries that America could be sure would support US foreign and strategic policy initiatives. In East Asia, this reinvigoration of Cold War alliance structures arose from the findings of a series of reports dealing with US engagement in Asia. These reports were published during the 1990s and were known as the East Asia Strategy Reports (EASRs).[5] The EASRs were written primarily to find a context for the US to remain militarily engaged in Asia following the end of the Cold War in 1991, and the collapse of the USSR in 1992. Some of the EASRs' most significant findings were that for the US to continue to execute the role of the 'strategic stabiliser' of East Asia, America would need to maintain a military/naval forward presence in the region of around 100,000 personnel.[6] Furthermore, it would need to ensure that its network of bilateral allies could contribute to maintaining this forward presence either in terms of lending logistics support when needed, or possibly through the deployment of their own military capabilities in support of any critical US military deployment.[7] This tasking of responsibilities to America's Asian alliances, particularly Japan and Australia, was neither clear nor easily put in place. During the early 1990s, the Japanese government's commitment to upholding the post-World War II constitutional limitations and legislation on the use of its Self Defense Forces (SDF) was not watered down sufficiently for it to play a significant role in support of the US. However, legislation was put in place to allow the deployment of the SDF to support *some* peacekeeping roles. The Japanese government, stung by international criticism for not proactively supporting the international military coalition for the 'liberation' of Iraqi-occupied Kuwait in 1991,[8] enacted the International Peace Cooperation Law (IPCL) the following year.[9] This law gave the Japanese government some measure of flexibility to deploy its military forces beyond the territorial confines of Japanese territory, but under very strict guidelines. For instance, the SDF could only be deployed for peacekeeping duties under the following conditions:

- A cease-fire must be in place;
- The parties to the conflict must have given their consent to the operation;
- The activities must be conducted in a strictly impartial manner;

- Participation may be suspended or terminated if any of the above conditions ceases to be satisfied; and
- Use of weapons shall be limited to the minimum necessary to protect life or person of the personnel;[10]

Since the enactment of the 1992 IPCL, the SDF has been actively involved in six peacekeeping operations (PKOs) – Cambodia and Angola (1992); Mozambique 1993; El Salvador 1994; the Golan Heights 1996; and East Timor 1999; as well as numerous international humanitarian and election monitoring missions.[11]

At the same time, Australia, while not being similarly constrained in deploying its military forces as Japan, only had a very limited military capability, most of which was orientated to the support of defence of Australia operations, that is, primarily guarding the maritime approaches to the mainland.[12]

In East Asia, while there was a general expectation that America would remain the central plank of the region's military stability and security in spite of the end of the Cold War, during the late 1980s and early 1990s there was enormous interest in the rise and consolidation of multilateral arrangements.[13] While it had been said that the Asia-Pacific was a region of great dynamism and instability,[14] the general trend during this period of time was one of exponential economic growth.[15] Indeed, so great was this economic growth that many Asia analysts were talking of the redundancy of the 'hard power' of military strength in the region as a medium for the conduct of international relations through the promotion of 'Asian values'.[16] The multilateral economic framework of the Association of Southeast Asian Nations (ASEAN, est. 1967) had demonstrated the ability of regional states in Southeast Asia to camouflage their outstanding territorial grievances in order to focus on the immediacy of economic activity. Military tension was viewed as a detriment to the free flow of capital, investment, trade and ultimately, economic profitability and growth. By ignoring or sidestepping sensitive 'hard power' issues in order to maintain the common purpose of furthering economic development, regional multilateralists convinced themselves that creating a web of mutual interests would curb the baser instincts of power politics and the potential for military conflict.[17]

American strategic power was nonetheless considered an important element in the short-to-medium term to allow multilateral forums to consolidate and mature as critical cogs in intra-regional development. But events were to conspire against the optimists of regional multilateralism. By the mid-1990s, the great multilateral experiment of the Asia-Pacific Economic Cooperation (APEC) forum (est. 1989) was being viewed by critics as a talk-shop.[18] So too was Asia's only multilateral security body, the ASEAN Regional Forum (ARF – est. 1994).[19] By 1996, neither organisation was seen to be making much headway in driving a multilateral regionalist agenda, critics suggesting these organisations were largely driven by national interests.[20] APEC's greatest claim to success was to economically engage the People's Republic of China (PRC), while the ARF claimed to have similarly strategically engaged the Chinese, especially over the heavily disputed Spratly Islands in the South China Sea.[21]

The Asian economic crisis of 1997 decimated many regional economies, unleashing political instability throughout Asia.[22] In Indonesia, the thirty-two year old dictatorship of General Suharto ended as a direct consequence of the collapse of the Indonesian economy. Security and hard power became important as governments either teetered on the brink of collapse or imploded, as in Indonesia's case. While the most immediate impact of this crisis was economic and political, the unravelling of political stability as a consequence of the economic meltdown in Southeast Asia saw the re-emergence of regional military forces as primary arbitrators of domestic political order, as a very real possibility. As the national capitals of Southeast Asia struggled to cope with the prospect of economic collapse, it was feared that long-standing, long-repressed ethnic tensions would come to the fore and violently tear these fragile nation-states apart, in a similar manner to events in the former Yugoslavia and Soviet Union between 1991 and 1996.[23]

American hard power was considered critical to maintaining a sense of external strategic order while the shock of the economic collapse overturned the sense of euphoria and invincibility of Asian economic growth, and the region's almost certain sense of being the future arbiter of its own destiny by exercising the soft power of economic might. While Japan, Australia and the US were all to greater or lesser degrees involved in the Asian multilateral experiments of the 1990s, they maintained a sense of distance. Indeed, Japan and Australia, having served as the 'high priests' of regional multilateralism during the early 1990s,[24] were aware of American concerns that multilateralism could hamper Washington's international freedom of movement. Tokyo and Canberra sought to balance between their competing interests of forging ahead with a new multilateral economic and security agenda, while at the same time remaining true to their respective longstanding bilateral economic and security ties to the United States.[25]

Japan as the region's economic titan and the country upon which much of Asia's economic strength lay, maintained its strong political and strategic attachment to the United States, parallel to its push for multilateralism. Japan also considered itself historically different from the rest of Asia, a difference highlighted by the fact that most of East Asia had neither forgiven nor forgotten Japan's role before and during World War II, and were reticent about allowing the country to develop a leadership role in the region commensurate with its economic strength.

Australia, during the early-mid 1990s, was trying hard to balance between the country's strong political and strategic ties to the United States and its desire to further build on its growing economic links with Asia.[26] The prime ministership of Paul Keating (1991–6) was characterised by this. He wanted Australia to be considered an Asian country in regional multilateral forums.

However, a strong undercurrent among conservatively minded Australians to maintain their unique, European-based identity thwarted Keating's goals.[27] Keating, having also incurred the ire of Malaysian prime minister Mahathir Mohamad, created a powerful enemy who did what he could to stymie Australia's efforts to formally tie itself to Asia;[28] a relationship that largely remains frosty to this day.

The United States, however, being an extra-regional power with global priorities, is neither part of the region, nor would it subsume its global leadership role to give East Asia 'special priority', although much was said during the Clinton administration of the future importance of the East Asian region. Being a global power, the US has the military ability to intervene anywhere. Its presence in Asia is critical to maintaining the regional balance of power.[29] It allows Japan the luxury of not having to become an independent military force as Tokyo remains under its strategic shield. America acts as a deterrent to the heavily militarised communist nation of North Korea and deters the PRC from using military force to unify with Taiwan. For the Japanese and Australian governments, the United States is of paramount importance on all three counts – politically, (as countries committed to upholding liberal-democratic values), militarily and economically. Multilateral arrangements, no matter how inclusive and integrated, were never considered viable alternatives to their bilateral links to the US. For the US government, Japan and Australia are two of many other allies and friends, though because of their steadfastness during the Cold War and immediate post-Cold War period, they are arguably two of America's most reliable allies in the Western Pacific.[30]

So the steady diminution of regional multilateralism post-1997, coupled with the growing importance of being able to act as facilitators for American military diplomacy in a region that was increasingly politically unstable, was viewed as critical to the enhancement of East Asia's geopolitical *status quo ante*, especially in Tokyo and Canberra. The conservative Koizumi and Howard governments of Japan and Australia further intensified this notion.

Japan and Australia: the new conservatism

More than any prime minister in recent years, Koizumi is keen on breaking away from some of Japan's self-limiting constitutional constraints on the use of military force. This, not so much to turn Japan away from its tight, long-standing bilateral alliance with the US, but to more properly adjust to a flexible, robust position in which Japan's Self Defense Forces could provide active rear-echelon support for US forces deployed to parts of Northeast Asia where the US could confront either North Korea or, possibly, the PRC. While this process has been underway since the Hashimoto government (1996–8)[31] and has been largely viewed as a consequence of a combination of external pressure from Washington (keen on Japan undertaking a larger security role) and bureaucrats in the Japanese Defense Agency (JDA) sympathetic to this American position, Koizumi represents the aspirations of a new generation of politicians and civil servants who want Japan to become known as a 'normal nation'. That is, a power that can exercise both economic and military strength to pursue its national interests. Past US governments have been actively encouraging Japan to be less attached to its constitutional limitations.[32] Japan has the largest navy in the Pacific with the exception of the US Pacific fleet. Furthermore, most of the military technology that the SDF utilises is either directly or indirectly drawn from US sources, making SDF and US forces highly interoperable.

The inauguration of a conservative government in Australia in 1996 on the other hand, has seen Canberra seeking ways in which to reposition Australia as an important cog in the network of US global bilateral alliances. For Howard, the stakes are both strategic and economic. Strategically, Australia is largely isolated from Southeast Asia and the Southwest Pacific. Its attempts at using regional multilateral forums such as APEC to tie itself to Asia more closely during the early 1990s did not produce expected results. The idea of finding a path towards security 'with and not against Asia' has not eventuated to the degree that it could have during the early to mid-1990s. Consequently, there is a feeling of drift in its Asian diplomacy, something that impacts on the country's overall security position.[33] Indeed, Howard's comments that he saw Australia acting as America's 'deputy sheriff' following Australia's successful leadership of the International Force East Timor (INTERFET) mission in 1999; his overt support of America's efforts to develop the controversial National Ballistic Missile shield; his defence of the Bush administration's position on not joining the Kyoto Protocols, the International Criminal Court (ICC) and its abrogation of the 1972 Anti-Ballistic Missile (ABM) Treaty, has incurred the criticism of many Asian countries. Malaysian prime minister Mahathir's earlier doubts that Australia was not committed to the goals espoused by Asian nations were vindicated by Australia's policy shifts under the Howard government. Australia's support of the Bush administration's War on Terror and the deployment of specialist Australian Defence Force (ADF) military capabilities to Afghanistan (2001) and Iraq (2003) were arguably a means by which Howard hoped to gain his ultimate political prize from Washington – an Australia-US Free Trade Agreement (FTA).[34] This goal, successfully accomplished in 2004, will bind Australia more closely to the US, but also significantly lessen the complications involved in trying to unilaterally re-open robust diplomacy with Asian capitals. Safe under America's military *and* economic umbrella, Australia need no longer fear isolation from its regional neighbours – many of whom are no longer considered as economically dominant and therefore politically not as important as they were during the 1980s and 1990s.[35]

For the US, in an international environment that has seen some dramatic shifts take place in terms of unfettered political goodwill being issued towards Washington, its main focus now is on attempting to get what were once tight, mutually exclusive bilateral allies such as Japan and Australia, to cooperate in new and innovative ways in order for them to more fully facilitate the continued forward US military presence in the region. The more unilateralist line disseminating from Washington has put a premium on trusted allies to substantiate and legitimise US foreign policy and strategic objectives. It is out of this concern (to use existing allies to maintain its international legitimacy) that the idea of developing a trilateral security forum between itself, Japan and Australia gained currency.

Shadow alliance?

Australian and Japanese officials began to privately discuss the idea of developing a new trilateral security dialogue with the United States in July 2001, during that year's session of the ARF in Hanoi, Vietnam.[36] Later that same month, at the Australia-US Ministerial (AUSMIN) meeting held in Canberra, Australian foreign minister Alexander Downer and US secretary of state Colin Powell, in response to questions posed by journalist Paul Kelly of the *Australian*, explained in brief terms what the advantages of developing a closer security dialogue between the three countries would mean. Downer emphasised the importance of closer Australian-Japanese collaboration as a means of fostering a more stable security regime in East Asia, while Powell spoke of the need to promote more comprehensive regional dialogue with and between its main Pacific allies – Australia and Japan. Both Downer and Powell stressed that any such security dialogue conducted by the three countries would be purely informal and would not develop into anything as substantial as an alliance structure.[37]

In a book written by US diplomat Robert D. Blackwill and co-authored by former Australian civil servant turned academic Paul Dibb, *America's Asian Alliances* (Cambridge MA: MIT Press, July 2000), the authors argued that America's geostrategic interests in East Asia might be better served by breaking down the tight, mutually exclusive network of bilateral US alliances and develop what Jimbo has called, 'bilaterally-networked multilateral security'.[38] What this relatively cumbersome term means is the development of a sort of 'expanded bilateralism' by utilising existing bilateral arrangements and expanding their connections so that all participating member-states acted as if they belonged to a multilateral arrangement. In the case of Japan and Australia, long considered by the US as the 'northern and southern anchors' of its presence in the Pacific (under existing bilateral ties with the US), these countries have been said to operate like the 'spokes' to the American security 'wheel'. Under the new paradigm of bilaterally networked multilateral security, the spokes such as Japan and Australia would coordinate more closely than they would under normal bilateral arrangements. This would give Washington a greater ability to facilitate a multilateral response to an East Asian security crisis, since two of its most valued bilateral allies in the Pacific would be able to share information between themselves and formulate a common approach in keeping with US policy objectives.[39] The advantage of this approach would be that it would not undermine the existing bilateral order. Indeed, there would be no need to formulate a new alternative security architecture to accommodate this process, at least not for the US. All that was required was a secure and comfortable venue where the Japanese and Australian foreign ministers could meet privately with the US secretary of state over a nice dinner and a bottle of red to discuss matters of mutual concern.[40] This would permit the participants to share ideas on mutual cooperation without giving it an overt official imprimatur, which might offend some influential Asian governments not privy to what was being discussed at these meetings.

Official yet subtle political-military and military-military linkages that have formed between Japan and Australia since 1994[41] give added weight to the trilateral dimension of such an informal arrangement because they allow both Tokyo and Canberra to not only talk about issues of mutual interest/concern, but actually to coordinate a joint response to issues such as peacekeeping. But there is a genuine concern by the Japanese, Australian and United States governments not to be seen to be developing any formalised and open alliance. While they are 'natural' allies in terms of purporting the virtues of liberal-democratic government, capitalism, and possessing similar levels of military technologies, any move to formalise defence linkages would have grave regional implications. For example, any moves that demonstrate a renewed closeness between Japan, Australia and the United States, especially in terms of security cooperation, might incur the anger and frustration of East Asian countries less enamoured with the direction of US strategic and foreign policies. For Japan and Australia this might mean that there is a very real danger of the two countries being perceived as agents of American regional hegemony and worse still, as possible staging bases for unilateral American strategic action.[42] At a time when Australia has already been heavily castigated by regional countries for its pro-US stance on the War on Terror, Iraq and North Korea, and while Japan is beginning to find novel ways around constitutional constraints preventing the deployment of its military forces outside of Japanese territory, both Japan and Australia, by following this path, might indeed preserve their status as 'regional outsiders' – liminal states that are of the region, but not part of it.[43]

Regional reaction

Upon the announcement of the possibility of an informal trilateral security dialogue between Japan, Australia and the US, the Chinese state-controlled media strongly condemned the development of such a move.[44] The rationale for the Chinese government's condemnation reflected the then ambivalent relationship between Beijing and Washington over a number of issues ranging from the perennial problem of human rights, the alleged Chinese proliferation and exportation of ballistic missile and nuclear weapons technologies (particularly to North Korea and Pakistan), the status of Taiwan, to the relevance of the 1972 Anti-Ballistic Missile (ABM) Treaty, US development of its National Ballistic Missile Defence scheme, and overt US spy flights close to mainland China which culminated in the Sino-American EP-3 spy plane incident in April 2001. Given the number of existing tensions between the People's Republic of China and the US, it was perhaps not surprising that Beijing took a hostile view to the proposed trilateral security dialogue, which it saw as the formation of a US-led policy of containment, designed specifically to hem in Chinese nationalist/strategic aspirations in East Asia.

While tensions between the US and China prevail, the government in Beijing is also apprehensive of Japan's rising nationalism and its attitude towards China, as reflected in the comments made by such high-profile politicians as Ishihara Shintaro (governor of Tokyo whose eyes are set on the prime ministerial position), who has openly expressed concerns about China's growing defence budget and its human rights records and has travelled to Taiwan, giving succour to that country's political regime. Moreover, Prime Minister Koizumi's visit in his official capacity to the Yasukuni shrine, (dedicated to Japan's war dead, including a number of war criminals), has also incurred the wrath of the Chinese leadership. Defence Agency director general Ishiba Shigeru and the prime minister himself, have raised the possibility of pre-emptive strikes against Japan's neighbours and have advanced the notion that Japan's Self Defense Force drop the official 'self defense' tag and become known as a 'normal' defence force. Given all these developments and historical distrust between the two nations, China would naturally see any new security structure that joins the two 'spokes' of the Pacific with its 'hub' to form a trio, as upsetting the power balance in the Asia-Pacific region and a clear threat to China's own desire for regional supremacy.

At a roundtable in the prestigious Qinghua University in Beijing where scholars, researchers and policy-makers participated, the Downer plan was called a 'little NATO' in the Asia-Pacific. The general consensus was that such a plan was not desirable, as it would create unstable conditions and be clearly regarded as a design against China and Russia, which could spark other kinds of alliances and break the strategic status quo. One of the participants went so far as to suggest that instead of the Australian proposed security structure, what could work better is a security system joining Japan, China, Russia and the US.[45]

But further afield in Southeast Asia too, some doubted the veracity of the trilateral security dialogue. Southeast Asian states have been comfortable with the existing loose regional security arrangement represented by the ASEAN Regional Forum (ARF)[46] that has sought to further develop a security culture based on ASEAN norms, which Haacke argues promotes the 'sovereign equality [of member-states], non-interference, the non-resort to the threat or use of force, quiet diplomacy, the non-involvement of the Association in the resolution of bilateral disputes and mutual respect'.[47]

The popularity of this 'passive' security culture in Southeast Asia remains in spite of criticism levelled at it for having failed to adequately address the widespread economic, environmental and security crises that hit the region between 1997 and 1999. Perhaps the most obvious problem during the period in question dealt with the issue of East Timor. The relatively muted response by ASEAN governments to the bloodshed in the Indonesian province during its referendum on independence in August 1999, demonstrated the problems of maintaining a security culture based on non-interference in the internal affairs of member-states in tandem with the reality of ASEAN's growing interdependence which, from a security perspective, allows the problems of one member-state to affect the security outlook of others.[48] Nonetheless, the development of the informal trilateral security dialogue was viewed in some quarters as an exclusive security club of wealthy, technologically advanced states. A club that would by its very existence further the impression of the impotence of the ARF as a regional security mechanism by introducing an unnecessary duplication of effort.[49] Furthermore, it was claimed that the formation of the trilateral security dialogue, due to its narrow membership base, would only help to re-enforce the image of Japan and Australia as historical/cultural 'outsiders'.[50]

Japanese and Australian contributions to US security initiatives since 9/11: bilateral cooperation or bilaterally networked cooperation?

To examine whether the notion of a trilateral security dialogue and cooperation between Tokyo, Canberra and Washington has developed in real and practical ways, it is important to analyse what both countries have done and whether there is evidence to support the existence of high-level cooperation/coordination between the Japanese and Australian governments.

Prime Minister Koizumi's reaction to the September 11 terrorist attacks against the World Trade Centre in New York and the Pentagon in Washington DC was uncharacteristically swift. In spite of previous Japanese governments having put into place improved mechanisms to increase the flexibility of the SDF in order for it to more actively support US military operations in and around Japanese territory, in past US military operations, notably the 1991 Gulf War, Japan was severely criticised by Washington for not having contributed anything to the liberation of Kuwait other than financial assistance to the tune of $US13 billion to help pay for the predominantly US military action. This action was regarded as particularly insufficient since Japan is highly dependent upon the free flow of oil out of the Persian Gulf to fuel its industries. Ten years later, in response to the September 11 attacks, Koizumi put into place a raft of measures designed to deflect potential US criticism of Japan's 'Peace Constitution'. Still working well within the limitations set on the application of Japanese military force inherent in the constitution, one week after the September 11 attacks, Koizumi pledged assistance to US authorities involved with the clean-up of 'ground zero';[51] promised financial inducements to Pakistan and India to help these countries fight terrorism; passed a domestic anti-terrorist law allowing the SDF to directly assist in the protection of US military bases in Japan against possible terrorist attack, and importantly, deployed five Maritime Self Defense Force (MSDF) ships to the Indian Ocean.[52] This was the first time that Japanese warships had been deployed for naval operations outside of Japanese territorial waters since World War II, thereby breaking the 1,000 nautical mile limit on the deployment of Japanese warships set in 1981, during the Suzuki administration. The ships were, however, not deployed in an aggressive manner. They were sent to collect intelligence on the movement of al-Qaeda/Taliban personnel out of Afghanistan to potential sanctuaries in East Africa or the Middle East, as well as supply Coalition ships on station or in transit through the Indian Ocean during Operation *Enduring Freedom* (October 2001).[53]

Australia's reaction to the events of September 11 was very different, possibly reflecting the difference between itself and Japan's limitations as a 'civilian power' constrained in the use of military force by its own constitution. Prime Minister Howard was in the United States when the September 11 attacks occurred, bringing to the Australian reaction a sense of immediacy and subjectivity absent from Japanese decision-making. On 14 September, Howard invoked Article IV of the ANZUS Treaty, which states:

> Each party recognises that an armed attack in the Pacific area on any of the parties would be dangerous to its own peace and safety and declares that it would act to meet the common danger in accordance with its constitutional processes.[54]

The fact that the attacks occurred on the US eastern seaboard, that is in the Atlantic area, arguably demonstrates that the invocation of ANZUS was largely symbolic. There was, however, nothing symbolic about Australia's military contribution. The Howard government deployed 1,500 ADF personnel to Operation *Enduring Freedom* – what was euphemistically called a 'niche capability'. The deployment of a significant element of the relatively small ADF to Operation *Enduring Freedom* concurrent to its then existing military commitments in East Timor, Bougainville, the Solomon Islands, and Operation Relex,[55] demonstrated a significant obligation to share the burden of fighting the threat posed by al-Qaeda.

The next most significant global security situation was America's war against Iraq, launched 19 March 2003, ostensibly to disarm that country and rid it of its alleged stocks of WMD. For the months leading up to the conflict, Prime Minister Koizumi played a relatively neutral hand. Mindful of the deep domestic antipathy against any prospective unilateral US-led strike against Iraq, the potential problems of backing such a strike in the face of steep Arab resentment of US foreign and strategic policies, as well as the doubts expressed by America's friends and allies such as France,

Germany and Russia, Koizumi was placed in a precarious political situation. He had to carefully navigate his way through a potential minefield and avoid upsetting his domestic constituents, while at the same time remain mindful of the sensitivities of his country's friends and significant trading partners in the Arab world and beyond. He also had to understand the position of the US administration's larger interests. Furthermore, as Curtin argued, for Koizumi to back a unilateral strike on Iraq would be to fundamentally undermine his populist credentials.[56] However, when the US finally launched its invasion on Iraq, Koizumi took a major political gamble and broke from his longstanding policy of neutrality to back the US position. According to Curtin, Koizumi's calculation was that while up to 80 per cent of Japanese voters were against a US-led invasion of Iraq, 100 per cent of Japanese voters were extremely concerned about the escalating crisis on the Korean Peninsula over North Korea's drive to develop a stockpile of nuclear weapons.[57] Indeed, it was figured that in any situation where North Korea had to be confronted over its nuclear ambitions, the US would be crucial to the resolution of any diplomatic or military impasse. By taking the step of supporting the Bush administration in its war against Iraq, Koizumi signalled that the Japanese government understood the critical nature of America's role as the primary stabilising influence in Northeast Asia, even if the majority of the Japanese people did not fully appreciate this. Japanese assistance to America's Operation *Iraqi Freedom* consisted of some medical and financial support.

In contrast to the Japanese example, the Australian government stood firmly behind the Bush administration's posturing against the Iraqi regime of Saddam Hussein. There was little doubt in the months preceding the war with Iraq, that Australia would contribute military forces to any American effort against Baghdad should a request for this type of assistance come from Washington. This, in spite of the fact that a clear majority of the Australian public was largely hostile to such a move, and the opposition and minor political parties in the federal parliament refused to give Prime Minister Howard bipartisan support for his 'pro-American' stance. Against this background of domestic political division, in January 2003 Howard gave the order to 'predeploy'[58] 2,000 ADF personnel to the Persian Gulf upon receiving a call from President Bush.

At no time were there any high-level trilateral discussions held between Japanese, Australian and American officials to coordinate a common position on either Operation *Enduring Freedom* or Operation *Iraqi Freedom*, leading to the conclusion that the notion of a trilateral security dialogue between Tokyo, Canberra and Washington flagged by Australian foreign minister Downer in July 2001, and given tacit support by former US secretary of state Powell and then Japanese foreign minister Tanaka, had been put onto the policy backburner by all three countries. Indeed, the Japanese and Australian foreign and defence policy positions, based on supporting America's efforts at suppressing international terrorism and invading Iraq, were largely derived from their own unique national perspectives. In strategic policy parlance it was more a case of old-style bilateralism that dominated the various national decision-making processes rather than the new-style bilaterally networked multilateralism.

Although no meeting at the ministerial level has taken place, nor has any coordinated trilateral response to recent wars in Afghanistan and Iraq emerged, it must be noted that low-level informal meetings between deputy foreign ministers (or their equivalent) of these three nations have been taking place. The third such meeting was held in Tokyo in June 2003 when former US deputy secretary of state Richard Armitage, Vice Foreign Minister Takeuchi Yukio of Japan and Secretary of the Australian Department of Foreign Affairs and Trade Ashton Calvert met and held a new round of 'security dialogue' that included topics such as North Korea and cooperation in Iraqi reconstruction.[59] Unfortunately, due to the subtle and opaque nature of these meetings it was not possible to get a detailed understanding of their content, nor a sense of their ultimate purpose in terms of developing a bilaterally networked multilateral agenda. One can only assume at this stage that this troika of Pacific powers is staying true to its original intent on keeping strategic dialogue between them as quiet as possible.

Conclusion

While the evidence strongly suggests that the trilateral security dialogue as first muted by Downer has not perceptibly changed the security architecture of the Western Pacific, there are signs that bilateral security cooperation between Japan and Australia is becoming tighter and more formalised. This was demonstrated by a number of measures taken by both countries since the 2001 Sydney Declaration for Australia-Japan Creative Partnership,[60] which opened the way to establishing a broader basis for cooperation between the two countries – a cooperation beyond trade and economics, which had formed the bedrock of bilateral Japanese-Australian relations since the early 1950s. This 'coming together' of Japan and Australia was emphasised recently when in May 2002, Koizumi visited Howard and the two prime ministers issued a joint statement reaffirming their commitment to growing bilateralism, including the 'non-traditional' areas of defence and security.[61] This official announcement by the two governments made plain their mutual desire to seek out ways to develop a broader basis for diplomatic complementarity.

So seemingly by default, and in a very unstructured way, bilateralism between Tokyo and Canberra on the one hand and between Tokyo-Washington and Canberra-Washington on the other, has driven a 'soft multilateral' dynamic between these three powers. In the wake of the Bali bombing, Japan and Australia spearheaded cooperative efforts to help fund and promote counter-terrorist measures among Southeast Asian states.[62] In

Operation *Iraqi Freedom* and in the post-Saddam counter-insurgency in Iraq, Japanese and Australian forces contributed what they could to preserve America's strategic interests in that beleaguered Middle Eastern state. Arguably the high point of Japanese and Australian military-to-military cooperation in Iraq came about from the deployment of SDF and ADF contingents to the Al-Muthanna province in early 2005.[63] This, along with Japanese coastguard involvement in the ongoing American initiated and internationally supported Proliferation Security Initiative (aimed at containing the flow of sensitive military technology into and out of North Korea), is demonstrating a more assertive Japanese role in international affairs. This role is largely supported by both the Bush administration and the Howard government. Indeed, 2005 seems to be a significant year in terms of consolidating the gains made by the trilateral security dialogue. What began as a set of informal talks between senior foreign office officials of Japan, Australia and the US has developed into a ministerial-level strategic dialogue.[64] As Secretary of State Rice explained:

> We agreed ... that we will intensify our dialogue. ... This will be sustained over time at the level of political directors, but it will give us an opportunity – the foreign ministers – to get together periodically to discuss the many issues of interest that we have in the Asia Pacific region, but also global issues of interest.[65]

Moreover, while Washington, Tokyo and Canberra are aware of regional concerns over the idea of establishing a formal trilateral security dialogue process and would not like to undermine regional multilateralism in the form of the ARF, all three countries are aware of and concerned at the rise of China, a rapidly modernising, nominally communist power with heavy autocratic leanings. As its strategic weight increases due to its industrial modernisation and growing wealth, China's capacity to eventually challenge the 'status quo' in the Asia-Pacific may become more pronounced. It is this prospect that arguably worries policy-makers in the US, Japan and Australia, since any near-term Chinese challenge to the status quo would likely destabilise Northeast Asia – a possibility with global implications.

The international system since the end of the Cold War is an increasingly fluid one. The current international order is one shaped around an established 'hyper power' – the US – and a growing number of lesser 'great powers' positioning themselves to undertake regional leadership roles. While the Bush administration has defended its recent military interventions in Central Asia and the Middle East in traditional Wilsonian terms, that is, speaking of America's indispensability to a just and moral international order, the reality is that the US is more concerned with maintaining a balance of power favourable to its ongoing geopolitical interests. As long-standing US allies in the Western Pacific, Japan and Australia share an interest in maintaining the primacy of US power, since the alternative is considered unpalatable. With China actively seeking out military cooperation with the Russian Federation, their first major post-Soviet military exercise dubbed 'Peace Mission' (August 2005), the likelihood of a deepening strategic relationship between Moscow and Beijing can only feed the concerns of Japan, Australia and the US. Moreover, as the US military streamlines both its domestic and overseas basing as well as its force structure, for American primacy to be maintained in Asia, reliable allies such as Japan and Australia could in time, under US guidance and support, develop into proactive bastions promoting a regional climate conducive to continuing US engagement in the Asia-Pacific.

Furthermore, now that a new American global military basing policy is being implemented by Washington, the possibility of Australia hosting a semi-permanent/permanent US military presence as a result of US troops being relocated from other parts of Asia, has been raised.[66] Were this to eventuate, the overt differences between Japan (which already hosts some 47,000 US military personnel) and Australia (which currently only hosts the 'joint' US-Australia intelligence facility at Pine Gap) would diminish further. With both countries acting as major regional staging bases for US forces in Northeast and Southeast Asia respectively, or, as Jain and Bruni contend – as America's 'unsinkable aircraft carriers',[67] the chances for greater coordination in security and defence matters between Tokyo, Canberra and Washington will increase significantly. Such a development, in tandem with growing bilaterally networked multilateralism may never turn this troika into a 'little NATO' as the Chinese fear, but into something far more sophisticated – a shadow alliance whose contemporary bilateralism is the only vestige of its existence.

Notes

1 This is a slightly revised and updated version of our article 'Japan, Australia and the United States: Little NATO or shadow alliance?', *International Relations of the Asia-Pacific*, vol. 4, 2004, 265–85. We are grateful to Oxford University Press for permission to reproduce the previously published material.
2 J. S. Nye Jr, 'US national interest and global public goods', *International Affairs*, vol. 78, no. 2, April 2002, 235–7; Nye, 'Limits of American power', *Political Science Quarterly*, vol. 117, no. 4, 2002–3, 545–59.
3 Ibid., pp. 235–7.
4 P. Jain, 'Turning to a new chapter on defence', *Advertiser* (Adelaide), 1 August 2001.
5 US Department of Defense (DoD) *The United States Security Strategy for the East Asia-Pacific 1998*, Washington DC: DoD, 1998, pp. 5–6.
6 Ibid., pp. 5–6.
7 Ibid., pp. 9–29.
8 This was despite Tokyo contributing some $US13 billion to help pay for the Coalition's military efforts. For Japan's response to the Gulf crisis, see T. Inoguchi, *Japan's Foreign Policy in an Era of Global Change*, London: Pinter Publishers, 1993, pp. 98–114.
9 S. Takai, 'Japan's contribution to UN peacekeeping', *Social Science Japan*, no. 6, February 1996, Institute of Social Science, University of Tokyo, http://web.iss.u-tokyo.ac.jp/newslet/SSJ6/takai.html (accessed 20 May 2003).

10 Ibid., p. 2.
11 The Ministry of Foreign Affairs of Japan (MOFA) 'Current issues surrounding UN peace-keeping operations and Japanese perspective', MOFA, January 1997, http://www.infojapan.org/policy/un/pko/issues.html (accessed 16 May 2003). See also Caroline Rose, 'Japanese role in PKO and humanitarian assistance', in T. Inoguchi and P. Jain (eds) *Japanese Foreign Policy Today*, New York: Palgrave, 2002, pp. 122–35.
12 During the 1990s, the Australian Defence Force (ADF) also contributed to a number of military and UN peacekeeping missions, for example: the deployment of three RAN ships to the Persian Gulf during Gulf War I 1991; peacekeepers to Cambodia and Somalia 1993; humanitarian assistance to Rwanda 1994; peace monitors to Bougainville (since 1989); INTERFET 1999.
13 R. Buckley, *The United States in the Asia-Pacific since 1945*, Cambridge and Cape Town: Cambridge University Press, 2002, pp. 181–215.
14 G. J. Ikenberry and J. Tsuchiyama, 'Between balance of power and community: The future of multilateral security co-operation in the Asia-Pacific', *International Relations of the Asia-Pacific: A Journal of the Japan Association of International Relations*, vol. 2, no. 1, 2002, p. 69.
15 W. R. Thomson, 'Asian economic growth', *Gold-Eagle.com*, April 2003, http://www.gold-eagle.com/editorials_03/thomson040903pv.html (accessed 25 April 2003).
16 For more on Asian values, see A. Milner, 'What's happened to Asian values?', Faculty of Social Sciences, Australian National University (ANU), 1998, http://www.anu.edu.au/asianstudies/values.html (accessed 27 May 2003).
17 J. Haacke, 'ASEAN's diplomatic and security culture: A constructivist assessment', *International Relations of the Asia-Pacific: A Journal of the Japan Association of International Relations*, vol. 3, no. 1, 2003, 57–88.
18 'APEC's free trade struggle', *BBC News: Business*, 6 April 2001, http://news.bbc.co.uk/1/hi/business/1251935.stm (accessed 27 May 2003).
19 Editorial, 'Time for action: Optimistic talk alone will not restore ASEAN's relevance', *Asiaweek.com*, 13 August 1999, http://www.asiaweek.com/asiaweek/99/0813/ed1.html (accessed 27 May 2003).
20 B. Buzan, 'The Asia-Pacific: What sort of regionalism in what sort of world?', in A. McGrew and C. Brook (eds) *Asia-Pacific in the New World Order*, London and New York: Routledge, 1998, pp. 68–86.
21 N. Morada, 'The United States and multilateralism in East Asia: American views and perspectives on the ASEAN Regional Forum', Occasional Paper, National Defense College of the Philippines (NDCP), March 2000, pp. 3–6, http://www.apan-info.net/ndcp/occasional_papers/HTML/morada-arf%20paper_opMarch2000.htm (accessed 23 March 2003).
22 See P. Jain, G. O'Leary and F. Patrikeeff (eds) *Crisis and Conflict in Asia: Local, Regional and International Responses*, New York: Nova Science Publishers, 2002.
23 D. Rohde, 'Indonesia unravelling?', *Foreign Affairs*, vol. 80, no. 4, July/August 2001, 110–25.
24 T. Murayama and P. Keating, 'Speech – joint declaration on the Australia-Japan partnership', 26 May 1995, pp.1–2.
25 For more on the importance of bilateral US-Japan/US-Australia ties for Tokyo and Canberra see S. Harris and R. N. Cooper, 'The US-Japan alliance'; and J. Baker and D. H. Paal, 'The US-Australia Alliance', in R. D. Blackwill and P. Dibb (eds) *America's Asian Alliances*, Cambridge MA and London: MIT Press, 2000, pp. 31–60, 87–110.
26 R. Dalrymple, *Continental Drift: Australia's Search for Regional Identity*, Aldershot: Ashgate Publishing, 2003, pp.74–94.

27 Ibid., pp. 97–107.
28 Ibid., p. 105.
29 Blackwill and Dibb, *op. cit.*
30 Ibid., 124–5.
31 G. D. Hook, J. Gilson, C. W. Hughes and H. Dobson, *Japan's International Relations: Politics, Economics and Security*, London and New York: Routledge, 2001, p. 139.
32 Hook *et al.*, *op. cit.*, pp.124–5.
33 Dalrymple, *op. cit.*, pp. 144–57.
34 M. Colvin, 'US to consider free trade agreement in 2004', Radio National, ABC, *PM programme*, 27 February 2003, http://www.abc.net.au/pm/s794463.htm (accessed 13 March 2003).
35 Although the Howard government has, after much public 'stonewalling' on the issue, pushed efforts to successfully gain Australia a seat at the multilateral East Asia Summit scheduled for late 2005; and in early 2005, successfully entered into negotiations with the Chinese government on a bilateral FTA.
36 Jain, 2001, *op. cit.*
37 Transcript, Secretary of State C. L. Powell, Secretary of Defense D. H. Rumsfeld, Admiral D. C. Blair, Foreign Minister A. Downer, Minister of Defence P. Reith and Admiral C. Barrie, AUSMIN joint press conference, 30 July 2001, Canberra, pp.1–10.
38 K. Jimbo, 'Emerging feature of bilateral-multilateral nexus on Asia-Pacific security: Search for a strategic convergence of major powers', paper presented at JIIA-APCSS meeting, Japanese Institute of International Affairs, December 2001, p. 2.
39 Ibid., pp. 2–5.
40 Interview with Hugh White, Director of the Australian Strategic Policy Institute (ASPI), Informal Trilateral Security Dialogue, 22 July 2002.
41 Interview with Air Commodore Peter McDermott, former Australian Defence Attaché to Japan, Informal Trilateral Security Dialogue, 23 July 2002.
42 P. Jain and J. Bruni, 'The lone ranger's regional posse', *Asia Times Online*, 3 August 2001, http://www.atimes.com/oceania/CH03Ah02.html (accessed 27 May 2003).
43 P. Jain and J. Bruni, 'Trans-Atlantic versus trans-Pacific alliances', *Asia Times Online*, 27 February 2003, http://www.atimes.com/atimes/Middle_East/EB27Ak02.html (accessed 24 May 2003).
44 Z. Xiao, ' "Mini NATO" in Asia-Pacific region plan by the US and Australia', *Beijing Review*, 9 September 2001, http://www.bjreview.com.au.cn/2001/200137/GlobalObserver-200137(B)htm (accessed 13 March 2003).
45 Song Nian Shen, 'Yutai huibahui chuxian "Xiao Beiyue" ' (Possibility of a 'little Nato' in the Asia-Pacific region), 8 May 2001, http://www.people.ne.jp (accessed 14 June 2001).
46 Interview, Indonesian Defence Attaché in Canberra, Informal Trilateral Security Dialogue, 24 July 2002.
47 Haacke, *op. cit.*, p. 59.
48 Ibid., p. 65.
49 Interview, Indonesian Defence Attaché in Canberra, 24 July 2002.
50 Ibid.
51 The term used to describe the area where the twin towers of the World Trade Center once stood.
52 T. Shinoda, 'CAPP hosts seminar on the Japanese response to terrorism', RAND Center for Asia-Pacific Policy (CAPP), 29 March 2003, http://www.rand.org/ nsrd/capp/events/japanresponse.html (accessed 27 May 2003).

53 Operation *Enduring Freedom* was designed to topple the Taliban regime from power and deny al-Qaeda, the group responsible for the September 11 attacks, a main base of operations.
54 'The ANZUS Treaty', *Australianpolitics.com*, http://www.australianpolitics.com/foreign/anzus/anzus-treaty.shtml (accessed 12 April 2003).
55 Operation Relex is designed to act as a deterrent to asylum seekers landing on Australian territory.
56 J. S. Curtin, 'Koizumi haunted by Blair's Iraq dilemma', *Glocom Platform* (Japanese Institute of Global Communications), 17 February 2003, http://www.glocom.org/debates/20030217_curtin_koizumi/ (accessed 7 March 2003).
57 J. S. Curtin, 'Japan's Iraq policy: It's North Korea, stupid', *Glocom Platform* (Japanese Institute of Global Communications), 26 February 2003, http://www.glocom.org/debates/20030226_curtin_japan/ (accessed 7 March 2003).
58 A word used by Howard to describe deploying military forces prior to hostilities.
59 The *Age* (Melbourne), 5 June 2003.
60 'Sydney declaration for Australia-Japan creative partnership', 30 April 2001, http://www.dfat.gov.au/geo/japan/aj_conf/statement.html (accessed 14 March 2002).
61 'Joint prime ministerial statement, Koizumi and Howard', 1 May 2002, http://www.pm.gov.au/news/media_releases/2002/media_release1623.htm (accessed 14 March 2002).
62 S. Green, 'Australia, Japan help neighbours combat terrorism', The *Age*, 8 November 2002, http://www.theage.com.au/articles/2002/11/07/1036308422515.html (accessed 20 May 2003).
63 With 450 ADF personnel sent to protect a contingent of 600 Japanese Ground Self Defense Force (GSDF) troops assigned to conduct humanitarian assistance to the southern Iraqi province.
64 This becoming public knowledge as a consequence of a meeting between US secretary of state Condolezza Rice and Australian foreign minister Alexander Downer on 4 May 2005.
65 Department of State Washington File: Transcript: *U.S. Security Talks with Australia, Japan To Intensify, Rice Says* *EPF304 05/04/2005.
66 'PM "would consider US bases" ', *Courier Mail* (Brisbane), 12 June 2003.
67 P. Jain and J. Bruni, 'America's "unsinkable aircraft carriers" ', *Asia Times Online*, 4 June 2003, http://www.atimes.com/atimes/Japan/EF04Dh02.html (accessed 6 June 2003).

6 Australia–Japan security cooperation

The Proliferation Security Initiative[1]

Andrew Newman and Brad Williams

Introduction

On 31 May 2003 in Krakow, Poland, President George W. Bush announced the Proliferation Security Initiative (PSI), an international partnership established to interdict the land, sea and air transport of weapons of mass destruction (WMD), their delivery systems and related materials.[2] PSI has variously been described as a 'political arrangement', an 'activity' and a 'new form of multilateralism',[3] and is intended to help overcome the inability of existing national and multilateral export controls to stop a 'thriving black market in [WMD] components, technologies and production materials'.[4] Since its inception, PSI has attracted fifteen *participating* members,[5] three countries have negotiated ship-boarding agreements[6] and more than sixty countries have expressed support for the initiative.[7]

This chapter is divided into four main sections. The first assesses PSI as a counter-proliferation tool and discusses why supporters of the initiative believe it is necessary, given the failure of more traditional approaches. The second section examines Australia–Japan PSI cooperation, both at the operational level of exercises, as well as actual interdiction and at the political level of conducting 'outreach' for the initiative in the East Asia region. Given Washington's critical importance to the success of PSI, US outreach activities in the region are also discussed.[8] The third section considers regional responses to PSI as a counter-proliferation tool and the effectiveness of Australian, Japanese and US outreach efforts. Some observers have focused on a perceived negative reception to PSI in the East Asia region. The authors do not underestimate both the practical difficulty of accurate and timely intelligence-gathering and the political and military risks of escalation that are implicit in forcibly and provocatively boarding shipping, grounding aircraft and stopping the land transport of WMD. However, they posit a more sanguine view of the prospects for PSI. They contend that opposition is neither as widespread nor deep-rooted in the region as may have been anticipated and outreach efforts have been successful in reinforcing PSI's underlying objective of preventing WMD proliferation; an objective that resonates in large parts of East Asia where there are genuine fears of these weapons falling into the hands of terrorist organisations. The fourth section focuses on the informal structure of PSI as an 'activity' rather than a 'treaty', which makes the initiative a more attractive option in East Asia, particularly as more states internationally become members. The importance of PSI's informal division of labor, which enables many states to participate and still distance themselves from the more operational aspects of the initiative that they may find untenable for political or technical reasons, is central to an understanding of PSI's structure. In conclusion, it is argued that appreciation of the WMD proliferation threat throughout the region combined with PSI's structure – and enhanced by outreach from Australia, Japan and the US – makes the lack of formal membership not only a poor indicator of regional support for PSI objectives, but also fundamentally misunderstands the initiative itself.

WMD proliferation and PSI

The last fifteen years have been decidedly mixed as far as preventing the spread of weapons of mass destruction is concerned. On the positive side, in 1990 Brazil and Argentina agreed to abandon their nascent nuclear programs, and in 1993 F.W. de Klerk's South Africa announced that it had dismantled the six nuclear devices it had manufactured. In the former Soviet Union, cooperative approaches to preventing proliferation helped to denuclearise Ukraine, Kazakhstan and Belarus by the end of 1996.[9] More recently, Libya renounced its WMD programs and has invited inspectors into the country to both verify and assist Tripoli in carrying out its pledge. On the negative side, in 1998 both India and Pakistan conducted nuclear tests.[10] Despite Washington and Pyongyang's negotiation of an 'Agreed Framework' to denuclearise the Korean peninsula in 1994, by late 2002 the settlement had broken down. While six-party talks are taking place, reports suggest North Korea has progressed from a 'proliferation risk to be prevented' to a 'nuclear weapons possessor to be managed or rolled back'.[11] Similarly Iran's purported nuclear ambitions have been a cause of great concern for the United States, the International Atomic Energy Agency and the European Union.

In the United States, the Bush Administration's approach to WMD proliferation was comprehensively expounded in the September 2002 *National Security Strategy*. The document was written largely by Condoleezza Rice's National Security Council and explains that during the 1990s, a small number of 'rogue states' emerged, determined to develop WMD to be used as threats or offensively to further their aggressive designs.[12] Just as important, it is feared that these states, who 'sponsor terrorism around the globe', may transfer WMD to their terrorist clients, giving America's enemies 'the means to match their hatred'.[13] Following the experience of September 11, it is this 'confluence of nefarious motives' that the administration is determined to prevent.[14]

The *National Security Strategy* outlines three reinforcing policies for combating WMD proliferation. First, proactive counter-proliferation capabilities such as detection, active/passive defences and counterforce capabilities. Second, strengthened efforts to prevent third-party acquisition of WMD materials, technologies and expertise. These include diplomacy, arms control, multilateral export controls and threat reduction assistance. Third, effective consequence management to respond to WMD use.[15] In February 2004, during a speech at the National Defense University, President Bush was more specific and noticeably more amenable to cooperative, multilateral approaches.[16] The key points are as follows:

- expanding the Proliferation Security Initiative;
- calling on all nations to strengthen the laws and international controls that govern proliferation;
- expanding nuclear threat reduction assistance;
- calling on the Nuclear Suppliers Group to refuse sale of enrichment and reprocessing equipment and technology to any state not already in possession of full-scale, functioning enrichment and reprocessing plants;
- restricting the importation of equipment for civilian nuclear programs to those countries that have signed the IAEA Additional Protocol;
- calling for the creation of a special committee of the IAEA Board to focus on safeguards and verification;
- prohibiting any state under investigation for violating nuclear non-proliferation obligations from serving on the IAEA Board of Governors.

The urgency evident in preventing the proliferation of WMD technologies and expertise is, in part, motivated by recent nuclear and missile trade revelations centred on North Korea and the A.Q. Khan network in Pakistan – revelations that prompted IAEA director-general Mohamed El Baradei to observe that 'international export controls have completely failed in recent years'.[17] PSI is a response to that failure; an admission that more traditional approaches to preventing proliferation have proven inadequate.

PSI is an aggressive counter-proliferation strategy that has been embraced, in particular, by Australia and Japan in the Asia-Pacific region. It is designed to complement a much broader non-proliferation effort that includes diplomacy, the enforcement of multilateral non-proliferation and arms control regimes, threat reduction cooperation, controls on the production and use of nuclear materials, export controls and sanctions, as well as pre-emptive military action.[18] PSI is an acknowledgement that in some cases, export controls and other supply-side non-proliferation efforts have and will continue to fail. It is also a sign of recognition that demand for weapons of mass destruction exists.

PSI is technically and politically challenging. Much of the current literature focuses on interdiction at sea, but PSI also incorporates land and air interdiction. Preventing smuggling by land is problematic given that many of the routes of greatest risk – presumably the border between North Korea and China as well as the regions surrounding Pakistan and Iran – fall within the territory of states not party to PSI. Further, interdicting suspect aircraft is both difficult and provocative in the extreme.[19] However, it has been suggested that, despite the operational difficulties, PSI may be sending a powerful political message to target states: by preparing to use instruments of military power to prevent the spread of WMD, PSI underscores US resolve and 'provides a surrogate for the more direct application of military force against North Korea and Iran, which many see as impractical or at least highly unattractive'.[20]

Pre-PSI efforts to interdict WMD-related trade were less than successful. For example, in December 2002 Spanish forces, acting on US intelligence, boarded a North Korean vessel, the *So San*, which was headed for Yemen with a cargo that included fifteen Scud missiles. But after officials protestations from the Yemeni government, as well as an assurance from Foreign Minister Abubakr Al-Qirbi that the missiles would not be transferred or sold to a third party, the freighter was released to complete its journey. At the time, White House spokesman Ari Fleischer explained that there was no international law prohibiting Yemen from receiving the missiles and no clear authority to seize the shipment.[21]

However, since its establishment, the initiative has had some significant, if somewhat under-publicised, successes. According to US under-secretary of state John Bolton, this is a quite deliberate strategy as it is feared that too much publicity could harm PSI.[22] Nonetheless, several interdictions have been confirmed. Most notably, in August 2003 Taiwanese officials, acting on US intelligence, boarded the North Korean vessel *Be Gaehung* – which was apparently en route from Thailand to North Korea – in Taiwan's largest port, Kaohsiung Harbour. Customs officials confiscated 158 barrels of phosphorus pentasulphide,[23] a chemical weapons precursor that may also be used in the manufacture of rocket fuel. In October 2003, German and Italian authorities interdicted a German-owned vessel, the *BBC China*, en route to Libya with centrifuge equipment for use in a uranium enrichment program.[24] Just as important as overt interdiction activities is the deterrent effect of PSI. As Bolton has observed, the illicit WMD deals not signed, shipments not sent and shipping routes no longer utilised are difficult to quantify but critical achievements nonetheless.[25]

PSI is an innovative approach to preventing WMD proliferation, but the concept is not new. Indeed, arguably the most famous interdiction strategy pursued by the United States in the post-Second World War period was the 'quarantine' imposed on Cuba in October 1962. More recently, following the 1991 Gulf War, a Maritime Interception Force was established to prevent smuggling in the Persian Gulf.[26] PSI was presaged briefly and somewhat obliquely in both the September 2002 *National Security Strategy* and the December 2002 *National Strategy to Combat Weapons of Mass Destruction*, although little detail was provided.[27] For example, the WMD strategy document declared that the United States must enhance the capabilities of 'military, intelligence, technical, and law enforcement communities to prevent the movement of WMD materials, technology, and expertise to hostile states and terrorist organizations'.[28]

PSI is also multilateralism of a peculiarly Bush administration brand. The Bush administration is sceptical, if not openly hostile, to arms control as traditionally practised through treaties and conventions. From the executive branch's perspective, the main problem is that these agreements serve mainly to constrain those who are already adhering to prescribed provisions rather than those who may be using the agreements as a smokescreen behind which to develop precisely those proscribed programs and provide little in the way of enforceable monitoring and verification procedures. This is why PSI consists of countries that support a set of principles rather than a formal grouping like NATO that carries obligations such as collective action.[29] As discussed below, and in stark contrast to more formal non-proliferation regimes such as the Biological Weapons Convention, this is one of the main strengths of PSI, particularly in the Asia-Pacific.

Australia-Japan PSI cooperation

The *Pong Su* incident

In April 2003, Australian special forces boarded a North Korean freighter in Australian territorial waters that was involved in an attempt to smuggle 125 kilograms of heroin with an estimated street value of A$200 million. While there were no WMD found on the *Pong Su*, the vessel's seizure and subsequent impoundment are not completely divorced from PSI. It is believed that North Korea uses the profits derived from the smuggling of drugs, arms and counterfeit money to help pay for its WMD development programs.[30]

A relatively unknown aspect of the *Pong Su* incident was the role Japan and the US played in the vessel's seizure. The *Pong Su*, which had docked in Japan on numerous occasions, was well known to Japanese authorities, who provided valuable information used to track and investigate the vessel.[31] It is plausible that Japanese assistance in this case was channelled through bilateral signals intelligence mechanisms, mostly managed by the US, as well as both countries' participation in the US Navy's Ocean Survey Information System outlined in Ball's chapter in this volume (see Chapter 9).

Pacific Protector

In September 2003, military and law enforcement personnel from Australia, Japan, the US and France conducted maritime interdiction training exercises in the Coral Sea off the coast of central Queensland. Dubbed *Pacific Protector*, the exercises were the first in a series of multilateral manoeuvres conducted under the PSI banner. The Australian government, in particular, strongly sought Japanese participation in the exercises and went to considerable lengths to facilitate this. Under Japanese law, the coastguard, which has conducted similar exercises with the Philippines and South Korea in the past but not with the US, Australia or France, is only authorised, in principle, to inspect Japanese-registered vessels outside its territorial waters. In order to circumvent this legal obstacle, Australian authorities proposed to stage the exercises so it was a Japanese-registered vessel – dubbed the *Tokyo Summer* – that would pose as the merchant ship suspected of carrying the dangerous cargo. Moreover, in consideration of Japan's desire to lessen *Pacific Protector*'s image as a military exercise, partly to avoid antagonising relations with North Korea, Australia decided to include one of its own customs vessels and lobby the US to have its coastguard also participate.[32] With the path to its participation cleared, the Japanese coastguard vessel *Shikishima* played a starring role in the *Pacific Protector* interdiction exercises, blocking the suspect vessel's escape and dispatching two helicopters, which lowered commandos onto the deck to search and secure its illicit cargo. A generally overlooked but symbolically important aspect of the exercises was the absence of a discernible public backlash in Australia over Japanese participation, which reflects the extent to which bilateral relations have moved beyond wartime animosity.

Outreach activities

Although not an exemplar of direct bilateral defence and security collaboration, authorities in Australia and Japan share a concern about focusing PSI outreach activities in East Asia.[33] This is, of course, understandable given their geographic location and the subsequent importance of the region to both countries' political, economic and security interests. As the only Asian country to be an original member of PSI, Japan has gone to considerable lengths to seek understanding and cooperation with the initiative from other states in the region, some of whom, rightly or wrongly, still harbour fears about a possible revival of Japanese militarism. In October 2003, Japan hosted the twelfth annual Asian Export Control Seminar, which focused on the pressing issue of adopting a regional approach to tightening export controls on WMD.[34] A coordinated approach to strengthening export controls in the region improves the likelihood of reducing incidents of WMD proliferation, which might spare some countries the dilemma of whether to carry out potentially controversial interdictions of vessels carrying contraband.

In November 2003, Japan also hosted the Asian Senior-level Talks on Non-Proliferation (ASTOP), which was attended by twelve Asian nations.[35] Australia and the US were also represented at the talks. ASTOP was the first senior-level dialogue among the Asian countries dedicated specifically to the discussion of the non-proliferation of WMD, their delivery means, and related materials and technology. During the talks, the participants reaffirmed their commitment to prevent terrorists or those who harbour them from acquiring or developing WMD, and were encouraged to prevent proliferation by reinforcing relevant national authorities in the respective countries. Participants discussed the need to further develop the national authorities, legislation and capabilities in order to strengthen the non-proliferation mechanisms of WMD. The meeting also acknowledged that some participating states may require technical assistance in implementing necessary measures to strengthen non-proliferation mechanisms, and called on participants to provide such assistance. The participants also received a detailed explanation of PSI from representatives of Australia, Japan and the United States, which they are reported to have appreciated.

During bilateral security talks with countries in the region, Australian government officials raise PSI as a matter of course as one of the tools available in addressing the WMD proliferation threat, as well as reinforcing existing multilateral non-proliferation regimes.[36] PSI also features on the agenda of multilateral fora such as the ASEAN Regional Forum. The importance of expanding support and, if possible, participation from countries in the region was highlighted in an address by the Australian Minister of Defence, Senator Robert Hill, to a PSI Operational Experts' Working Group in Sydney in November 2004. Among the factors contributing to the region's significance, Senator Hill noted, were its high trade volumes, standing as a major transhipment hub and growing production base in dual-use commodities, the presence of several terrorist organisations and, as outlined in greater detail below, evidence of WMD-suitable materials and missile parts and technology being diverted through front companies.[37]

Particularly illustrative of the concern Australia has regarding regional sensitivities to PSI is the case of China. In what can also be seen as Canberra's acknowledgement of China's status as an influential regional power, the Australian government dispatched its deputy secretary of foreign affairs, Paul O'Sullivan, to Beijing immediately following the Coral Sea exercises to explain the details of PSI.[38]

Mirroring Australia and Japan's outreach activities, the US has also made attempts to keep countries in the region abreast of PSI developments. During regular bilateral security discussions with Chinese officials held in Beijing in July 2003, US Under-Secretary of State for Arms Control and International Security Affairs, John Bolton, conveyed the thinking of PSI members to his Chinese interlocutors. In particular, Bolton described PSI members' concerns about so-called rogue states and terrorist groups obtaining WMD, their obligations and responsibilities, and identified what they are prepared to interdict, against whom they are prepared to interdict and to delineate some of the circumstances under which some of the interdictions would take place.[39] The absence of a discernible demonstration of opposition suggests Bolton was able to gain a measure of Chinese understanding regarding PSI.[40]

In January 2004, Bolton travelled to Malaysia to discuss PSI and other security issues. These talks were conducted against the backdrop of allegations by US and British intelligence that a Malaysian firm linked to the son of Prime Minister Ahmad Badawi, supplied parts crucial to the construction of Libya's now-defunct secret nuclear program. These allegations highlighted the inadequacy of Malaysia's current export control regime for WMD technology, forcing the government to backtrack somewhat from earlier statements regarding its satisfactoriness.[41] Bolton's global PSI lobbying activities brought him to Moscow soon after for talks with senior Russian officials. Despite its initial caution, Russia had reportedly displayed an interest in learning more about PSI and even raised the possibility of future participation in the initiative.[42] One commentator noted the irony attached to the possibility of Russia joining PSI in light of US accusations of widespread Russian WMD proliferation,[43] either through poor security at nuclear facilities or nuclear cooperation with 'rogue' states such as Iran. The irony was accentuated with Russia's decision in May 2004 to join PSI, leaving China as the only permanent member of the UN Security Council not a member.

Varying regional responses to PSI

While it is difficult to take issue with the underlying objective of PSI, some observers such as Ralph Cossa have noted the 'less-than-enthusiastic reception' it has received in Asia.[44] While one can argue that PSI has received a cool response from some quarters in the region, evidence indicates that opposition to it is neither as widespread nor deep-rooted in the Asia-Pacific region as some may have anticipated. The following section provides an overview of the various responses to PSI from the major countries in the region.

Japan

Japan's prominent role in both the operational aspects and outreach activities associated with PSI is indicative of an increasing activism in international security matters in recent times. This more assertive posture is reflected in Japan's response to suspected North Korean WMD proliferation in its territorial waters. Since June 2003, Japan has subjected North Korean cargo and fishing boats docking in Japanese ports to rigorous inspections and is reportedly considering measures to limit financial transfers to Pyongyang by *Chongryun* Koreans estimated to be anywhere between US$40 to 400 million annually.[45] These moves led one observer to make the erroneous claim that Japan has been the first country to initiate PSI.[46] PSI is broadly congruent with Tokyo's basic two-track strategy of applying 'pressure' (*atsuryoku*) and pursuing 'dialogue' (*taiwa*) in an attempt to normalise relations with North Korea. Given Pyongyang's reliance on exports of

WMD, their delivery systems and related materials as an important foreign currency earner and Japan's geographic location, which gives it control of access points from North Korea's eastern ports to the Pacific Ocean and the East China Sea, Japan is expected to play an increasingly active role in the operational aspects of PSI in the future. This was evidenced in late October when Japan coordinated the multinational PSI exercise 'Team Samurai 2004' in the Pacific near Tokyo Bay. Japan's coastguard and Maritime Self Defense Forces hosted more than a dozen participants in a simulated inter-diction.[47]

Singapore

Apart from Japan, the most salient example challenging the notion that Asian countries are opposed to PSI is Singapore, whose government became a participating member in March 2004. PSI falls neatly within the Framework Agreement for the Promotion of a Strategic Cooperation Partnership in Defence and Security that President Bush and then Prime Minister Goh agreed to negotiate during the former's visit to Singapore in October 2003. Indeed, Singapore has displayed a willingness to cooperate with several US initiatives in the context of the war against terror in recent times. It was the first Asian country to join the US-sponsored Container Security Initiative, which aims to prevent terrorists from using cargo containers to launch attacks mainly on the US – possibly with WMD.[48] Connected to over 600 ports in 123 countries, Singapore is the world's largest transhipment hub and the principle centre for shipping activities in Southeast Asia. The scale of activity makes Singapore a prime target for terrorists seeking to transport WMD or themselves worldwide by sea. In a sign of further cooperation, Singapore has also reportedly agreed to assist the US in the Regional Maritime Security Initiative (RMSI) – a plan to deploy marine and special operations forces on high-speed vessels to combat transnational threats in the form of terrorism and trafficking in humans and drugs in the pirate-infested waters of the Malacca Straits.[49] Allegations that the explosives used in the attacks on the US embassies in Kenya and Tanzania in 1998 and Bali in 2002 were transported by ship[50] underscore the necessity of such maritime counter-terrorism initiatives, which were relatively low on the US security agenda in the period shortly following the airborne attacks of 9/11.

The Philippines

Although not a participating member, the Philippines is supportive of PSI. According to the Minister and Consul General of the Philippines Embassy in Australia, Laureano C. Santiago, 'the PSI is an easy proposition for the Philippines government to support'.[51] The Philippines' receptivity to the initiative is indicative of its attempts to ally itself more closely with the US in a post-9/11 environment. The Philippines contributed a humanitarian contingent to the US-led war in Iraq and is also the only country in Southeast Asia where hundreds of US troops are stationed to train local soldiers to battle Islamic insurgents in its troubled southern regions.[52] One can surmise that the Philippines' unsuccessful attempts to eliminate this insurgency and the subsequent fear generated by domestic groups such as Abu Sayyef obtaining WMD is a contributing factor behind its support for PSI.[53]

Taiwan

Like the Philippines, while Taiwan is not a participating member, it is supportive of PSI. Taiwanese president Chen Shui-bian has declared that his country will cooperate with the international community to crack down on terrorists and to prevent such groups and rogue states from obtaining WMD. Taiwan's non-participation in PSI probably derives more from a US reluctance to incorporate it formally into the program for fear of unnecessarily antagonising relations with mainland China rather than Taipei's disinclination to join. In fact, according to an official from the Taipei Economic and Cultural Office in Australia (Taiwan's unofficial embassy), Taiwan did have aspirations to join PSI in some capacity.[54] As its aforementioned boarding of a North Korean freighter in August 2003 demonstrates, Taiwan's formal exclusion from PSI has not prevented it from cooperating with the US to prevent WMD proliferation. Despite lack of formal membership, Taiwan's participation in PSI may also serve a larger political purpose beyond counter-proliferation, that is gaining a degree of understanding and acceptance for Taipei's entry into other international organisations which, in turn, serves to legitimate Taiwanese sovereignty.[55]

North Korea

The most vocal opposition to PSI has come from North Korea, which has responded to the initiative with its customary doses of bellicose rhetoric. During the *Pacific Protector* exercise conducted in the Coral Sea in September 2003, North Korea's state-run news agency issued a blunt warning that such military exercises were 'intolerable. . . . as it [*sic*] was a prelude to nuclear war'.[56] Pyongyang's outburst was not surprising given that, despite official pronouncements to the contrary, it is commonly acknowledged that *Pacific Protector* and other planned PSI-related exercises in the Asia-Pacific are directed at North Korea.

Strong evidence has emerged in recent years regarding the scope of North Korean WMD proliferation. For instance, North Korea has exported ballistic missiles and related technology to Iran, Pakistan and Yemen. Its missile sales to Pakistan were allegedly carried out in exchange for technology to assist in the production of nuclear weapons using highly enriched uranium.[57] North Korea has also emerged as a possible supplier in a clandestine nuclear network through which it is alleged to be a likely source of nearly two tonnes of uranium that Libya bought for its now-scrapped weapons program.[58] According to David Albright, former nuclear inspector and current head of the Institute for Science and International Security, this deal suggests North Korea is much closer than previously thought to be being able to develop nuclear weapons through uranium enrichment.[59] North Korea's involvement in this clandestine and illicit commerce not only provides much needed foreign currency for its moribund economy, but in the case of nuclear technology imports, also serves to add bite to the bark of its bellicose rhetoric and is Pyongyang's sole means of regime survival in the face of the US policy of possible pre-emptive interventionism. PSI threatens to disrupt this economically and strategically profitable trade.

China

Like Russia and South Korea, China shares a land border with North Korea. Moreover, the key air routes between North Korea and its WMD trading partners in South Asia and the Middle East pass through Chinese airspace, making China's cooperation in anti-proliferation measures vitally important. In recent times, the Chinese government has grown increasingly aware of non-traditional security threats such as that posed by the proliferation of WMD. This recognition is reflected in the release of a White Paper by China's State Council in December 2003 entitled 'China's non-proliferation policy and measures'. The White Paper – China's first on the subject – emphasises Beijing's firm opposition to the proliferation of all kinds of WMD and their means of delivery and elaborates on the country's various non-proliferation measures. It further declares that '[China] will constantly increase consultations and exchanges with the multinational non-proliferation mechanisms, including the Nuclear Suppliers' Group [which Beijing joined on 28 May 2004],[60] the Missile Technology Control Regime (MTCR), the Australia Group, and the Wassenaar Arrangement'.[61] PSI is a notable omission from the above list of multilateral non-proliferation regimes. China has adopted a fairly ambivalent approach towards PSI. On the one hand, the Chinese government has expressed an understanding for the concern of PSI participants regarding the spread of WMD and their means of delivery, as well as agreement on PSI's principles and objectives. On the other hand, Beijing has tempered this display of understanding by emphasising the importance of resolving proliferation issues through peaceful means[62] – something the operational aspect of PSI has the potential to undermine.

Beijing's ambivalence towards PSI may be a reflection of competing interests among government organisations. For instance, the People's Liberation Army (PLA) is probably more inclined to participate in WMD proliferation as it relies to a large extent on external funds and sources for funding and therefore sees commercial merit in the sale of nuclear, chemical and biological weapons. In this context, an alarmist and polemical account of the PLA and its threat to US security accuses 'Chinese arms dealers . . . [of] transfer[ing] nuclear, chemical, and biological weapons to the most depraved tyrannies of the late twentieth century'.[63] The alleged list of customers of Chinese arms merchants is extensive and includes every state the US State Department identifies as a terrorist regime: Iran, Iraq, Syria, Libya, Sudan, North Korea and Cuba.[64] At the same time, the Ministry of Foreign Affairs, which is charged with the task of maintaining cooperative relations with China's foreign partners, may be less supportive of a commerce that threatens to complicate its efforts in this regard. It is important to note that in what may provide substantiation for those with a more benign view of China, the government has not dismissed PSI with the barrage of bellicose rhetoric that it might have in the past, but rather has agreed to continue dialogue with the US on the matter.[65]

Malaysia

In light of the accusations of a burgeoning trade in WMD, their delivery systems and related materials between North Korea and China, on the one hand, and countries in South Asia and the Middle East, on the other hand, and the probability of vessels loaded with these weapons passing through the Malacca Straits – a body of water linking the Pacific and Indian Oceans through which more than 50,000 vessels per year pass, carrying a third of the world's commerce and half its oil supply – Malaysia has an important role to play in any regional WMD counter-proliferation initiative. Malaysia's position on the non-proliferation of WMD has come under the spotlight in recent times with allegations concerning the involvement of the Prime Minister's son in a clandestine network that supplied parts crucial to Libya's formerly secret nuclear program. In a setback to PSI's proponents, Malaysia has publicly and vehemently opposed its operational variant, the RMSI. In response to earlier comments by US Defense Secretary Donald Rumsfeld about hoping to have US troops fighting terror in the region, which fuelled speculation that Washington wanted to deploy forces in the Malacca Straits, the Malaysian government declared that American patrols would infringe on littoral states' sovereignty.[66] While opposed to the possibility of US patrols in the Straits, Malaysia's Deputy Prime Minister and Defence Minister, Najib Razak, did not completely dismiss RMSI, indicating that Malaysia would support a plan in which it, Singapore and Indonesia shared military and other intelligence with the US and other parties concerning the Malacca Straits. However, he emphasised that 'the actual interdiction will be done by the littoral states'.[67] In fact, Malaysian and Indonesian concern at the prospect of US forces operating in the Malacca Straits, which they believed would attract more terrorists, is believed to be a motivating factor behind an agreement these two countries concluded with Singapore in July 2004 to coordinate patrols in the narrow waterway.[68]

Indonesia

Another of the littoral states of the Malacca Straits, Indonesia also has an important role to play in any regional WMD counter-proliferation initiative. As a member of ASEAN, Indonesia has acceded to several of the aforementioned international disarmament and non-proliferation conventions. In February 2004, Indonesia co-chaired (with Australia) the Bali Ministerial Meeting on Counter-Terrorism, which issued a recommendation that states adopt measures to prevent terrorists from acquiring WMD, their means of delivery, and materials and technology related to their manufacture.[69] However, despite these displays of concern for WMD proliferation and having witnessed spiralling sectarian violence and high-profile terrorist attacks in recent years, Indonesia is opposed to PSI. According to Indonesia's ambassador to Australia and a diplomat vastly experienced in proliferation issues, Mr Imron Cotan, Jakarta's resistance to PSI is based on the perception of it as a unilateral (that is, US-led) regime that falls outside international norms. Indonesia sees an inherent hypocrisy in the US non-proliferation policy of demanding non-nuclear states renounce these weapons while, at the same time, continuing its own nuclear weapons development, as well as denying developing countries the benefits derived from dual-use technology, particularly in the fields of agriculture and medicine. In what may be interpreted as an indication of flexibility on the matter, Mr Cotan did not completely discount the possibility of Indonesia participating in PSI sometime in the future, but preconditioned this upon the UN assuming control of the initiative.[70] While the UN Under-Secretary General for Disarmament Affairs has raised the possibility of the initiative becoming 'a foundation or framework for coordinated, multilateral action to enforce non-proliferation norms',[71] a reluctance on the part of some of its members, including the US, to over-institutionalise PSI makes UN control problematic.[72]

South Korea

Given the raft of allegations concerning North Korea's involvement in WMD proliferation, there are perhaps no countries in the Asia-Pacific region whose position on PSI is as delicate as South Korea. Thus far, South Korea has decided to refrain from declaring its formal policy, preferring instead to adopt a wait-and-see approach towards PSI.[73] South Korea's measured approach towards PSI can be explained by its special relationship with North Korea. With its capital located a mere seventy kilometres from the DMZ and within range of at least 300 of North Korea's artillery pieces dug into the surrounding hills, South Korea has every reason to be cautious of initiatives that its northern neighbour has threatened could spark war on the peninsula.[74] South Korea's reluctance to fully back PSI is also reflective of a desire to ease tensions in relations with Pyongyang within the framework of the 'Sunshine Policy' initiated by former president Kim Dae-jung and extended as the 'Policy of Peace and Prosperity' by President Roh Moo Hyun – policies that have at times resulted in a divergence of attitudes with the US over how to deal with the North's suspected nuclear weapons program.

South Korea's reluctance to officially declare its hand in response to PSI, however, should not be construed as outright opposition to the initiative and its broader objectives. South Korea has acceded to most international disarmament and non-proliferation conventions. Since becoming a member of the UN in 1991, South Korea has joined the Nuclear Suppliers Group, the Zangger Committee, the Australia Group, the Wassenaar Arrangement, the MTCR, the Nuclear Nonproliferation Treaty, the Chemical Weapons Convention and the Biological Weapons Convention.[75] Although not a participating member of PSI, South Korea is a close military ally of the US and it is likely that non-operational aspects of cooperation such as intelligence sharing extend to both countries' attempts to counter WMD proliferation in the region.[76]

PSI division of labor

Purnendra Jain claims that 'any exclusive high-level trilateral security dialogue centred around Japan, the US and Australia will incur suspicion from many East Asian nations as being a platform for unrestrained US unilateralism and exceptionalism and will impact negatively on both Australia and Japan in the region'.[77] Yet, apart from a few of the aforementioned cases, PSI has not encountered the widespread or deep-rooted opposition in the region some might have anticipated. Moreover, if ASEAN's decision in April 2004 to resurrect Canberra's long-held and frequently thwarted objective of a free trade deal is any indication, PSI does not appear to have caused the type of negative fallout that would harm important national interests.[78] There are two key factors that explain this positive outcome.

First, it is difficult to argue against the notion that the absence of expressions of visceral opposition to PSI among Asian countries (apart from North Korea) stems from a belated and growing recognition of the threat posed by the unfettered spread of WMD to nations in the region – many of which, particularly in Southeast Asia, are faced with Islamic insurgencies and are believed to be constituent parts of a regional terrorist network. However, at the same time, one cannot underestimate the impact of genuine attempts by the US, Australia and Japan to make PSI as inclusive as possible and seek the understanding of countries in the region regarding the initiative's objectives and functions as a contributing factor in alleviating regional opposition.

Second, one of the main reasons PSI has proven an attractive counter-proliferation proposal for many in the Asia-Pacific is that its structure offers an effective division of labor amongst both participants and supporters. It is not expected that all participating nations will carry out the same functions. In its 'Statement of Interdiction Principles', the PSI group expresses its desire to involve *in some capacity* all concerned states and looks forward to working on measures they are *able and willing* to take. This enables supporters to engage in the aspects of PSI that are operationally feasible without the requirement to be associated with the more provocative activities, such as interdiction operations, that may be politically untenable. Such flexibility is critical to an understanding of the support of, but not participation in, PSI offered by countries like South Korea. Indeed, even the resistance of key regional players such as Indonesia and Malaysia may not be the impediment to achieving PSI goals that it appears at first glance. The willingness of Malaysia, Indonesia and Singapore to patrol the Malacca Straits fits within the broad international PSI consensus that encourages countries to use their own laws and resources to halt the spread of dangerous technologies to and from states and non-state actors of proliferation concern.[79] It also suggests that there is scope for cooperation on an ad hoc basis. Collaboration on such activities as informal intelligence sharing fits within the PSI's broad objective of 'working with all concerned states on measures they are able and willing take in support of the PSI'.[80]

Conclusion

The Proliferation Security Initiative is an aggressive strategy designed to prevent the further spread of WMD technologies and expertise to both state and non-state actors; a problem that has gained currency with the confluence of the September 11 attacks, al-Qaeda's apparent interest in WMD and revelations concerning illicit nuclear and missile trade networks stemming from A.Q. Khan in Pakistan and North Korea. PSI has attracted broad international support, particularly from European nations strongly opposed to the use of force in Iraq in 2003. It has also found a receptive audience in East Asia, and even those countries opposed to PSI on the grounds that it infringes on regional states' sovereignty and smacks of US unilateralism do not dispute the seriousness of the WMD proliferation problem and are, in their own ways, taking actions that can be seen to augment PSI's broad nonproliferation objectives. A concerted outreach effort by Australia, Japan and the US has been essential in facilitating such support in the region. Equally as important, PSI's status as an activity rather than a formal treaty – which by its nature creates both rights and obligations – has enabled states to 'calibrate' their support to what is technically possible and politically tolerable. The principal examples of this division of labor are South Korea and Taiwan, both of whom support PSI's goals and activities but are reluctant to become participating members for fear of antagonising relations with their most important neighbours. As the discovery of centrifuge components in Libya of Malaysian origin has demonstrated, WMD-related materials trade is a reality in East Asia. PSI is one strategy, within a broader framework, to prevent such proliferation, and the lack of formal membership in the region is by no means an accurate indicator of support for the activity's underlying objectives.

Notes

1 This is a revised version of our article 'The Proliferation Security Initiative: The Asia-Pacific Context' published in *The Nonproliferation Review*, vol. 12, no. 2, 2005. We are grateful to Taylor and Francis (http://www.tandf.co.uk) for permission to reproduce the previously published material.

2 White House, 'Remarks by the President to the people of Poland', Wawel Royal Castle, Krakow, Poland, Office of the Press Secretary, 31 May 2003, http://www.whitehouse.gov/news/releases/2003/05/20030531-3.html (accessed 18 June 2003).

3 W. Boese, 'The Proliferation Security Initiative: An interview with John Bolton', *Arms Control Today*, 33, December 2003, 37; US Department of State, 'Proliferation Security Initiative: Chairman's conclusions at the 4th meeting', London, 10 October 2003, http://www.state.gov/t/np/rls/other/25373pf.htm (accessed 18 February 2004); Interview with a senior Defense Department official, 9 March 2004.

4 Boese, *op. cit.*, p. 37.

5 These are: Australia; Canada; France; Germany; Italy; Japan; the Netherlands; Norway; Poland; Portugal; Russia; Singapore; Spain; the UK; and the US.

6 Liberia, Panama and the Marshall Islands.

7 Australian Department of Foreign Affairs and Trade (DFAT), 'Proliferation Security Initiative', http://www.dfat.gov.au/globalissues/psi/index.html (accessed 2 February 2004).

8 For a discussion of the concept of Japan and Australia as 'northern and southern anchors' of the US regional alliance system in East Asia, see William Tow and Russell Trood, Chapter 4 in this volume.

9 G. Allison, A. Carter, S. Miller and P. Zelikow, *Cooperative Denuclearization: From Pledges to Deeds*, CSIA Studies in International Security no. 2, Center for Science and International Affairs, Harvard University, 1993, pp. 13–14; A. Newman, 'Cooperative threat reduction: "locking in" tomorrow's security', *Contemporary Security Policy*, vol. 22, April 2001, p. 91.

10 For Pakistan, this was public confirmation of its membership in the nuclear club. India had already conducted a so-called peaceful nuclear explosion in 1974.

11 The six parties to these talks are China, Japan, North Korea, Russia, South Korea and the United States.

12 J. Mann, *Rise of the Vulcans: The History of Bush's War Cabinet*, New York: Viking, 2004, p. 316; White House, *The National Security Strategy of the United States of America*, Washington DC, September 2002, p. 14.

13 The White House, 'President delivers State of the Union Address', 29 January 2002, http://www.whitehouse.gov/news/releases/2002/01/20020129-11.html (accessed 4 February 2002).

14 'The international aspects of terrorism and weapons of mass destruction', remarks of John Bolton, Under Secretary of State for Arms Control and International Security, to the Second Global Conference on Nuclear, Bio/Chem Terrorism: Mitigation and Response, Washington DC, 1 November 2002, http://usembassy-australia.state.gov/hyper/2002/1101/epf502.htm (accessed 8 February 2003).

15 White House, September 2002, *op. cit.*, p. 14.

16 All information is taken from 'Remarks by the President on weapons of mass destruction proliferation', Fort Lesley J. McNair – National Defense University, Washington DC, 11 February 2004, http://www.whitehouse.gov/news/releases/2004/02/20040211-4.html (accessed 11 February 2004).

17 I. Traynor, 'Nuclear chief tells of black market in bomb equipment', *Guardian*, 26 January 2004, http://www.guardian.co.uk/international/story/0,3604,1130956,00.html (accessed 30 January 2004).

18 White House, *National Strategy to Combat Weapons of Mass Destruction*, Washington DC, December 2002, pp. 3–5.

19 For an analysis of the difficulties in applying PSI to North Korea see Michael Levi, 'Uncontainable: North Korea's loose nukes', *The New Republic*, 26 May 2003, http://www.brook.edu/views/articles/fellows/levi20030526.htm (accessed 27 May 2003).

20 International Institute for Strategic Studies, 'The Proliferation Security Initiative: An interdiction strategy', *Strategic Comments*, vol. 9, issue 6, http://www.iiss.org/stratcomfree.php?scID = 282 (accessed 15 March 2004).

21 'US lets Scud ship sail to Yemen', *CNN.com*, 12 December 2002, http://edition.cnn.com/2002/WORLD/asiapcf/east/12/11/us.missile.ship/ (accessed 15 June 2004); R. Marquand, 'Ship's seizure sends warning to N. Korea', International Institute for Strategic Studies, *Strategic Comments – The Proliferation Security Initiative: An interdiction strategy*.

22 Boese, *op. cit.*, p. 37.

23 Marquand, *op. cit.*

24 White House, 'Remarks by the President on weapons of mass destruction', Fort Lesley J. Mcnair – National Defense University, 11 February 2004, http://www.whitehouse.gov/news/releases/2004/02/20040211-4.html (accessed 11 February 2004); S. Squassoni and A. Feickert, *Disarming Libya: Weapons of Mass Destruction*, CRS Report for Congress, Congressional Research Service, RS21823, 22 April 2004, p. 3.

25 'The Proliferation Security Initiative: A vision becomes reality', remarks of Under-Secretary for Arms Control and International Security John Bolton to the first anniversary meeting of the Proliferation Security Initiative, Krakow, Poland, 31 May 2004, www.state.gov/t/us/rm/33046pf.htm (accessed 8 June 2004).

26 K. Pollack, *The Threatening Storm: The Case for Invading Iraq*, New York: Random House, 2002, p. 66.

27 White House, September 2002, *op. cit.*, p. 14; White House, December 2002, *op. cit.*, p. 2.

28 While House, December 2002, ibid., p. 2.

29 Interview with a senior Defense Department official, Washington DC, 9 March 2004.

30 It has been suggested that the *Pong Su*'s seizure was conducted under a separate program known as the DPRK Illicit Activities Initiative. See M. Richardson, *A Time Bomb for Global Trade: Maritime-related Terrorism in an Age of Weapons of Mass Destruction*, Singapore: Institute of Southeast Asian Studies, 2004, pp. 105–6.

31 Ibid., p. 105. Australian foreign minister Alexander Downer acknowledged Japanese assistance in a press conference in Tokyo in May 2003. DFAT, 'Tokyo press conference', 15 May 2003, http://www.dfat.gov.au/media/transcripts/2003/030515_tokyo_pressconf.html (accessed 4 January 2005).

32 *Asahi Shimbun*, 14 September 2003, p. 3.

33 Australian Department of Foreign Affairs and Trade official (name withheld by request), interview by authors, Canberra, 15 April 2004.

34 'Tairyō hakai heiki no yushutsu soshi: Ajia demo "wakugumi" ' ('Stopping the export of weapons of mass destruction: A "framework" also in Asia'), *Asahi Shimbun*, 22 October 2003, p. 2.

35 This paragraph draws from the Ministry of Foreign Affairs of Japan, 'Asian Senior-level Talks on Non-Proliferation, Tokyo, 13 November 2003, Chairman's summary',http://www.mofa.go.jp/policy/un/disarmament/arms/astop/summary03 11.html (accessed 15 June 2003)

36 Australian Department of Foreign Affairs and Trade official (name withheld by request), 'PSI', email (11 January 2005).

37 Department of Defence, 'Opening address Proliferation Security Initiative: operational experts' working group', delivered by Minister for Defence Senator Robert Hill, Sydney, 30 November 2004, http://www.minister.defence.gov.au/HillSpeechtpl (accessed 11 January 2005).

38 Department of Foreign Affairs and Trade, 'Minister for Foreign Affairs, Alexander Downer, doorstop interview, Perth', 15 September 2003, http://www.dfat.gov.au/media/transcripts/2003/030915_doorstop_perth.html (accessed 29 May 2004).

39 US Department of State, 'Press conference on U.S.-China security dialogue', 28 July 2003, http://www.state.gov/t/us/rm/22917pf.htm (accessed 29 May 2004).

40 Under-Secretary Bolton's role in the broader effort to denuclearise the Korean peninsula has been somewhat more confrontational. Bolton, who prior to his appointment served as senior vice president of the conservative American Enterprise Institute, was foist upon Secretary of State Colin Powell by the vice president's office and his political outlook is aligned more closely with senior members of the Pentagon and White House than with his ostensible boss. On a visit to South Korea and Japan in mid-2003, Bolton 'got out in front' of his departmental colleagues, who had been instructed to push for negotiations, and took a hard line with Pyongyang. The North Korean Foreign Ministry was apoplectic, reportedly calling Bolton 'human scum' and a 'bloodsucker'. 'Spokesman for DPRK Foreign Ministry slams U.S. mandarin's invective', *Korean Central News Agency of the DPRK*, 4 August 2003, http://www.kcna.co.jp/index-e.htm (accessed 8 July 2003); Interview with one of the authors, Washington DC, 3 February 2004.

41 Australian Department of Foreign Affairs and Trade official (name withheld by request), interview by authors, Canberra, 15 April 2004.

42 C. Giacomo, 'U.S. presses Russia to join arms body', *Moscow Times* online edition, 19 January 2004, http://www.themoscowtimes.com/stories/ 2004/01/29/012.html (accessed 4 June 2004).

43 Ibid.

44 R. Cossa, 'Putting a lid on proliferation', *Japan Times*, 23 October 2003, http://www.japantimes.co.jp (accessed 25 February 2004).

45 G. McCormack, *Target North Korea: Pushing North Korea to the Brink of Nuclear Catastrophe*, Sydney: Random House Australia, 2004, p. 171. In addition, Japanese authorities have been monitoring attempts by trading houses set up by *Chongryun* Koreans in early 2003 to export high-tech items capable of being used for the development of WMD. In a move clearly directed at Pyongyang, the Japanese Diet also passed legislation in June 2004 enabling it to ban vessels from specific countries docking in Japanese ports for a certain period of time. 'Nyūkō kinshi-hō ga seiritsu: Kitachōsen e no seisai dainidan' ('Law forbidding port entry approved: Second stage of sanctions on North Korea'), *Hokkaidō Shimbun*, 15 June 2004, http://www.hokkaido-np.co.jp (accessed 15 June 2004).

46 Suzuki Yūji, 'Kakusan Anzen Hoshō Inishiatibu (PSI)' ('The Proliferation Security Initiative'), *Kaigai Jijō*, 52, January 2004, 150. In April 2002 French authorities, acting on a German government tip-off, ordered a French ship suspected of carrying components for high-speed centrifuges to unload its cargo in an Egyptian port.

47 Undersecretary for Arms Control and International Security John Bolton, 'Stopping the spread of weapons of mass destruction in the Asian-Pacific region: The role of the Proliferation Security Initiative', Tokyo, 27 October 2004, http://www.state.gov/t/us/rm/37480.htm (accessed 6 December 2004).

48 M. Richardson, 'It's full steam ahead in hunt for terror arms shipments', *The Straits Times*, 23 October 2003, http://web.lexis-nexis.com (accessed 12 February 2004).

49 'US war on terror goes to water', *The Australian*, 5 April 2004, p. 13.

50 See for instance, 'Liberia lets US search ships', *China Daily*, 14 February 2004, http://www.chinadaily.com.cn/English/doc/2004-02/14/content _ 306091.htm (accessed 24 February 2004)

51 Interview with the authors, Canberra, 13 April 2004.

52 'US war on terror goes to water', *The Australian*, 5 April 2004, p. 13. The Philippines government withdrew its troops from Iraq in July 2004 one month ahead of schedule in response to demands by insurgents who had kidnapped and threatened to execute one of its nationals.

53 In March 2004, Philippine police arrested six suspected Abu Sayyaf militants and confiscated 'readings on biological and chemical warfare'. Global Security Newswire, 'Philippine police find chemical weapons information in hands of Abu Sayyaf militants', *Nuclear Threat Initiative*, 24 May 2004, http://www.nti.org (accessed 27 May 2004)

54 'PSI', email (5 March 2004).

55 Dr Chen Jie, lecturer in the School of Social and Cultural Studies at the University of Western Australia, observed that when it considers joining international organizations, Taiwan is interested in the 'symbolism and trappings of sovereignty, more often than not treating the substance of the organization as [a] secondary issue'. Any organization that doesn't force Taiwan to use the demeaning label 'Taipei, China' is even more welcome. Chen Jie, 'Taiwan and PSI', email (5 May 2005).

56 Korean Central News Agency, 'KCNA assails U.S.-led multinational naval blockade exercises', 17 September 2003, http://www.kcna.co.jp/index-e.htm (accessed 25 February 2004)

57 See S. A. Squassoni, 'Weapons of mass destruction: trade between North Korea and Pakistan', *CSR Report for Congress*, 11 March 2004, pp. 1–14. As North Korea does not participate in the MTCR, its missile sales to Pakistan and Yemen do not, strictly speaking, violate international law. Nevertheless, it has been sanctioned for such sales while Yemen has not.

58 G. John, 'Suspected nuclear sale of uranium to Libya raises concerns of North's role in nuclear black market', Associated Press, 23 May 2004.

59 Ibid.

60 'China joins the Nuclear Suppliers Group', Embassy of the People's Republic of China in the United States of America, http://www.china-embassy.org/eng/xw/t122871.htm# (accessed 15 June 2004)

61 Information Office of the State Council of the People's Republic of China, *China's Non-Proliferation Policy and Measures*, Beijing: New Star Publishers, 2003, p. 23.

62 A Chinese Foreign Ministry spokesperson issued a statement to this effect following talks between Vice-Foreign Minister Zhang Yesui, and US Under-Secretary of State for Arms Control and International Security Affairs, John Bolton, in February 2004. China's emphasis on attaining the goal of non-proliferation through peaceful means is also featured in the White Paper. See Ibid., pp. 4–5.

63 E. Timperlake and W. C. Triplett II, *Red Dragon Rising: Communist China's Military Threat to America*, Washington DC: Regnery Publishing, 1999, p. 92.

126   *Andrew Newman and Brad Williams*

64 Ibid., p. 98.
65 See for instance, 'Liberia lets US search ships', *China Daily* online edition, 14 February 2004, http://www.chinadaily.com.cn/English/doc/2004-02/14/content_306091.htm (accessed 24 February 2004).
66 Malaysian National News Agency, 'Singapore, Japan pledge to work for safer straits', 11 June 2004, http://www.bernama.com/bernama/v3/printable.php?id = 72726 (accessed 16 June 2004)
67 Malaysian National News Agency, 'Malaysia, US to discuss security in Melaka Straits soon', 6 June 2004, http://www.bernama.com/bernama/v3/printable.php?id = 71715 (accessed 16 June 2004)
68 S. Powell, 'Navies unite to fight piracy in a dire strait', *The Australian*, 21 July 2004, p. 8. It should also be noted that problems related to the joint command of these patrols remain unresolved.
69 Australian Government, Department of Foreign Affairs and Trade, 'Bali Regional Ministerial meeting on counter-terrorism: Co-chairs statement', 5 February 2004, http://www.dfat.gov.au/icat/2004_conference/cochair_statement.html (accessed 3 March 2004)
70 Mr Cotan remarked that Indonesia would be happy to join PSI if it was under UN control. Interview with the authors, Canberra, 13 April 2004.
71 These comments were made in an address to a conference entitled 'Challenges to non-proliferation and disarmament norms in East Asia', held in South Korea on 3 December 2003. See http://disarmament.un.org:8080/speech/03dec2003.htm (accessed 9 June 2004)
72 In any event, the Bush administration's disdain for the United Nations in general makes any such eventuality unlikely at best.
73 Political attaché, Embassy of South Korea, Australia, 'PSI', email (5 May 2004).
74 M. O'Hanlon and M. Mochizuki, *Crisis on the Korean Peninsula*, New York: McGraw-Hill, 2003, p. 66.
75 The South Korean National Assembly ratified the NPT in 1975 and the BWC in 1987. Ministry of Foreign Affairs and Trade, South Korea, 'Disarmament and non-proliferation', 29 September 2003, http://www.mofat.go.kr/en/for/e_for_view.mof (accessed 5 April 2004).
76 Former South Korean unification minister, Jeong Se-hyun, is reported to have expressed caution over pressuring North Korea through PSI during a speech he delivered in New York in October 2003. *Asahi Shimbun*, 2 October 2003, p. 2.
77 Remarks of Professor Purnendra Jain at the Symposium on Regional Security and Australia-Japan Cooperation, sponsored by the Monash University Japanese Studies Centre and the Consulate General of Japan, Melbourne, 27 February 2004, Clayton.
78 ASEAN's decision is more significant in light of the criticism that involvement in the war in Iraq had inflicted mortal damage to Australia's standing in the region. See P. Kelly, 'A door opens in Asia', *The Weekend Australian*, 24–5 April 2004, p. 30.
79 The White House, 'Statement on Proliferation Security Initiative', statement of the press secretary, 4 September 2003, http://www.whitehouse.gov/news/releases/2003/09/20030904-10.html (accessed 18 February 2004)
80 Department of Foreign Affairs and Trade, 'Proliferation Security Initiative: Statement of interdiction principles', undated, http://www.dfat.gov.au/globalissues/psi/psi_statement.html (accessed 18 February 2004).

7 Japan and the War on Terror

Opportunity costs

David Wright-Neville

Introduction

One of the most remarkable features of the post-1945 strategic landscape in East Asia was the speed with which Japan was transformed from an adversary characterised in wartime propaganda as the epitome of Oriental evil into that of a key ally, a bulwark against the spread of a new evil.[1] The context within which this evolution occurred was, of course, the rapid spread of Cold War hostilities from Europe into the Asia-Pacific, and the shared interest of both Tokyo and Washington in containing the spread of Soviet and Chinese influence throughout the region. Looked at through a wider historical lens, this speedy rapprochement is a useful reminder of how shifting international political forces can generate new national interest calculations that overwhelm quickly old antipathies and hostilities.

The events of 11 September 2001 provided a tragic example of how constantly evolving political dynamics are again at work, particularly with respect to the emergence of religiously and culturally motivated violence as an organising principle within international politics. Against this background, the War on Terror launched by the Bush administration in the wake of the attacks has also presaged a fresh set of international political forces that could once again reconfigure Japan's relevance to the United States and to the international community more generally. The precise shape of this reconfiguration is still not clear, largely because of seemingly intractable debates within Japan itself about how best to respond to these changes.

Along with Australia, Japan has loomed as one of Washington's major Asia-Pacific supporters in the War on Terror. As with Australia, for the past fifty years Japan's military relationship with the United States has provided the fulcrum upon which national security planning has rested. Like Australia, Japan has also suffered directly from recent terrorist attacks, notably in Bali where two Japanese and eighty-eight Australians were killed in the attacks by Jemaah Islamiyah on two nightclubs on 12 October 2002, and in Iraq, where Japanese nationals have been the victims of kidnappings and executions. It is therefore not surprising that Japan's response to the Bush administration's War on Terror has mirrored that of Australia, with both countries playing a leading role in coordinating multilateral counter-terrorism initiatives among the broader East Asian and Southeast Asian regional community and in lending military and other support to US-led operations in Afghanistan and Iraq. In this latter case, however, Japan's ability to contribute to multilateral military operations has been limited by constitutional constraints in place since the end of the Second World War that place significant restrictions on Tokyo's ability to deploy troops overseas in combat roles. Indeed, in Southern Iraq teams of Japanese engineers involved in reconstruction efforts are currently protected by several hundred Australian military personnel in an operation that underscores the extent to which both countries can work together.

The most overt expression of the mutual interests of both countries is contained in a 'Joint Statement on Cooperation to Combat International Terrorism', which was signed by representatives from both countries in July 2003. The Joint Statement's Action Plan resolves both countries to cooperate in a range of key counter-terrorism areas, including better intelligence exchange, including more regular visits by senior officials, enhanced cooperation between the respective bureaucracies of both countries in helping other countries in the region, notably in Southeast Asia, to meet their obligations under new United Nations counter-terrorism protocols and to build their counter-terrorism capabilities in areas such as border control, the establishment of financial intelligence units across the region to better monitor terrorist financing, cyber-security and the protection of critical national infrastructure.[2]

However, although these initiatives are valuable in their own right, Canberra, along with Washington, would like Japan to play a more active military role. Although it would not say so publicly, Australia has been privately supportive of the gradual erosion of Japan's post-war pacifist instincts. For several decades, successive Australian governments have wanted Japan to translate its economic clout into a more muscular strategic role in the East Asian region where it might work alongside the United States in keeping China and North Korea in check. However, a wish to avoid offending the sensitivities of many older Australians, whose experiences in the Pacific theatre of the Second World War still feeds a deep animus towards Japan, and a desire not to be seen to be involving themselves in what remains an extraordinarily delicate domestic issue within Japan itself, means that Canberra's ambitions for Tokyo have been muted. Reinforcing Australia's reluctance to be seen to be too vocal in supporting a more assertive Japanese role in regional security issues in general, but in the War on Terror in particular, has been a fear that such a stand would risk alienating some of Japan's neighbours, especially China as well as South and North Korea, all of whom have expressed deep reservations and even hostility towards the prospect of a strategically resurgent Japan.

In short, while Australia and Japan will continue to work cooperatively in combating terrorism with the wider Asia region and around the world, the relationship is unlikely to deepen. This is because debates within Japan itself about Japan's role in the world and the opposition to a more assertive Japan within North Asia more generally are issues over which Canberra has little control. Hence, there is little that Australia can do except wait for these issues to develop and then act with diplomatic creativity to tailor bilateral initiatives that sit comfortably with Japan itself as well as with other regional players.

Japan and terrorism

Japan's military role in regional and global affairs has been a highly divisive issue for more than half a century. However, since the 1970s, a growing number of Japanese have begun to jettison the historical baggage of the early 1940s and urge their government to assume a more proactive strategic role on the international stage. The pervasiveness of this mood within Japan has traditionally varied according to wider international developments, with support for overhauling Japan's post-war constitution to allow a more proactive military and strategic role seemingly dependent on assessments as to whether the international environment would punish or reward Japan for such a move. This ambiguity has been again brought into sharp relief by the growing threat of terrorism. On the one hand, a growing number of Japanese have responded to the post-9/11 world convinced that it is time that Japan abandon the restrictions placed on its military capabilities by the post-war constitution and play a more assertive role in international affairs. Within this group, there are those who see a more strategically formidable Japan as playing a more proactive role alongside the US in policing fundamental aspects of the international neo-liberal order. This is a view of Japan that Washington has long advocated. Becoming especially evident in the 1980s, successive US administrations have chafed at Japan's reluctance to translate its economic muscle into greater strategic clout designed to relieve the burden on the US in containing China, policing (as much as possible) the unpredictable regime in North Korea, and more recently combating terrorist networks in the region. A more belligerent variation on this theme is epitomised by the maverick governor of Tokyo, Ishihara Shintaro, whose Pan Asian antipathy towards Washington underpins a vision of Japan as a nuclear weapons-capable state – an Asian power in its own right.[3] However, although Ishihara's pugnacious rhetoric touches the nationalistic sentiments of a new generation of Japanese, most appear uncertain (even uneasy) about transforming the rhetoric into reality.[4]

The lack of a public consensus about Japan's place in the contemporary world has also coloured Tokyo's response to the War on Terror. While Prime Minister Junichiro Koizumi has embraced Washington's initiatives as a vehicle for engineering a proactive strategic role for Tokyo, suspicions about the costs such a strategy might impose on Japan remain deeply embedded and have thus contributed to a situation whereby Koizumi's own pro-US rhetoric has not been matched by concrete policy shifts.

Even so, there have been some subtle but important changes, not least in Koizumi's successful efforts to amend key elements of Japan's post-war pacifist constitution to allow for a more proactive use of the nation's Self Defense Forces in support of Washington's global military endeavours. This chapter will explore these dynamics within the context of the War on Terror, arguing that while Koizumi's reforms have created space for a more energetic Japanese security role, there remain significant institutional and attitudinal obstacles that will impede the realisation of this vision for the foreseeable future. As a result, Japan's contribution to US-led efforts to combat the spread of religiously motivated terrorism will continue to rely mainly on its soft rather than hard power. It is possible to discern the shape of these policies by examining Japan's counter-terrorism role in Southeast Asia, where Tokyo has played a leading role in helping to coordinate a series of measures designed to boost the region's ability to deal with the myriad problems that have facilitated the spread of terrorist networks across the region.[5]

Japan is no stranger to terrorism, in either its 'new' or 'old' varieties.[6] In the 1960s, members of the extremist left-wing Japanese Red Army carried out a series of attacks in both Japan and overseas, often in league with Middle Eastern counterparts. More recently, Japan was also a tragic victim of the new variety of mass-casualty terrorism when in April 1995 the Aum Shinrikyo religious cult launched a sarin gas attack on the Tokyo subway.[7] Coupled with a long tradition of state monitoring of religious and ethnic minorities, the experience of these different forms of terrorism meant that by the time of the 9/11 attacks on the United States, there was already in place in Japan a system of policing and surveillance that other wealthy democracies have only recently begun to replicate.[8]

However, there is less Tokyo can do about the threat to Japanese interests outside its own borders. Japanese nationals were among those killed in the 9/11 attacks, while two of its citizens were also victims of the terrorist bombings in Bali barely twelve months later. Nor has Japan been spared in the anarchy that has slowly engulfed Iraq in the wake of the US-led invasion to topple Saddam Hussein. The deaths in 2003 of two Japanese diplomats, and the 2004 capture and videotaped intimidation of several Japanese aid workers by terrorists linked to the al Qaeda-linked Jordanian terrorist Abu Musab al-Zarqawi, caused widespread anxiety within Japan. Demands by the kidnappers that Tokyo withdraw its small contingent from Iraq within forty-eight hours of the kidnapping were not acceded to by the government of Junichiro Koizumi, and negotiators managed to secure their release. Another Japanese national, Shohei Koda, was not so fortunate. Kidnapped by the same group later that year, his decapitated body was found several days later by a US military patrol.

The external focus of Japan's counter-terrorism concerns has been further reinforced by signs that anger at the counter-terrorism policies of the Bush administration has struck deep roots outside the Middle East, manifesting itself in particular among Muslim communities in Southeast and South Asia, East and North Africa, and among Muslim diasporas in the developed world. The metamorphosis of this anger into a fragmented collection of self-contained terrorist cells, such as that responsible for the July 2005 attacks on the London public transport system, is also a major concern to Tokyo, as it is to Canberra and many of Washington's other allies. Reports that a convicted French terrorist, Lionel Dumont, who was a member of the so-called Roubaix Gang of Islamist militants, had lived in Japan from July 2002 to September 2003 emphasised to Japanese officials that despite their vigorous immigration controls they are not immune to this global phenomenon.[9] Even so, from a domestic counter-terrorism perspective, Japanese officials consider that extensive state surveillance of minority groups (mainly ethnic Koreans, foreign workers, and religious sects), coupled with notoriously strict immigration controls, have served it well and continue to provide a level of protection that other wealthy democracies are now struggling to replicate.

As mentioned above, Japanese policy-makers are much more concerned about the threat posed by terrorism to Japanese interests outside its national borders. Especially worrying are reports that these networks could adjust their tactics from land and air-based violence to maritime targets. In light of Japan's heavy dependence on trade, especially oil imports from the Middle East, the 2000 attack against the USS *Cole* in Aden harbour, the 2002 bombing of the oil tanker *Limburg*, and reports that the Philippines-based Abu Sayyaf group (which has links to Jemaah Islamiyah, the group responsible for the attacks in Bali) has organised for members to receive diving instruction, have reinforced Tokyo's sense of vulnerability to the spread of terrorist violence. Added to this has been the dramatic increase in the incidence of piracy in Southeast Asian waters, especially in the Straits of Malacca (through which most of Japan's oil supplies from the Middle East pass) by individuals and groups linked to Indonesian rebels.[10]

However, enhancing the protection of its overseas interests from terrorist attack through supporting Washington's international counter-terrorism initiatives has presaged a number of important foreign policy decisions for Japan. In particular, it is becoming increasingly clear that Japan's high-profile support for Washington's 'War on Terror' is not cost-free, and as a result Tokyo has been forced to make complex diplomatic calculations designed to calibrate the national benefits it accrues by dent of its support for the Bush administration against costs imposed as punishment for this support. These costs are measured in terms of the potential targeting of Japanese nationals or interests abroad by different elements of a disaggregated international terrorist community, as well as by criminal gangs operating in the Middle East and Southeast Asia. In the latter case, kidnapping-for-ransom syndicates, many of whom on-sell their hostages to terrorist groups, are of particular concern to Tokyo.

Domestic changes

An important first step in understanding how Japan has attempted to nuance its approach to counter-terrorism at the international level is to examine debates within the context of recent changes in Japan's domestic political scene. In particular, the changes to Japan's domestic policy environment overseen by Prime Minister Koizumi have been critical, especially in terms of Tokyo's uncharacteristically rapid policy response to the attacks on the United States on 11 September 2001. Indeed, the speed with which Koizumi responded to the attacks suggest a determination to capitalise on anxieties generated by the attacks to assert a more energetic style of leadership and cut through the atrophied and overly bureaucratic foreign policy-making habits of the past. To this end, Koizumi has earned the respect of Washington and other regional allies, notably Australia, but this support means little within the context of Japanese domestic politics.

Despite Japan's post-1945 status as a bulwark of the US-sponsored global capitalist system, in areas of defence and security Tokyo has been a cautious player, satisfying itself with a quiet form of diplomacy wherein its growing financial clout was used to buy diplomatic support for broader Western policy objectives. To this end, for most of the post-1945 era, Japanese foreign policy has been content to support wider US strategic interests through financial measures rather than an assertive use of diplomatic or military muscle. Generally speaking, this preference for soft power was underpinned by two attitudinal phenomena. At the domestic level, the highly divisive nature of debates over Japan's possession and use of military power has complicated efforts to rebuild a post-war military posture commensurate with Japan's international economic clout. In particular, the conservative instincts of Japan's foreign policy bureaucracy, coupled with its extraordinary influence over the policy-making process, meant that Tokyo's international initiatives were rarely flamboyant and often highly predictable.

However, the early 1990s saw growing momentum for change as a new generation of politicians replaced those whose tenure began during the post-war reconstruction phase of the 1950s. In particular, a series of electoral reforms instituted in 1994 conferred more power upon younger politicians, especially from the dominant Liberal Democratic Party (LDP), to set out on reformist paths independent of an overly cautious but highly interventionist bureaucracy and the deadening hand of deep intra-party factional rivalries. It was this group of politicians that were to prove instrumental in Koizumi's ascendancy to the premiership in 2001.

A second wave of political reforms was introduced in 1999, during which time the LDP shared government in a shaky coalition with the Liberal Party, the latter headed by a former LDP powerbroker, Ichiro Ozawa. To secure Ozawa's support, the LDP was forced to concede to a set of demands from Ozawa which were designed to strengthen the power of cabinet members and reduce the influence of senior bureaucrats in the policy-making process.

Among the most important of these initiatives was the abolition of a practice whereby bureaucrats could be called upon to answer questions posed to their respective ministers on the floor of the Diet or in parliamentary committees. The effect of these reforms was to reduce politicians' dependence on bureaucratic advisors, and the prime minister has henceforth been forced to consider ministerial appointments based more on competence and ability than on factional manoeuvrings within the ruling party.

These reforms were followed in 2001 by further adjustments to the policy process through amendments to the Cabinet Law. These changes were designed to alter the functions of the powerful cabinet secretariat and through this change to enhance the power of the prime minister in a number of important policy areas. From a foreign policy perspective, an important outcome of these 2001 reforms was a diminution of the influence of the Ministry of Foreign Affairs in the cabinet process and an increase in the influence of both the Ministry of Finance and, more interestingly from a counter-terrorism perspective, the Japanese Defense Agency.

Against this background, Koizumi assumed the premiership in early 2001 at the end of a decade-long process of institutional reform that effectively empowered the position of prime minister and allowed its incumbent to act with a degree of flexibility that had eluded most of his post-1945 predecessors. Substantially released from the ossifying influence of an activist but highly conservative bureaucracy, Koizumi was therefore well positioned to use the office of prime minister to give voice to the increasingly self-confident international ambitions of a new generation of Japanese. To this end, the events of 9/11 provided Koizumi with a useful opening.

Steering a more assertive path

To this end, Koizumi moved with extraordinary speed to place his own stamp on Japan's response to the attacks and to any subsequent response by Washington. As Shinoda has observed:

> Forty-five minutes after the incidents, he [Koizumi] established a liaison office at the Situation Centre of the Cabinet (later upgraded to the Emergency Anti-Terrorism Headquarters) headed by the prime minister. He then called a cabinet-level meeting of the National Security Council for the first time since 1998. At a press conference after the meeting, Koizumi announced the government's initial action plan, and described the terrorist attacks as 'grave challenges not only to the United States, but to the entire democratic society'.[11]

In terms of coordinating Japan's overall response, officials from the Japanese Defense Agency, rather than the Ministry of Foreign Affairs, were given a leading role. Underscoring the extent to which defence, rather than diplomacy alone, would play a key role in Japan's response, Koizumi announced plans to dispatch ships and C-130 aircraft from the Japanese Self Defense Forces to help protect US military facilities in Japan, gather signals intelligence on terrorist activities in the region, move supplies (including guns and bullets) to boost Washington's ability to launch retaliatory military actions against al Qaeda's training camps in Afghanistan (considered at the time to have been the source of the 9/11 attacks), provide search and rescue operations for missing US military personnel, supply field hospitals near the Afghanistan-Pakistan border, and facilitate the provision of more conventional forms of humanitarian relief.

At a diplomatic level, Tokyo followed its military commitments by offering foreign aid, a long-standing weapon in Japan's diplomatic arsenal, to both India and Pakistan to help secure their cooperation in any future actions against the Taliban in Afghanistan. Just two weeks after the attacks Koizumi called on the president in Washington and used the meeting to undertake to implement quickly Tokyo's response. From the American side, Bush pressed Koizumi to offer Tokyo as host for a planned international donors' conference dedicated to soliciting funds for the reconstruction of Afghanistan. In his opening address, Koizumi pledged $500 million to be dispersed during the first thirty months of reconstruction and used primarily for the resettlement of refugees, the eradication of landmines, as well as children's and women's health.

However, before Koizumi could deliver on his strategic undertakings, he needed to secure parliamentary approval for a revision to the Self Defense Force Law, to confer on Japanese forces the legal right to take pre-emptive military measures to secure US military bases from terrorist attack and to provide logistic and supply support to US military operations in the Indian Ocean.[12] In both instances, the proposed amendments raised issues long considered taboo in both a domestic political and diplomatic context.

Posing particular problems was post-1945 Japan's deeply embedded suspicion of militarism and the corresponding support for Article 9 of the post-war constitution, which strictly proscribes any military activity not related to the self-defence of the Japanese homeland. Reinforcing this non-belligerent tradition within Japan has been the residual hostility of several of Japan's neighbours, most notably China and South and North Korea, to the prospect of Japanese rearmament and a more assertive strategic role for Tokyo in the region. In the case of the latter, while it is true that sensitivities over the brutality of Japanese aggression during the first half of the twentieth century remain a factor in sustaining this hostility, more recently the legacy of the imperialist inclinations of Japan more than half a century ago has been gradually displaced by more concrete, realist calculations, with governments in Beijing, Pyongyang, and to a slightly lesser extent Seoul, using generational anger with Tokyo as an instrument to justify what are more fundamental concerns over a relative diminution of their own power should Tokyo assume a more proactive diplomatic and security posture. Even so, the strident criticism directed at Tokyo by its neighbours at any sign of a revitalisation of an offensive Japanese military capability, has worked to reinforce concerns at home that the costs in terms of external hostility towards Japan generated by departing from the spirit of post-war pacifism will outweigh any benefits in terms of national well-being.

Against this background, Koizumi's response to the tragedy of 9/11, whereby he defined terrorism as 'Japan's own security issue', presaged a potentially divisive debate within Japan over its role in international affairs. Yet, Koizumi's ability to link his response to the events of 9/11 to Japan's obligations as a signatory to the UN Charter and a series of Security Council resolutions on combating terrorism, helped him circumvent objections that the amendments to the Self Defense Force Law breached constitutional and other legislative restrictions designed to limit Japan's military operations to air and sea defence around its own territorial borders. This connection was made clear in comments Koizumi made to the Diet when introducing the amendments: 'If we say "No, we can't do this and that" at a time when everyone is gearing up to crush terrorism . . . Japan will never get respect in the international community'.[13] More flamboyantly, in a speech to voters involved in a by-election in the northern Japanese prefecture of Miyagi, Koizumi drew on the words of John F. Kennedy to tell voters that the amendments to the Self Defense Force Law should be supported because, 'it is high time Japan began actively considering what it can do for the world rather than what the world will do for Japan'.[14] In the end, Koizumi failed to secure the support of key opposition parties in the Diet, but in the face of opinion polls showing majority support for the initiatives he challenged political convention by deciding to push the amendments through the parliament regardless. As a result, the legislative changes required to facilitate Japan's proactive support for Washington were passed into law less than a month after being introduced into the parliament, without the lengthy and often debilitating debates that had slowed and diluted much less ambitious proposals in the past.

However, it soon became obvious that Koizumi had not exhausted his desire to use 9/11 as lever with which to pry further reforms out of the Diet. In April 2002, his government introduced into the Diet a package of 'contingency bills' designed to further amend the Self Defense Forces Law to enable the prime minister and Security Council of Japan to deploy the Japanese military to deal with 'emergency situations'. The move proved significantly more controversial than the initiatives announced in the immediate wake of the 9/11 attacks, with opposition groups in parliament charging that the amendments constituted a 'secret war plan' and were indicative of Koizumi's deeper urge to whittle away Article 9 of the constitution, which provides the legal basis for limits on Japan's defence posture, in favour of a more assertive military posture.[15] However, in the face of these further reforms opposition to Koizumi's policies began to reassert itself, with the opposition parties presenting a vigorous front in the Diet and opinion polls showing a dramatic fall in public support for the initiatives,

from around 70 per cent support for the first wave of reforms in the immediate wake of 9/11, to just over 50 per cent by mid-2002.[16]

Japan and the 'global war on terror': guilt by association?

Overall, the response included a range of military, diplomatic and humanitarian initiatives that marked a significant departure from Japan's cautious
assistance to US-led security operations in the past. Until then, Tokyo's preference had been to avoid igniting pacifist sentiments at home and stymie
charges of resurgent militarism from its neighbours, principally Beijing and
Seoul, by using its financial muscle to help bankroll US initiatives without
making any tangible material contributions to US-led operations. However,
by the 1990s this balancing act was becoming increasingly untenable as both a
growing number of Japanese and the United States itself pressed for a more
robust contribution to global security, one commensurate with Japan's
economic status as a global power. The difficulties in maintaining this balance
were driven home by both domestic and US criticism of Tokyo's contribution
to the first Gulf War, which amounted to a $13 billion contribution out of the
$61 billion total cost of the war, but a failure to commit members of the Self
Defense Forces to the international coalition sanctioned by the United
Nations to forcibly end Saddam Hussein's occupation of Iraq.[17]

However, not everything has gone Tokyo's way, with public anxieties over
the dramatic kidnapping in Iraq of the Japanese aid workers by Iraqi insurgents, and an outpouring of anti-Japanese sentiment in China and South
Korea underscoring the extent to which entrenched attitudinal obstacles can
continue to impede a more assertive Japan in the world.

In the domestic context, the ensuing debate within Japan took a familiar
path, with pacifist and left-leaning groups questioning the utility of violence
as an answer to terrorism, and arguing that the Bush administration's
response to the terrorist threat would only unleash a cycle of violence and
that Koizumi's support for this strategy therefore risked dragging the nation
into an elevated conflict within which Japan risked being rendered a target
for retaliatory violence. It was in this vein, that on 25 September 2001 the
Japan Times editorialised:

> there is a deep undercurrent of popular sympathy for Islamic fundamen-
> talism in regions . . . there is also the danger of retaliatory counterstrikes
> from bin Laden's international terrorist network . . . if Japan in any way
> gets involved in U.S. military strikes against Islamic forces, its security
> principles could collapse from their foundations. Japan will probably
> find itself in unintended antagonism with the global Muslim
> community.[18]

Against this view, conservative and more nationalist elements supported
Koizumi's initiatives as addressing a major gap in the government's ability to

secure Japan from a new and dangerous external threat. Although not a unanimous view among conservatives, the majority also stressed the need for Japan to do more to express solidarity with the United States, Tokyo's major ally and the leader of democratic nations, and shoulder more of the burden in maintaining international security. A variation on this theme advocated by more extreme nationalist circles, such as Ishihara Shintaro's supporters, placed less emphasis on Tokyo's obligations to Washington and couched their defence of Koizumi's initiatives more in terms of a vision of Japan as a global player in its own right.

As the debate progressed in the following months, opposition to Koizumi's vision of a more robust strategic capability to respond to international crises spread as memories of the 9/11 attacks faded and attention turned to a possible invasion of Iraq. This turnaround in public opinion reflected both a revival of Japan's post-war tradition of pacifism, as well as the civilisational turn that the war rhetoric had taken under the influence of conservative Western governments, especially the United States. As Sakai notes:

> [w]hen war came to be seen as unavoidable . . . the traditional mind-set of Japanese pacifism started to set in, and a rejection of the 'clash of civilizations' thesis began to be expressed in public discourse. However, they did not reject the idea itself, but rejected its adoption by Japan; that is, Japan was seen to be outside of the two worlds in conflict.[19]

Reinforcing this view were periodic reports that groups linked to al Qaeda were planning attacks within Japan. For example, in November 2003 several Arabic language newspapers reported receiving information that in the wake of several attacks against two synagogues in Istanbul, al Qaeda was planning to follow up with further attacks against the United States and its major allies, including Japan.[20] Concerns generated by these threats were reinforced by the tragic deaths, also in November, of two Japanese diplomats at the hands of Iraqi insurgents. Despite these fears, and a loss of seats to the opposition in the November elections, at a rhetorical level Koizumi continued to press ahead with his reforms, which included the dispatch of ground forces to help protect Japanese officials and aid workers in Iraq, which Koizumi, taking his lead from Washington, argued was integral to the wider global War on Terror.[21]

Trouble with (some of) the neighbours

Despite the speed with which it became clear that Koizumi would use the War on Terror as a vehicle for developing a more assertive strategic and military posture, initial responses from Japan's two most vocal protagonists on this front, China and South Korea, were muted. Part of the reason for this was an apparent reluctance by Beijing and Seoul to antagonise the United

States, which at the time was placing significant pressure on countries such as Japan to carry more of the counter-terrorism burden. The little criticism that did filter into the public realm was muted, with some South Korean commentators for instance accusing Tokyo of being 'in more than a hurry than would seem necessary' to make a military contribution to the US War on Terror[22] and a South Korean academic warning that Koizumi's efforts were 'a bone that sticks in our throat'.[23]

Japan met much less resistance in Southeast Asia, an area considered much more problematic in terms of terrorist threats more generally. Indeed, it is in this region that Tokyo has been an energetic player, avoiding the problematic issue of military assistance to the United States and working bilaterally with regional governments to forge better counter-terrorism relationships in areas such as intelligence sharing, counter-terrorism capacity building, and in providing the financial and technical assistance needed to fulfil their obligations under UN counter-terrorism protocols. Meanwhile, at the multilateral level Japan has been an active partner of the ten-member Association of Southeast Asian Nations (ASEAN), but also within the ASEAN Plus Three format (which brings together ASEAN, China, Japan and South Korea into a semi-regional multilateral body), in the ASEAN Regional Forum (a wider multilateral body including ASEAN members and their dialogue partners), as well as within the largely economically oriented Asia Pacific Economic Cooperation (APEC) forum.

With specific regard to ASEAN, in December 2003 Tokyo hosted a Japan-ASEAN summit that adopted a series of measures designed to boost the individual and collective counter-terrorism capabilities of all states in the region. This initiative followed from the ASEAN-Japan Joint Declaration, issued in December 2004, designed to enhance counter-terrorism cooperation between the parties. Meanwhile, in APEC Japan has played a key role within the Counter-Terrorism Task Force, including formulating and proposing key elements of the Santiago Declaration adopted by APEC leaders at their meeting in Chile. Of particular note was the role played by Japan in pushing for the issuance of machine-readable travel documents, as a step towards addressing the capacity for terrorist and criminal groups to exploit loopholes in Southeast Asia's often-arcane system of immigration control.

Combating terrorism in Southeast Asia

The sudden revival of US strategic interest in Southeast Asia after a decade-long decline was one of the first consequences of 9/11. The region's status as home to almost 250 million Muslims, a number of ethno-nationalist insurgencies in the region, some of which have attracted the interest of groups inked to al Qaeda, and the fact that several Southeast Asian Islamists had hosted individuals linked to the 9/11 attacks meant that the area quickly re-entered onto Washington's strategic radar. However, the Bush administration's efforts to rally Southeast Asian support and cajole regional states into a more disciplined counter-terrorism regime has not been without its problems, and beneath the facade of polite diplomatic-speak it is possible to discern a degree of American frustration that grand counter-terrorism initiatives have not progressed as smoothly as hoped. US frustration has been especially evident in its relationship with Indonesia, a country that looms as the key to US counter-terrorism strategy in Southeast Asia. Although the burst of Indonesian activity unleashed by the terrorist attacks in Bali on 12 October 2002 appeared to have shaken Jakarta from its lethargy and inspired a greater cooperative ethic, former president Megawati Sukarnoputri's clumsy attempts to balance an apparently genuine desire to cooperate with Washington against rising anti-US sentiment among the country's 210 million Muslims resulted only in a pattern whereby prolonged periods of political atrophy were shaken temporarily by frenetic and poorly targeted counter-terrorist activity.

Similar problems occur in other regional states belie the budding counter-terrorism arrangements between Washington and other Southeast Asian states. In their attempts to capitalise on Washington's invigorated post-9/11 interest in Southeast Asia, the Malaysian and Philippines governments have been forced to into some deft political manoeuvring lest a revival of popular anti-US and anti-Western sentiment at home weaken their domestic support. In Thailand, the administration of Prime Minister Thaksin Shinawata has avoided these problems largely by giving counter-terrorism cooperation with the United States a lower public profile. Even so, significant anti-US and anti-Western sentiment lurks beneath the surface of Thai politics, as it does in the newer ASEAN members of Cambodia, Laos, Myanmar and Vietnam, although in these cases their relatively small Muslim communities have allowed Washington to put momentarily on the backburner the need for matching albeit smaller counter-terrorism initiatives in mainland Southeast Asia. Even so, the a more assertive and more visible US presence in Southeast Asia poses a delicate set of problems for both Washington and those Southeast Asian governments eager to work with it in combating terrorist networks in the region. Indeed it is only Singapore, where a close security relationship with the United States is both long-standing and domestically unproblematic – except perhaps among the small but politically impotent Muslim community – which offers the US its only trouble-free Southeast Asian counter-terrorism partner. It is in this regard that Japan's status as a key ally of Washington in the War on Terror has come to the fore.

Especially important has been Japan's ability to capitalise on its long standing economic and financial relationships with the region to exercise a more effective form of quiet diplomacy, using foreign aid and regional assistance programs to address operational shortcomings in key counter-terrorism areas. Especially noteworthy has been Tokyo's work in the area of capacity building. Between early 2002 and early 2005 Tokyo dedicated around ¥3 billion to providing training assistance and technical support to Southeast Asian states in areas such as improved immigration controls, aviation security, port and maritime security, customs cooperation, export controls, law enforcement cooperation, anti-terrorist financing, and in the promotion of international counter-terrorism protocols.[24] Japan has also played a leading role in urging Southeast Asian states to accede to a series of international counter-terrorism protocols, and has matched this diplomatic effort with financial and technical assistance to regional states to facilitate their ability to meet international requirements in terms of aviation and port security, the monitoring and detection of illicit financial transactions, and in other key areas. Japan's initiatives in these domains have allowed Washington to avoid having to harangue Southeast Asian states in key counter-terrorism areas. In terms of Washington's efforts to balance its sense of strategic urgency against the need to cultivate a better public image among Islamic communities in Southeast Asia, Japan's efforts have played a critically important role both in terms of helping the US better calibrate its public diplomacy in Southeast Asia, while at the same time ensuring that there is forward movement in important areas of counter-terrorism capabilities.

Japan has also played an important role at the multilateral level, using its influence within the ASEAN Regional Forum and ASEAN Plus Three to tackle the suspicion of US counter-terrorism efforts among Southeast Asia's 'closed regionalists'. Constituted by ASEAN's newer members, especially Laos, Mynamar and Vietnam, and to a lesser degree Cambodia and Malaysia (especially on strategic issues), closed regionalists are much less optimistic about the benefits that can accrue to the region through coordinating policies with larger external powers, especially the United States. These countries tend to see the outside world through a hostile lens and view globalisation as a revival of neo-colonial and neo-imperialistic forces that threaten to overwhelm small states and empower larger countries, especially those of the West, to reimpose their will on their former colonies. For these states, ASEAN's worth is measured by its ability to keep the outside world at bay, to dilute and even repel the unwanted attention of larger international actors. Equipped with such a world-view, Southeast Asia's closed regionalists view US efforts in the area of counter-terrorism through a suspicious lens, as a vehicle for forcing them to adapt to a US-centric view of the world and in ways that are not always consistent with their own interests. Rather than working multilaterally with the US on counter-terrorism, their instinct is to work against the US.

ASEAN itself is caught between these competing world-views, and since the organization's expansion to ten members in the late 1990s, the regular rhetorical flourishes expressing regional unity have been belied by a lack of concrete multilateral initiatives. Japan's status as an Asian power, coupled with its less belligerent form of diplomacy and willingness to match its diplomatic efforts with financial incentives, has conferred upon it an ability to overcome a degree of this institutional atrophy, and especially through the

ASEAN Plus Three to help engineer higher levels of multilateral counter-terrorism coordination.

It would be naive to assume that Japan's efforts represent a panacea for Southeast Asia's problems, and Washington continues to have serious reservations about the commitment of many regional states to the counter-terrorism agenda. Moreover, there is little that Japan can do to redress the severe damage caused to Washington's reputation in Southeast Asia by dent of its ill considered invasion of Iraq and its continued flaunting of international law in the way that it detains and prosecutes terrorist suspects. Even so, without Tokyo's proactive approach to fostering support and enhancing counter-terrorism capabilities in the region, Washington would have cause for a great deal more pessimism over the region than is currently the case.

Conclusion

For a growing number of Japanese, the struggle against terrorism represents a test of Japan's ability to leave behind the unusual strictures imposed at the end of the World War II and assume its place as 'normal' member of the international community, exercising a level of strategic muscle more commensurate with Japan's economic might in ways that both promote Japan's own national interests and advance the interests of the international community more generally. Looked at in this way, the events of 9/11 brought to the fore a debate that had been simmering with steadily increasing intensity since the late 1980s. As yet, it is still far from clear that Koizumi's vision of a more robust Japanese security capability – an objective shared by most of Japan's major allies – will be realised during his tenure as prime minister. To be sure, the traditional obstacles posed by post-1945 Japanese society's deeply rooted suspicion of militarism, its aversion to becoming embroiled in larger conflicts not of its making, and the hostility of several of its immediate neighbours continue to loom as major impediments to this vision.

At the same time, however, it is perhaps inevitable that a growing number of Japanese born after 1945 will see little reason for Japan to continue to deny itself a strategic role commensurate with its economic power. To this end, Tokyo's counter-terrorism initiatives with Australia and other countries in the wider Asian region will provide a useful indicator of how the on-going transition from strategic 'quietism' to activism will play out over the next decade. But it will not be without difficulty as strategic rivalries between Tokyo on the one hand, and Beijing, Seoul and Pyongyang on the other, play themselves out in Southeast Asia.

Based on its achievements thus far, it would be shame if these tensions were permitted to distract Tokyo from its counter-terrorism efforts in Southeast Asia. Although the region is far less of a hotbed of terrorist activity than has been portrayed by some of the more panicked accounts,[25] it remains the case that simmering ethno-nationalist and religious conflicts in the region will continue to attract the attention of groups linked to or inspired by networks such as al Qaeda, and as such pose a threat to the security and well-being of both Southeast Asians themselves, and to the interests of outsiders, including Japanese and Americans, for many years to come.

Notes

1 See J. Dower, *Embracing Defeat: Japan in the Wake of World War II*, New York: W.W. Norton and Co., 2000.
2 Ministry of Foreign Affairs of Japan, 'Australia-Japan joint statement on cooperation to combat international terrorism', 2003, http://www.mofa.go.jp/region/asia-paci/australia/pmv0307/terrorism.html (accessed 4 May 2005).
3 I. Shintaro, *The Japan That Can Say No: Why Japan Will Be First Among Equals*, New York: Simon and Schuster, 1991.
4 See J. Kingston, *Japan's Quiet Transformation: Global Change and Civil Society in the Twenty First Century*, London and New York: Routledge, 2004.
5 J. Cotton, 'Southeast Asia after September 11', in D. Martin Jones (ed.) *Globalisation and the New Terror: The Asia-Pacific Dimension*, Cheltenham: Edward Elgar, 2004; International Crisis Group, *Jemaah Islamiyah in Southeast Asia: Damaged But Still Dangerous*, ICG Asia Report no.63, Brussels and Jakarta, 16 August, 2003.
6 The distinction between 'new' and 'old' terrorism is used by scholars such as Hoffman and Juergensmeyer to contrast the targeted and restrained violence of mainly secularly motivated groups such as the Irish Republican Army, the Palestinian Liberation Organisation, and the various Red Army factions active in Europe and Japan in the 1960s and 1970s, and on the other hand the mass casualty violence perpetrated by a 'new' generation of religiously motivated groups such as al Qaeda which emerged in the 1980s and 1990s. See B. Hoffman, 'Terrorism: Trends and prospects', in I. O. Lesser, B. Hoffman, J. Arquilla, D. Ronfeldt and M. Zanini (eds) *Countering the New Terrorism*, Washington DC: RAND, 1999; M. Juergensmeyer, *Terror in the Mind of God: The Global Rise of Religious Violence*, Berkeley: University of California Press, 2001; and M. Juergensmeyer, 'The religious roots of contemporary terrorism', in C. W. Kegley Jr (ed.) *The New Global Terrorism: Characteristics, Causes, Controls*, Upper Saddle River NJ: Prentice Hall, 2003.
7 R. J. Lifton, *Destroying the World to Save It: Aum Shinrikyo, Apocalyptic Violence, and the New Global Terrorism*, New York: Henry Holt and Company, 1999.
8 S. Furuya, 'Migrants, national security and September 11: The case of Japan', *Race and Class*, vol. 44, no. 4, 2003, pp. 52–62.
9 E. Blanche, 'Arrests of Western converts indicate new security fears', *Jane's Intelligence Review*, 19 January 2005, http://jir.janes.com/ (accessed 3 April 2005).
10 A. Harris and S. Fidler, 'Pirates hold Malacca Strait shipping hostage to fortune', *Financial Times* (UK) 23 June 2005, p. 20.
11 T. Shinoda, 'Koizumi's top-down leadership in the anti-terrorism legislation: The impact of political institutional changes', *SAIS Review*, 2003, p. 28.
12 K. Sakai, '11 September and the clash of civilizations: The role of the Japanese media and public discourse', *Arab Studies Quarterly*, vol. 25, nos. 1 and 2, 2003, p. 160.
13 G. Wehrfritz and H. Takayama, 'Bringing up the rear: An embarrassed Japan tries to join the fight', *Newsweek (International)*, 15 October 2001, p. 47.
14 Kyodo World News Service, 'Koizumi asks nation to consider ways to counter terrorism', 27 October 2001.

15 Y. Tatsumi, 'Let Japan's defence debate be heard', *International Herald Tribune*, 1 May 2002.

16 Shinoda, *op. cit.*, p. 30.

17 Wehrfritz and Takayama, *op. cit.*, p. 47.

18 *Japan Times*, 14 September, 2001.

19 Sakai, *op. cit.*, p. 159.

20 Kyodo World News Service, 'Terror threats investigated, officials urge vigilance', 17 November 2003.

21 N. Onishi, 'Koizumi reaffirms Iraq plan for troops: Japanese leader says he won't be deterred by killing of envoys', *International Herald Tribune*, 1 December 2003.

22 Wehrfritz and Takayama, *op. cit.*, p. 47.

23 D. Struck, 'As alliances shift, Japan's military role is widening', *Washington Post*, 28 September 2001.

24 Ministry of Foreign Affairs of Japan, 'Japan's international counter-terrorism cooperation', 2005, http://www.mofa.gov.jp/policy/terrorism/cooperation.html (accessed 2 February 2005).

25 R. Gunaratna, *Inside Al Qaeda: Global Network of Terror*, New York: Columbia University Press, 2002; Z. Abuza, *Militant Islam in Southeast Asia: Crucible of Terror*, Boulder CO: Lynne Rienner, 2003.

8 Perspectives on UN peacekeeping collaboration between Japan and Australia

Katsumi Ishizuka

Introduction

This chapter examines UN peacekeeping policy in Japan and Australia. International peacekeeping operations (PKO), which were initiated as a replacement for the totally ineffective post-World War II collective security environment, have played a vital role in the maintenance of international peace and security, even in the current post-Cold War period. The continuing significance of UN peacekeeping operations for conflict resolutions can be recognised by the fact that there are currently more than 60,000 military and civilian police forces serving in sixteen operations around the world.[1] Both Australia and Japan have adopted a 'UN-centred policy', and therefore always aspire to be a positive contributor to peacekeeping operations. However, this chapter points out a significant difference in the historical records, culture, and basic political approach towards peacekeeping operations between Japan and Australia. This difference stems from their own diplomatic positions in international affairs and several domestic factors that influence troop mobilisation, peacekeeping and national character. However, despite these disparities, are there any possibilities for collaborative peacekeeping operations between Japan and Australia? This chapter begins by introducing the two key foreign policy approaches to UN peacekeeping for contributing states, and will then apply them to the cases of Japan and Australia. Finally, it explores the cases of cooperation in peacekeeping operations between Japan and Australia, and suggests further possibilities in this area for the future.

UN peacekeeping as a foreign policy

It is relatively easy to understand that participation in PKO is considered to be an important component of foreign policy for contributing states. When one considers the theory of peacekeeping from the viewpoints of the contributing sides, the following two points should be considered. First, UN PKO can provide each member state within an opportunity to contribute in their own way. That is to say, all UN member states have an equal chance to participate in peacekeeping insofar as they have the will and capability to do so. In fact, according to statistics from the Department of Peacekeeping Operations, there is a nearly equal distribution of contribution to peace-keeping among states.[2]

Second, and more importantly, the UN has a non-persuasive nature in deciding which states contribute. As Alan James notes,

> it is a great mistake to conceive of the UN as the prime mover ... It is very far from the case that the world organisation simply speaks, and the relevant states then hasten to comply with its wishes, in the manner of ciphers.[3]

It is normally state contributors rather than the UN which show a keen interest in participating in peacekeeping missions. It is true that contributing states are usually authorised by the UN Security Council, followed by host states' approval of the candidate states' status as peacekeepers, and that an official invitation is always made by the UN. However, formal invitation is always based on the understanding of some informal discussion that has already taken place between UN officials and delegates from the member states that are keen to participate. Therefore, the policy of PKO adopted by the dispatching side depends on the discretion of the governments of the contributing states. In sum, a strong motivation to commit to peacekeeping operations will enable any state to become a positive contributor.

How are states motivated to participate in peacekeeping? In answering this basic question, one can apply a basic theory of international relations, that is, the classical debate between idealists, who advocate a collective approach to international conflict, and realists who favour the self-help approach.

In terms of the idealist perspective, it is generally agreed that state policy is essentially 'good and altruistic', and therefore states are 'capable of mutual aid and collaboration though reason and ethically inspired educa-tion'.[4] PKO, which sometimes lead to enormous casualties, must also have a sense of 'altruism'. Likewise, a peacekeeping operation is an activity of international 'aid and collaboration', providing civilian and military personnel to areas in conflict. Idealists believe that universal moral princi-ples can guide policy, and therefore international organisations such as the UN will address the major problems facing the world today. In reality, the majority of international PKO have been authorised and operated by the UN. Therefore, according to basic theory, UN PKO has to be based on an idealistic approach. Idealists expect international PKO to be an appropriate instrument for the improvement of long-term global peace and security rather than one aimed at short-term stability.

Andreas Anderson argues that in regard to state participation in PKO, there is a viable alternative to explanations based on *Realpolitik*. He empha-sises that the purpose of peacekeeping is not only to end conflict but also to prevent its recurrence by promoting democracy. He mentions that among the substantial contributors to peace support operations, well consolidated democracies show the greatest propensity to participate. He also notes that among the states in conflict, non-democratic states undertake a disproportionate number of operations.[5]

According to the idealist perspective, states participating in PKO in a positive manner should be regarded as 'internationalist' rather than 'nationalist'. Their peacekeeping policies are the result of governments' overall foreign policy direction. In other words, as David Wainhouse claims, 'Participation in a peacekeeping operation is a voluntary act and if a state has no special interest in a situation it will usually have a fairly high degree of general interest.'[6] A similar premise is posited by Boutros Boutros-Ghali: 'all states . . . have a strong interest in preventing a global pattern of violence, in checking the disease of conflict, and in deterring would-be aggressors'.[7]

Meanwhile, the school of political realism is influenced by the notion of the 'national interest'. National interest is seen as an analytical tool used to identify foreign policy objectives. In other words, once a government identifies the national interest, it establishes objectives, which then direct state policies. Therefore, a state consistently adhering to its national interests is likely to maintain its political balance and continue to progress towards its goal.[8] Contributions to PKO can also be supported by this realist theory. Alan James argues that in PKO the question of which states should be invited to contribute to an operation, or whose offers should be accepted, is often intensely political. He is clear that in relation to any decision to establish PKO, political factors are both most visible and most important, and that without such authorisations, PKO would not exist at all.[9]

David Bobrow and Mark Boyer consider PKO as 'impure public goods' that have continued to be provided by the self-interests of contributing states associated with maintaining some modicum of international system stability. In addition, they insist that UN PKO are 'club goods'; some highly supportive participants remain members of the UN PKO-relevant club for reasons pertaining to their status within the UN.[10] These goods are, therefore, not universally motivated.

Laura Neack also strongly supports the realist account regarding a state's participation in PKO. She focuses on the fact that peacekeeping forces seem heavily dominated by one group of states, the so-called 'middle powers' that are willing to put considerable resources into their participation. Her main argument is that the particular interests that have been served by UN peacekeeping operations are those of Western states, who benefit from the status quo, and of a few non-Western states that lay claim to some prestige in international affairs through their UN activities. Interestingly, she points out that such middle-power states are among the top thirteen major weapons exporters to the developing world, which has frequently requested and accepted international PKO at the same time. She sees arms sales and peacekeeping as tied to the same mission: the pursuit of national interests.

Furthermore, the term 'national interests' was explicitly mentioned by the US in the context of PKO. On 4 May 1994, Presidential Decision Directive 25 (PDD-25) was signed by US president Bill Clinton. PDD-25 thoroughly pursued national interests, ensuring that US peacekeeping policy would become more selective and cost-effective.[11]

Thus, one can identify both liberalist and realist influences on contributing states' peacekeeping policies. Each contributing state has adopted both perspectives, and whether its peacekeeping policy focuses more on liberalism or realism depends on the state in question. The next section explores the nature of PKO policy in Japan and Australia.

Japanese peacekeeping policy as a new and realistic form of political power

It is generally accepted that the first significant domestic controversy over a Japanese military role in international affairs was brought about by the Iraqi invasion of Kuwait in August 1990 and the subsequent Gulf crisis. After the commencement of air strikes on Iraq by the international coalition in January 1991, Japan's 'non-bloodshed' policy was the subject of much criticism from the international community. US pressure on Japan was particularly significant. Former US secretary of state James Baker declared during a speech to the Japan Institute for International Affairs in Tokyo in November 1991, 'your checkbook diplomacy like our dollar diplomacy of an earlier era is clearly too narrow'.[12]

In Japan, the clamour for a larger role in world affairs was pervasive. The Foreign Ministry White Paper of 1991 stated that military personnel contributions were indispensable. According to the prescription of Prime Minister Miyazawa, Japan's international contribution 'should include some "sweating" or dispatch of personnel to assist UN PKO rather than relying solely on "a lavish scattering around of aid"'.[13] Gradually, a consensus was developing among the main political parties and the Japanese public that Japan should play a more active role in maintaining international peace and security rather than simply contributing money to solve global problems.

On 6 June 1991, the ruling Liberal Democratic Party (LDP) created a 'Special Study Group on Japan's Role in the International Community' chaired by the party's general secretary Ichiro Ozawa, which was simply called 'the Ozawa Commission'. This commission claimed that the Preamble of the Japanese Constitution made clear provision for Japan's pursuit of peaceful cooperation with all nations,[14] and therefore the dispatch of the Self Defense Forces (SDF) to UN forces under Articles 42 and 43 of the UN Charter would be constitutional. The commission also maintained that on the subject of so-called 'multi-national forces' authorised under UN Security Council resolutions, like the one regarding the Gulf War, Japan would be able to contribute a logistical unit. Its conclusion, which was published in November 1991, strongly recommended Japan's participation in UN PKO.

This bill, the International Peace Cooperation Bill, the so-called 'PKO' bill, was finally presented to the Diet by the government in September 1991.

This bill required the approval of the Diet in the case of the dispatch of the Self Defense Forces (SDF). Furthermore, the bill included the so-called 'Five Principles' for the participation of a Japanese contingent in PKO:

1   Agreement on the ceasefire shall have been reached among the parties to the conflict.
2   The parties to the conflict, including the territorial states, shall have given their consent to the deployment of a peacekeeping force and Japan's participation in the force.
3   The peacekeeping force shall maintain strict impartiality, not favouring any party to the conflict.
4   Should any of the above guideline requirements cease to satisfy the government of Japan, she may withdraw its contingent.
5   Use of weaponry shall be limited to the minimum necessary to protect personnel's lives, etc.[15]

The PKO bill became law in June 1992 after stormy deliberation and resistance from the Socialist Party. Thus, the new International Peace Cooperation Law (the PKO Law) became the legal authority for SDF participation in all UN peacekeeping operations. Consequently, the Japanese government dispatched 600 SDF to the United Nations Transitional Authority in Cambodia (UNTAC), as an engineering unit, in September 1992. It was extremely significant that this debate was the first opportunity for both the Japanese Diet and public to seriously discuss the possibility and perspectives of their country's first 'physical commitment' to international peace and security. This issue was something they preferred to avoid raising in consideration of their country's desire to continue its consistent commitment to an economically oriented society, and of its wish to maintain amicable diplomatic relations with its Asian neighbours. However, international criticism of Japan in the aftermath of the Gulf War urged Japan to seek a consensus on how she could win international respect in terms of conflict management on the world stage.

The September 11 terrorist attacks on the US have had an enormous impact on perspectives of how international peace and security should be maintained in the future. The day after the attacks, Japanese prime minister Koizumi ordered his cabinet members to consider the possibility of dispatching the SDF for counter-terrorist activities in the near future.[16] On 13 September 2001, he also mentioned in a press interview that Japan would fully support the US and not hesitate to provide the necessary assistance and cooperation to the international community.[17] The secretary general of the LDP, Taku Yamazaki, also stated in a television interview:

> it is against the national interest not to use the SDF for counter-terrorism measures. It is possible under the current PKO Law for the

SDF to conduct humanitarian activities even in non-peacekeeping areas under UN resolutions, as long as international organizations actually ask Japan to do so.[18]

On 23 September, the government and the LDP reached a consensus on creating a new law to enable the SDF to join counter-terrorism operations. Thus, the prompt response of the Japanese government to the September 11 incident demonstrated not only the government's strong desire to overcome the 'trauma' of the 1991 Gulf War but also its commitment to contributing to the international community in this crisis.

On 29 October 2001, the SDF Anti-terrorism Bill was passed after exceptionally speedy deliberations in the Diet, during which Prime Minister Koizumi said, 'The focus of the legislation was whether we think of the terrorist incidents in New York and Washington on September 11 as other people's business or as our own affair.'[19] This Anti-terrorism law covered such activities as providing supplies and services, including medical treatment to US forces and their allies. It also made it legally possible for the SDF to engage in search-and-rescue activities and to provide humanitarian relief to refugees overseas with the consent of host governments.

In September 2001, the Japanese government held an initial meeting to discuss sending SDF personnel to the UN peacekeeping operation in East Timor (United Nations Transitional Administration in East Timor, UNTAET). Japan's role of simply providing logistical support in UN PKO had been long debated since the establishment of the PKO Law in 1992. This issue was viewed as increasingly more urgent from September 2001. This was because the government was expected to seek a broader role for the SDF by dispatching it to Afghanistan and neighbouring states as a peacekeeper.

The Five Principles in the 1992 PKO Law were reassessed after the September 11 terrorist attacks. For example, 'the consent of the parties to the conflict', one of the Five Principles, was questioned as to its practicality, since there might be a case in which one could not clearly identify the parties to the conflict. The bill to amend the 1992 PKO Law was finally passed in the Upper House on 7 December 2001, allowing the government to expand the scope of the SDF's participation in UN peacekeeping operations. The bill was supported by the three ruling parties: the LDP, the New Clean Government Party, and the New Conservative Party, and by a majority of the largest opposition group, the Democratic Party. The revised legislation lifted a freeze on SDF participation in UN peacekeeping forces engaged in such activities as monitoring ceasefires, disarming local forces, patrolling demilitarised zones, inspecting the transport of weapons, and collecting and disposing of abandoned weapons.

How does participating in PKO serve Japan's national interests? One motive would be to express Japan's international policy more distinctively as a new political power. PKO could provide Japan with the opportunity to imbue its diplomacy with some originality. For example, the reason why Canada and Ireland have been consistent international peacekeepers is based on the belief that they need to establish an original diplomatic policy to counterbalance their 'overbearing neighbours', the US and UK, respectively. Unlike multi-national forces, UN PKO are a form of conflict resolution in which superpowers have not been actively involved. In sum, political realists consider Japan's recent activism in PKO as a strategy aimed at balancing its bilateral relationship with the US.

Japan's consistent commitment to UN peacekeeping broadens its diplomatic options on the international political stage. It is significant for Japan to have a more influential voice at the UN since it has maintained a 'UN-centred policy'. This is very important for Japan in the current post-September 11 period, characterised by a US unilateralism which bypasses the UN. While Japan inevitably complies with the decisions and policies of the US to a considerable extent, participation in UN operations ensures that Japan maintains a balance between valuing its alliance with the US and its UN-centred policy. Therefore, Japan's participation in peacekeeping is limited to UN-sponsored and commanded operations.

The political difficulties experienced by North Korea, Afghanistan, India-Pakistan, China-Taiwan, and Sri Lanka mean that Asia is potentially one of the most insecure areas in the world. Regional stability in Asia is in the interests of Japan for economic and political reasons, and can be promoted through its commitment to PKO. In fact, the dispatches of the SDF to UNTAC in Cambodia, and UNTAET and UNMISET in East Timor were on a major scale in terms of personnel (1,216 in UNTAC and 1,370 in UNTAET and UNMISET). Asia does not have a regional military alliance such as NATO. This means that regional peacekeeping operations, such as the NATO-led Stabilisation Forces (SFOR) in the former Yugoslavia, cannot be established in Asia. Multi-national forces led by European troops might be one option. However, in many cases, multi-national forces are deployed only when local situations are too volatile for peacekeeping. They are interim measures, and therefore they are normally replaced by UN peacekeepers after situations become more stable, as in East Timor in 1999.

The terrorist attacks of September 11 led the US to adopt a much more hawkish policy that marginalised PKO. For example, President Bush's National Security Adviser, Condoleezza Rice, stated in an interview with the *New York Times*:

> The US is the only power that can handle a showdown in the Gulf, mount the kind of force that is necessary to protect Saudi Arabia, and deter a crisis in the Taiwan Strait. And extended peacekeeping detracts from our readiness for these kinds of global missions.[20]

Therefore, Japan's physical commitment to Asian security will need to be high; and its participation in peacekeeping in Asia will enhance its political status as a regional power. This will also play a role in regional confidence-building.

Japan's peacekeeping policy is motivated by more realistic concerns. The Japanese government has been convinced that Japan's new role as a consistent contributor to UN PKO will positively influence its bid for a permanent seat on the UN Security Council. For example, the Japanese SDF's commitment to the UN Disengagement Observer Force (UNDOF) in the Golan Heights was motivated by a desire to create a positive image as a suitable candidate for permanent membership of the Security Council. The US Senate also passed a resolution threatening not to support Japan's bid for a permanent seat unless it lived up to its full commitment to PKO.[21]

On the whole, Japan's peacekeeping policy, which was initiated fairly late in the 1990s, rapidly developed following the 1991 Gulf War and the September 11 attacks in 2001. It was the international community, especially the US, and three remarkable legal reforms: the PKO Law, the Anti-terrorism Law, and the amended PKO Law, which provided the impetus for the formulation of Japan's peacekeeping policy. This was based on its realist motivations as outlined above. As far as its motivations are valid, Japan will continue to participate in PKO.

Australian peacekeeping policy as a liberalist middle power

Australia's peacekeeping policy differs greatly from that of Japan. Australia has a much longer history of participating in PKO than Japan. Australia's first peacekeepers were dispatched to the UN Commission for Indonesia (UNCI) as military observers in 1947. In 1948, Australian military observers were sent to Korea to the UN Commission on Korea (UNCOK). In 1950, Australian military observers and air transport were deployed to the UN Military Observer Group in India and Pakistan (UNMOGIP). After the dispatch of medical units to the UN Operation in the Congo (ONUC) from 1960 to 1964, Australian troops were dispatched to the UN Temporary Executive Authority (UNTEA) in West Irian in 1962, the UN Yemen Observation Mission (UNOPOM) from 1963 to 1964, and to the UN Force in Cyprus (UNFICYP) where they have been deployed continually since 1964. In the case of UNFICYP, the Australian government dispatched peacekeeping forces (PKF) instead of military observers for the first time. Furthermore, Australian peacekeepers were dispatched to the India-Pakistan border (UN India-Pakistan Observer Mission, UNIPOM) in 1965–6, the Sinai Peninsula (UN Emergency Force II, UNEFII) in 1973–9, Syria (UNDOF) in 1974, and to South Lebanon (UN Interim Force in Lebanon, UNIFIL) from 1978 to the present.[22] Thus, it can be said that the history of UN PKO from the late 1940s to the 1970s, has been almost identical to Australia's record of committing to UN PKO.

Why was Australia so eager to participate in UN PKO during this period? Several factors can explain this. First, Australian participation in UN PKO was strongly demanded by the UN. During the Cold War, the superpower confrontation prevented their satellite states and close allies from participating in UN peacekeeping, since such UN operations required adherence to the principle of neutrality. Therefore, the UN was highly reluctant to invite close Western allies such as NATO members and the East European states. Thus, during the Cold War, several neutral states such as Austria, Sweden, Finland and Ireland were enthusiastically requested to contribute to UN peacekeeping. Australia, which was quite pro-US but not strongly allied like Japan and NATO members, was also encouraged to participate. During the Cold War, in particular, most of the missions conducted by Australian contingents in UN PKO were not in the form of PKF but as military observers. Military observer missions did not require troops to be as heavily armed and coercive as PKF troops. They promoted peace indirectly by ensuring that neither side in a conflict could violate a ceasefire or commit atrocities without the UN knowing about it. The strong demand for and popularity of Australian troops in UN peacekeeping was explained by the fact that many newly independent and non-aligned countries were still militarily unprepared and were not mature enough to send contingents to UN peacekeeping operations. At present, many African and Asian states are very keen contributors to PKO, although they began to participate following the end of the Cold War.

Another factor explaining the Australian enthusiasm for peacekeeping stems from the country's status as a middle power. Many middle powers, such as Canada, Norway and Australia, have traditionally aspired to play the role of a 'good international citizen'. The main diplomatic areas for middle powers include positive participation in international organisations, arms control efforts, international and humanitarian aid, and international peacekeeping.[23] In terms of international peacekeeping, the great powers, such as the permanent members of UN Security Council, are basically unsuitable as contributors to peacekeeping for the political reasons mentioned above. They are better suited to dealing with militarily hard issues such as nuclear proliferation. Their military training also focuses more on conventional warfare than peacekeeping. However, peacekeeping operations require a high degree of morale and sophisticated military equipment; they are therefore unsuitable for troops from developing countries, even though these might be politically neutral. Furthermore, since some peacekeepers from developing countries are financially motivated to participate, it is widely known that their professional attitude and performance has, on occasion, not compared favourably with troops from developed countries. Thus it can be concluded that middle power states are the most ideal troop contributors. Although Laura Neack considers that the middle powers have utilised peacekeeping as a tool on the basis of their realist approach, this case can challenge this argument.

Australia's peacekeeping performance has gradually evolved and expanded. Since the 1970s, Australia's contribution to PKO has increased in size and scope. In 1979, an Australian infantry force of 150 soldiers participated in the Commonwealth Monitoring Force as Zimbabwe achieved independence. Australian troops monitored the Rhodesian (now Zimbabwean) security forces, the cantonments of guerrillas, and the return of civilian refugees. In 1989, an even larger contingent, composed largely of engineers, assisted a UN operation with a similar role in Namibia (UN Transition Assistance Group, UNTAG). For a period in 1993, Australia had over 2,000 peacekeepers in the field, with large contingents in Cambodia (UNTAC) and Somalia (Second UN Operation in Somalia, UNOSOM II). In UNTAC, Australian peacekeepers played a leading role in the search for a settlement to factional strife in a country still suffering the effects of the genocidal Pol Pot regime of the 1970s. In Somalia, despite the failure of international efforts, a battalion-level Australian contingent successfully secured the delivery of humanitarian aid to the Baidoa area.[24] Australian troops were involved in a new type of operation, so-called 'peace enforcement', which requires troops to be more heavily armed and occasionally runs the risk of losing neutrality in highly belligerent areas. This gradual evolution and improvement of Australia's peacekeeping performance stands in contrast to the case of Japan, which sent several hundred troops on its first mission to UNTAC.

Australia has also adopted a 'UN-centred policy' like Japan. According to a paper written by the Australian Department of Foreign Affairs and Trade:

> The commitment of Australian forces to UN PKO increases our potential influence on a range of issues of concern to Australia that are before the international community and reflects our willingness to support the UN in its wider responses to security problems around the world.[25]

Furthermore, like Japan's peacekeeping policy, Australia has been deeply concerned about regional security, particularly in East Timor, Bougainville, the Solomon Islands, and Fiji. However, Australian peacekeeping policy has varied greatly from that of Japan in that Australia itself played a leading role in the rapid creation of a non-UN peacekeeping force, sending troops to extremely volatile areas. For example, in 1997 Australia took the initiative in establishing a Peace Monitoring Group (PMG) in the Papua New Guinea province of Bougainville, which was in a state of civil war involving the Bougainville Revolutionary Army, which sought independence, and the Papua New Guinea Defence Force. In September 1999, in response to a strong request from the international community, the Australian government played a leading role in establishing the International Force for East Timor (INTERFET), dispatching as many as 5,500 troops in order to establish security, assist refugees and help humanitarian efforts.

INTERFET, commanded by Australian Major General Peter Cosgrove, achieved significant success before authority was handed over to the UN mission, UNTAET. Furthermore, the establishment of an International Peace Monitoring Team (IPMT) in 2000 was based on Australia's desire to assist the Solomon Islands recover from ethnic and civil conflicts. In many ways, these interventions by Australia are similar to some of those initiated by the big powers to stem conflict in their own backyards, such as the US intervention in Haiti (UNMIH and MNF) in 1993, Russia's peacekeeping in Abkhazia and Tajikistan, and Nigeria's involvement in Liberia (ECOMOG) in 1990.[26] In this sense, Australia might be regarded as a regional power which plays the role of a regional policeman. Although such initiatives in the sphere of non-UN peacekeeping might reflect regional powers' national interests, their large financial and physical commitment cannot be explained simply by a realist approach. In the post-September 11 period, Australia's role as a regional peacekeeper has become more crucial since the US and NATO members are now focused more on the 'war on terror' than on the maintenance of other regions' security. For example, US involvement in UNTAET was minimal, and apart from Portugal, a former colonial power, most of the contributing states to UNTAET were regional countries such as Australia, New Zealand, ASEAN, South Korea, and Japan.

It should also be noted that the achievement and experience of Australian peacekeepers can be recognised by the fact that the past six UN and non-UN operations have been commanded by Australians.[27] The operational success of Australian peacekeeping contingents can also be understood when seen in terms of the very small number of Australian fatalities: just nine deaths in more than fifty years of peacekeeping.[28]

On the whole, Australian peacekeeping policy has been permissive and liberal. This is partly because Australia, unlike Japan, does not have legal restraints on participation in PKO, and also because Australia and the UN have needed each other, especially during the Cold War era; Australia sought a UN-centred policy, and the UN, lacking suitable troop contributors, also needed Australia to consistently contribute peacekeepers. Although Australia has several motivations based on a realist perspective, it is more appropriate that its approach be characterised as idealist and internationalist. In the post-September 11 milieu, Australia will also be expected to play the roles of an ideal regionalist and a regional policeman.

The history and further possibility of cooperation in peacekeeping between Japan and Australia

Thus, there is a significant difference between a realist Japan and a liberalist Australia in terms of peacekeeping policy. As Colonel Mark Hoare of Australia has observed, 'there is considerable potential for Australia and Japan to co-operate more closely in peacekeeping, but more substantive bilateral co-operation in this area will take time to develop'.[29] In fact, in the past, there has been very little such cooperation between Australia and Japan. The first case of close cooperation between the two powers was in

Cambodia. The two countries provided key components – communications and engineers – to UNTAC in 1992. The UNTAC commander, Lieutenant General Sanderson of Australia, worked very carefully with the Japanese SDF to ensure that Japan's first contribution to UN peacekeeping would be successful.[30] The Japanese SDF appreciated Sanderson's interest and assistance, and afterwards he was invited as a guest speaker to the symposium 'UN Peacekeeping and Japan's Role' organised by the National Institute for Defense Studies in Tokyo in 1994.[31]

Australia and Japan also cooperated in the UN mission in East Timor, coordinating support among key member states in the United Nations Assistance Mission to East Timor (UNAMET) in 1999. Australia and Japan, as well as New Zealand, the United Kingdom and the United States, constituted a Core Group of coordinating support. Coordination ranged from practical efforts to get UNAMET established to the critical day-to-day diplomacy geared towards the referendum of August 1999. Each of the five countries contributed personnel as well as funding to UNAMET, enhancing their engagement and information; and their ministers, ambassadors, or senior officials visited East Timor during the referendum term.[32]

Similarly, the next case of cooperation between Australia and Japan was expected to be under INTERFET in East Timor, again, in September 1999. However, one can identify clear differences in policy regarding the establishment of a peace-making operation in East Timor, between a realist Japan and an idealist Australia. The former, which still valued its diplomatic relations with Indonesia, insisted that an international or regional peace-making operation in East Timor should require the consent of the host government in Jakarta. Japan's foreign minister, Masahiko Komura, said that while Japan would 'strongly urge' Indonesia to maintain security in East Timor, 'now is not the time to discuss measures about what to do if it doesn't'.[33] Meanwhile, the Australian army had already begun preparing for its contribution to a peacekeeping force with a 1,200-strong unit under training near Darwin in early September 1999. Australia had already considered that the mission should be a short-term one aimed at restoring security prior to the establishment of a UN force; and the force had a strong regional component.[34] The Australian government also raised the possibility of a 'coalition of the willing' with President Habibie.[35]

Therefore, although Australia and Japan consulted each other prior to the INTERFET intervention, the above difference in policy towards East Timor made cooperation difficult. Furthermore, the constitutional restraints imposed by the current PKO Law prevented the Japanese SDF from participating in INTERFET on the grounds that East Timor was still a combat zone and that INTERFET was not a UN-commanded operation. Some Australian planners initially misunderstood the limitations placed on Japan and were disappointed that Japan did not directly contribute to INTERFET.[36] Furthermore, the Australian leadership role in INTERFET was considered to be 'aggressive' by Japan. Australian pressure on Japan to bankroll the peace-making process in East Timor created tension between Canberra and Tokyo. This tension was due to Japanese reluctance to pursue 'cheque-book diplomacy' as a result of the 1991 Gulf War experience.[37] However, since INTERFET, which was not a UN operation, had to be funded by the contributing states themselves and several sponsoring states, Japan's financial support to INTERFET was desperately requested. Therefore, Japan's final decision to make a substantial financial contribution, US$100 million, to the UN Trust Fund for INTERFET,[38] was coordinated through diplomatic channels between Canberra and Tokyo. Furthermore, in November 1999, Japan airlifted humanitarian relief supplies for displaced persons from Surabaya to Kupang.

INTERFET was replaced by the UN-commanded UNTAET in October 1999. In fact, Japan's decision to send peacekeeping personnel to UNTAET was initiated during consultations between the Japanese and Australian governments. Australia's foreign minister Alexander Downer told his Japanese counterpart, Tanaka Makiko, in Tokyo on 28 May 2001, that Canberra wanted Japan to participate in PKO in East Timor in addition to providing financial assistance to the area.[39] Responding to this request, Japan dispatched a 690-strong engineering battalion to UNTAET in March 2002. Also, in recognition of Japan's role in UNTAET, Akira Takahashi was appointed in charge of humanitarian assistance and emergency rehabilitation as one of two deputies to Sergio Viera De Mello, the Special Representative of the UN secretary general. Australia, as a leading state, provided the largest contribution (2,000 personnel) to UNTAET to assist in East Timor's transition to independence from Indonesia and to protect the border with West Timor. During the UNTAET mission, on 1 May 2002, a joint statement issued by Australian prime minister John Howard and his Japanese counterpart Junichiro Koizumi referred to the collaboration of the two states on UN policy. They confirmed their wish for closer cooperation in peacekeeping in the region, continued collaboration on implementation of the Brahimi recommendations, and the need for Security Council- and other reforms.[40]

Following the independence of East Timor on 20 May 2002, UNTAET was replaced by the United Nations Mission of Support in East Timor (UNMISET), which is similar to the NATO-led Stabilisation Force (SFOR) in the former Yugoslavia, concentrating more on stability and security-building than the comprehensive operation of UNTAET. In UNMISET, Australia accepted the basic responsibility for the initial training of the East Timor Defence Force, the F-FDTL. It pledged an A$26 million funding package over a five-year period. The East Timor Defence Force Training Centre at Metinaro was completed at a cost of A$7.5 million. This training centre was funded by the Australian government and built by the Australian Army's 19th Chief Engineer Works.[41] It is also significant that even after starting the downsizing of UNMISET in 2003, Australia's military contribution to UNMISET remained about a quarter of the total.[42] Prime Minister

Howard said that his country's contingent would stay until East Timor was considered stable.[43] Even after the complete withdrawal of UNMISET, Australia will deploy a so-called 'guardian force' near the border with West Timor. Japan's contribution to UNMISET was also remarkable. In May 2004, UN Secretary General Kofi Annan appointed Japanese UN senior officer, Sukehiro Hasegawa, as his Special Representative of the UNMISET. It was the first time that Japan would provide a Special Representative to a UN peacekeeping operation. The operational relationship between Hasegawa and the Australian troops and civilian police in UNMISET was a new type of collaboration.

What kind of collaborative relations between Australia and Japan might be possible in terms of PKO in the future? The first suggestion is the establishment of a joint peacekeeping training centre. A peacekeeping training system needs to be established in Japan. Currently, Japan's peacekeeping training is conducted under the auspices of the Prime Minister's Office or Defense Agency, depending on the category of mission and the rank of personnel dispatched. However, it has been suggested that a training centre specifically for PKO should be established, such as those in operation in the Nordic states, Canada and Ireland. In this context, the author has suggested that Australia and Japan create a Joint Peacekeeping Training Centre, which should be located in Japan with the cost borne by the Japanese government. In this training centre, experienced and skilled Australian officers would provide peacekeeping training to Japanese SDF and some other troops from the Asia-Pacific region. For the Japanese side, this training program would act as an incentive for SDF personnel and assure neighbouring states that Japan's participation in PKO is not motivated by militaristic objectives or neo-imperialism. For the Australian side, training Asian soldiers, including the Japanese SDF, would benefit it as a regional peacekeeping power, since such potential peacekeepers trained in the program would positively participate in UN or non-UN operations to maintain peace in their own region. In fact, the argument for establishing a peacekeeping training centre in Japan is supported by Mr Yasushi Akashi, Special Representative of the UN Secretary General in UNTAC,[44] and even the Director of Japanese Studies at the Korean Institute for Defence Analysis.[45]

Colonel Hoare has suggested that Australia and Japan could cooperate in the establishment of so-called 'guardian forces' for longer-term peace operations. As the security environment becomes more secure following successful peace efforts in the region, rules of engagement (ROE) can also be changed according to the new security environment:

> 'Guardian forces' with a constabulary rather than peace-enforcement role can then be deployed and follow on with different capabilities and ROE. Japan [and Australia] might consider contributing to such 'second wave' or 'guardian forces' with tasks such as civil reconstruction and maintaining civil order rather than the more dangerous and sensitive

roles of the forces that must initially enforce peace. Such a course of action may allow Japan to broaden its participation in peacekeeping even under the existing interpretation of Article 9 [of the Japanese Constitution] and defence legislation.[46]

Professor Susumu Takai from Japan's National Institute for Defense Studies (NIDS), has suggested the rather novel idea of joint peacekeeping cooperation between Australia and Japan for the maintenance of regional security. He advocates joint ocean-peacekeeping (OPK) operations initiated by the two states in the Asia-Pacific region. There are several territorial disputes in this region, such as those involving the Paracel Islands, the Spratly Islands and Pedra Branca Island.[47] Furthermore, the incidents of piracy in ASEAN waters are very serious; nearly 50 per cent of all incidents of piracy in the world occurred in this region from January 2000 to September 2003.[48] In fact, the availability of secure sea-lanes in these areas is very important for Japan and Australia, both of which are heavily dependent on international trade, including crude oil from the Persian Gulf. In this sense, OPK, which calls for conducting joint monitoring activities to protect the maritime environment and resources, would be highly effective. The specific activities of OPK include monitoring fishing conditions in designated waters – for instance, when, where, who, from what states and how many fishing boats are in operation in accordance with regional arrangements or agreements; and at the same time collecting data on various marine phenomena such the emergence of red tide (an environmentally hazardous algal bloom) and other marine data.[49] Thus, OPK should be coordinated by the regional maritime forces, led by the Japanese and Australian forces, to assure the regional security of the oceans. In fact, the concept of OPK has already been applied in the case of the Mediterranean, as the Mediterranean Action Plan Mediation Unit (MEDU) established in Athens with the support of the Greek government.[50]

Meanwhile, it is considered that Japan and Australia have considerable potential to contribute to the post-conflict state-building operations of the UN. Although state-building missions originated as early as the 1960s, the demands of state-building have increased in the post-Cold War period as a number of internal conflicts in Asia and Africa have necessitated the building of newly democratised states. UN state-building operations require not only security-building but also capacity-building and confidence-building. In the post-9/11 period, security-building emphasises human security issues such as refugee repatriation and the protection of human rights, as well as state security mainly by peacekeeping force. Capacity-building in UN operations should include a variety of elements such as good governance, low enforcement and judicial frameworks, democratisation, social and economic development, infrastructure, and medical and education services. Confidence-building will also be needed by local people in the post-conflict peace process. Therefore it can be said that post-conflict UN state-building is multi-functional, requiring input from a variety of non-military and civilian sectors. In this sense, state-building is a highly suitable UN operation to which Japan would be willing to commit. In December 2002, the so-called 'Meeting for International Peace and Co-operation' was chaired by Yasushi Akashi, and its final report was submitted to Prime Minister Koizumi. This meeting advocated the consistent involvement of Japan in conflict resolution, from preventive measures to state-building.[51] UN state-building requires strong civil-military relations. In fact, as Michael William put it, 'One of the most striking features of second-generation interventions (multi-functional peacekeeping including state-building) was their unique and previously unknown configuration of civil-military relations.' In this context, Australia, which has been a consistently active troop contributor to UN peacekeeping operations, should be an ideal partner to a Japanese civilian contingent in state-building. Furthermore, since state-building operations require a strong regional commitment to confidence-building, a post-conflict peace process in the Asia-Pacific region requires Japan-Australia cooperation for regional peace and security. The case of UNTAET and UNMISET in East Timor provides an ideal stepping stone to the enhancement of this function.

Furthermore, it is possible that Australia and Japan could take an initiative in a multi-national standby arrangement for peacekeeping operations in the Asia-Pacific region. The capability for rapid deployment of forces for peacekeeping operations has been a significant issue in the UN. The so-called 'Brahimi Report' of August 2000 also suggested that the UN should define rapid and effective capabilities as the ability to fully deploy traditional peacekeeping missions within thirty days of the adoption of a Security Council resolution, and within ninety days in the case of more complex peacekeeping operations.[52] The UN Standby Arrangement System (UNSAS) had also been created as one of the major pillars in the reform of UN peacekeeping operations advocated by several contributing states such as Poland, Sweden, Malaysia, Canada, the Netherlands and Austria in 1994. Furthermore, in 1995, Denmark established a working group comprising a number of like-minded member states, all with extensive experience and high standards in the field of peacekeeping, to explore the option of creating a rapid deployment force within the framework of the UNSAS. Thus, a Multi-national Standby Force High Readiness Brigade for UN Operations (SHIRBRIG) was established in 1996. SHIRBRIG complements the UNSAS with a complete, integrated unit that has a projected response time of 15–30 days. Currently, sixteen nations (Argentina, Austria, Canada, Denmark, Finland, Italy, Ireland, Lithuania, the Netherlands, Norway, Poland, Portugal, Romania, Slovenia, Spain and Sweden) have signed one or more SHIRBRIG documents.[53] However, no nation from the Asia-Pacific region has yet signed. Meanwhile, when INTERFET was established in an urgent manner in September 1999, Australia had difficulty in requesting its neighbouring states to deploy their troops to East Timor. Thus, a rapid reaction capability, of either UN or regional peacekeeping forces, is needed in the Asia-Pacific region. Several states in this region have consistently contributed to UN peacekeeping (for example Pakistan, Bangladesh, India and Nepal)[54] as providers of peacekeeping forces (PKF). Japan has a remarkable record as a UN peacekeeper in providing logistical support such as engineering and transportation units. From its long-standing experience, Australia is capable of providing a force commander. Most of the ASEAN states have also traditionally dispatched their troops to UN peacekeeping operations, and China and South Korea are emerging as new peacekeeping powers. Therefore, it is strongly recommended that Australia and Japan, as regional powers, advocate the creation of a standby arrangement system of peacekeeping forces in the Asia-Pacific region.

Conclusion

On the whole, Japan and Australia, both of which aspire to be regional powers, consider international or regional peacekeeping as an important measure in promoting international peace and security, especially in their own region. This is clear from their recent peacekeeping policy and commitments in the Asia-Pacific region. However, the differences in tradition and political motivations regarding peacekeeping between the two countries lead one to suggest that Australia should further make available its own know-how, experience and skills of peacekeeping to Japan. The cases of UNTAET in East Timor and UNAMSIL in Sierra Leone, for example, indicate that current UN PKO consist of regional and neighbouring contributors. In this context, Japan's more significant role as a peacekeeper in the Asia-Pacific region would also be beneficial to Australia, which would be able to reduce its own burden as a regional leader of peacekeeping. Japan might also ultimately adopt a more liberal-oriented internationalist approach to UN PKO. However, it should be noted that in the case of INTERFET, UNTAET, and UNMISET, Japan, which was initially an extremely passive peacekeeper, gradually expressed greater commitment to peace-building in East Timor, and finally in UNMISET a Japanese UN official was appointed as a head of the UNMISET. This was remarkable progress in Japan's role as a promising contributor to UN peacekeeping operations. However, one should not forget that Australia's assistance and initiative contributed to such progress, as was evident in Cambodia and East Timor. This chapter has also suggested that peacekeeping can be reviewed from broader perspectives. Guardian forces, ocean-peacekeeping operations and UN state-building operations shared by Japan and Australia in the Asia-Pacific region would not only accord with these countries' own military doctrines, but are also necessary in order to mitigate current regional security concerns. Australia and Japan should advocate the creation of a training centre and a standby arrangement system of peacekeeping operations in the Asia-Pacific region. Both countries' support for the US-led 'war on terror' convinced Japan and Australia that they should protect their own region by themselves and further promote security dialogues, including PKO, to this end. On the whole, promoting a joint PKO policy would be a significant preventive measure for Japan and Australia to take in the context of a volatile Asia-Pacific region.

Notes

1 United Nations Department of Peacekeeping Operations (DPKO), 'Information note', New York, February 2005, http://www.un.org/Depts/dpko/dpko/bnote.htm (accessed 18 March 2005).
2 United Nations Department of Peacekeeping Operations (DPKO), 'Contributors', New York, February 2005, http://www.un.org/Depts/dpko/dpko/contributors (accessed 19 March 2005).
3 A. James, 'Comparative aspects of peacekeeping, the dispatching end, the receiving end', paper written for the National Centre for Middle East Studies, Cairo and the Jaffee Centre for Strategic Studies, Tel Aviv University, 1996, p. 1.
4 C. W. Kegley and E. R. Wittkopf, *World Politics: Trend and Transformation*, New York: St Martin's Press, 2001, p. 29.
5 A. Anderson, 'Democracy and UN peacekeeping operations, 1990–1996', *International Peacekeeping*, vol. 7, no. 2, summer 2000, p. 1.
6 D. W. Wainhouse, *International Peacekeeping at the Crossroads*, Baltimore MD: Johns Hopkins University Press, 1973, p. 562.
7 B. Boutros-Ghali, 'UN peacekeeping: An introduction', *Brown Journal of World Affairs*, vol. 3, no. 1, 1996, pp. 17–21.
8 C. O. Lerche Jr and A. A. Said, *Concepts of International Politics in Global Perspective*, 3rd edn, Englewood Cliffs NJ: Prentice-Hall, 1979, p. 28.
9 A. James, *Peacekeeping in International Politics*, London: Macmillan, 1990.
10 D. B. Bobrow and M. A. Boyer, 'Maintaining system stability: Contributions to peacekeeping operations', *Journal of Conflict Resolution*, vol. 41, no. 6, December 1997, pp. 723–9.
11 US State Department, 'The Clinton administration's policy on reforming multi-lateral peace operations', 16 May 1994, p. 801, Washington DC: USGPO.
12 *Daily Yomiuri*, 12 February 1992.
13 *Mainichi Daily News*, 20 October 1991.
14 The Preamble starts thus:

> We, the Japanese people, acting through our duly elected representatives in the National Diet, determined that we shall secure for ourselves and our posterity the fruits of peaceful cooperation with all nations and the blessings of liberty throughout this land, and resolved that never again shall we be visited with horrors of war through the action of government, do proclaim that sovereign power resides with the people and do firmly establish this Constitution.

15 The Defense Agency, *Defense of Japan: The White Paper of the Defense Agency*, Tokyo: The Japan Times, 1995, p. 99.
16 *Yomiuri Shimbun*, 13 September 2001.
17 *Yomiuri Shimbun*, 14 September 2001.
18 *Yomiuri Shimbun*, 16 September 2001.
19 *Yomiuri Shimbun*, 30 October 2001.
20 Cited in K. Ishizuka, 'Peacekeeping operations after 9/11', *The Newsletter of the British International Studies Association*, no. 74, July 2002, p. 13.
21 H. Dobson, *Japan and United Nations Peacekeeping*, London: RoutledgeCurzon, 2003, p. 140.

22 Australian Government, Department of Veteran's Affairs, 'Table of Australian participation in multinational peacekeeping operations to 2000', Canberra, February 2005,http://www.dva.gov.au/commen/commac/studies/anzacsk/res1.htm (accessed 18 March 2005).
23 C. Bell, 'Political objectives,' in F. A. Mediansky (ed.) *Australian Foreign Policy*, South Yarra VIC: Macmillan, 1997, pp. 67–8.
24 Australian War Memorial, 'Australians and peacekeeping', Canberra, February 2005, http://www.awm.gov.au/atwar/peacekeeping.htm (accessed 21 March 2005).
25 Department of Foreign Affairs and Trade, 'Australia and the United Nations', Canberra, February 2005, http://www.dfat.gov.au/un/aus _ un13.html (accessed 19 March 2005).
26 K. Ishizuka, 'Peacekeeping and national interests: Positive factors influencing potential contributing states', *Kyoei University Journal*, vol. 1, no. 1, 2002, pp. 19–20
27 They are:
   1   Lieutenant General Robert Nimmo, Chief Military Observer in Kashmir with the UN Military Observer Group in India and Pakistan, 1950–66.
   2   Lieutenant General John Sanderson, Force Commander with the UN Transitional Authority in Cambodia, 1992–3.
   3   Brigadier David Ferguson, Force Commander with the Multinational Force and Observers (in the Sinai), 1994–7.
   4   Richard Butler, who led the UN Special Commission (in Iraq) from 1997 to 1999; Supervision Organisation from 1998 to 2000.
   5   Major General Timothy Ford, Chief of Staff with the UN Truce Supervision Organisation, 1998–2000.
   6   Major General Peter Cosgrove, who commanded the International Force for East Timor (INTERFET) from 1999 to 2000.
           (Australian War Memorial, 'Australians and peacekeeping', Canberra, February 2005, http://www.awm.gov.au/atwar/peacekeeping.htm (accessed 24 March 2005)).
28 Ibid.
29 M. Hoare, 'The prospects for Australian and Japanese security cooperation in a more uncertain Asia-Pacific', Working Paper no. 123, Land Warfare Studies Centre, Canberra, September 2003, p. 17.
30 Ibid., p. 25.
31 Interview with Professor Susumu Takai at the National Institute for Defense Studies, Japan, 27 December 2004.
32 I. Martin, *Self-determination in East Timor: The United Nations, the Ballot, and International Intervention*, Boulder CO: Lynne Rienner, 2001, p. 130.
33 *International Herald Tribune*, 9 September 1999.
34 N. J. Wheeler and T. Dunne, 'East Timor and the new humanitarian intervention', *International Affairs*, vol. 77, no. 4, 2001, p. 807.
35 *The Times*, 6 September 1999.
36 Ibid., p. 26.
37 D. Walton, 'Japan and East Timor: Implications for the Australia-Japan relationship', *Japanese Studies*, vol. 24, no. 2, September 2004, pp. 233–43.
38 Statement from the Ministry of Foreign Affairs of Japan, 'Japanese contribution to the United Nations Trust Fund for the multinational force in East Timor', Tokyo, 4 October 1999.
39 P. Gorjao, 'Japan's foreign policy and East Timor, 1975–2002', *Asian Survey*, vol. XLII, no. 5, September/October 2002, p. 768.
40 Prime Minister of Australia John Howard, News Room, 'Joint Statement with Prime Minister Koizumi: Australia-Japan creative partnership', 1 May 2002,

Canberra,httm://www.pm.gov.au/news/media_releases/2002/media_release1623.h tm (accessed 2 July 2004).

41 D. Ball, 'The defence of East Timor: A recipe for disaster?', *Pacific Review*, vol. 14, no. 3, October 2002, 179–80.

42 Agence France-Presse (AFP), 12 May 2004.

43 Agence France-Presse (AFP), 18 December 2003.

44 T. Jinyo, *Kokusai Heiwa Kyōryoku Nyūmon* (*Introduction to International Co-operation*), Tokyo: Yuhikaku, 1995, p. 263.

45 M. Leitenberg, 'The participation of Japanese military forces in UN peace-keeping operations', Maryland/Tsukuba Papers on US-Japan Relations, June 1996, p. 40.

46 Hoare, *op. cit.*, p. 37.

47 In the dispute over the Paracel Islands, China, Vietnam and other countries neighbouring the islands claim territorial jurisdiction over them, and China has already constructed a sizeable airfield on Woody Island, the largest among these islands. As for the dispute over the Spratly Islands, China, Taiwan and Vietnam claim territorial jurisdiction over all the islands, while the Philippines, Malaysia, and Brunei over some of them. China has constructed permanent facilities on Mischief Reef and has deployed troops on the reef for patrol and monitoring. Taiwan is said to have dispatched warships to Itu Aba Island, the largest of the Spratly Islands. The Philippines has established effective control of the Thitu Island, and Vietnam, six islands in the southwest including Namyit Island. As far as the dispute over Padra Branca Island, Singapore and Malaysia claim jurisdiction over the island. In July 2003 the two countries agreed to refer the dispute to the ICJ, which is currently examining the case. The National Institute for Defense Studies (NIDS), Japan, *East Asian Strategic Review 2004*, Tokyo: NIDS, 2004, p. 34.

48 Ibid., p. 37.

49 S. Takai and K. Akimoto, 'Ocean-peace keeping and new roles for maritime force', *NIDS Security Reports*, no. 1, March 2000, p. 63.

50 The National Institute for Defense Studies (NIDS), *op. cit.*, p. 53.

51 A. Yamanaka, 'Why Japan needs to contribute to international peace now', *Gunshuku Mondai Shiryō* (*Journal for Disarmament Issues*), March 2003, p. 35.

52 UN Document A/55/305-S/2000/809, identical letter dated 21 August 2000 from Secretary-General to the President of the General Assembly and the President of the Security Council, 21 August 2000, para. 91.

53 Multi-national Standby Force High Readiness Brigade For UN Operations, 'Introduction to SHIRBRIG', Birkered, Denmark, February 2005, http://www.shirbrig.dk/shirbrig/html/sb _ intro.htm (accessed 8 March 2005).

54 In this context, it is highly significant that, as of 31 January 2005, the top ranking of military and civilian police contributions to UN operations are: (1) Pakistan (8,183); (2) Bangladesh (7,942); (3) India (5,154); and (4) Nepal (3,453). United Nations Department of Peacekeeping Operations (DPKO), 'Contributors', New York, January 2005, http://www.un.org/Depts/dpko/ dpko/contributors/ (accessed 4 February 2005).

9 Security cooperation between Japan and Australia

Current elements and future prospects

Desmond Ball

Introduction

Cooperation between Australia and Japan with respect to 'hard' security matters began, in secret, in the mid-1970s, at the instigation of the Australian Secret Intelligence Service (ASIS), and was essentially limited to secret intelligence exchanges for more than a decade. However, its purview began to be substantially expanded at the beginning of the 1990s, albeit with very tentative initial steps, to include reciprocal visits by senior defence officials, official dialogues on security matters of mutual concern, and modest cooperation in some maritime fields (including joint exercises between elements of the respective Australian and Japanese navies). It was given a critically important public dimension when, in May 1990, Yoso Ishikawa became the first Japanese defence minister to visit Australia, and Senator Robert Ray, the Australian minister for defence, visited Tokyo in September 1992. Minister Ishikawa's visit 'had little policy content', but that it 'took place without incident or any negative publicity in Australia ... was extremely reassuring to those who wanted a strategic dialogue and the opening of defence contacts between the two countries'.[1] The close cooperation between the Australian Defence Force (ADF) and the Japan Self Defense Force (JSDF) in the peacekeeping operation in Cambodia in 1992–3 added a further dimension to the security relationship.

By around 1996–7, a fairly comprehensive range of cooperative measures had been institutionalised, including regular reciprocal visits by senior defence officials (including chiefs of the defence forces), annual political-military dialogues, expanded intelligence exchanges, joint naval exercises and reciprocal port visits and some maritime surveillance operations. A researcher from the National Institute for Defense Studies (NIDS), Naoko Sajima, thought in 1996 that 'a new security partnership' was being forged between Canberra and Tokyo, although she recognised that it had been largely defined by the alliances which each of them had with Washington.[2] By this time it had become common to refer to Japan and Australia as 'the Northern and Southern Anchors of the Free World or Western position in the western Pacific'.[3] (From a Chinese perspective, they were the two claws of a US 'crab' grasping Asia.)[4]

The security relationship has been further intensified and expanded since the terrorist attacks against the US homeland on 11 September 2001. The bilateral connections have been strengthened, but most of the new cooperative activity has derived from the respective relationships with the US, and particularly their supportive roles in the 'war on terror' and their common concerns about the proliferation of weapons of mass destruction in Asia.

The security relationship between Australia and Japan has now grown to the extent that, if the range of cooperative activities could be summated, Japan would be in the top ten of Australia's security partners – after the US, UK, New Zealand, Indonesia (where the relationship was shattered in 1999 but is now being reconstructed) and perhaps some of the other ASEAN countries (i.e. Singapore, Malaysia and Thailand). Australia would probably rank in the top five or six in Japan's list of security partners.

This chapter describes the principal constituent elements of security cooperation between Australia and Japan and provides some assessment of the prospects for this relationship. In addition to the bilateral activities (such as the intelligence exchanges, reciprocal visits, dialogues and joint exercises), it also discusses the principal common endeavours in multilateral fora and coalitions in the region, as well as some of the most important cooperative activities arising from their respective alliances with the US (including their commitments to participating in US missile defence and counter-proliferation programs). It argues that progressive further strengthening of security links is likely, but they will still remain fairly modest in sum, and that the primary dynamics derive from their coincidence of interests and partnership in multilateral activities rather than direct bilateral factors.

The Australia-Japan bilateral security relationship

Two points should be made at the outset. The first is that it is often difficult and sometimes even impossible to distinguish purely bilateral activities from the myriad multilateral activities in which Australia and Japan are engaged, and particularly from collaborative activities undertaken as part of the respective alliance arrangements with the United States. These arrangements provide a framework for bilateral connections between Tokyo and Canberra as well as between Tokyo and Washington and Canberra and Washington. This is especially the case with some of the most important cooperative activities, such as some aspects of intelligence cooperation (particularly those involving technical collection operations), maritime surveillance activities, the major joint exercises, and peacekeeping operations (PKO).

The second point is that there are real resource constraints on expansion of cooperative activity, at least on the Australian side. The ADF is only a small force – perhaps about a sixth of the size of the JSDF. Australia's defence budget (US$6.75 billion in 2001) is about 17 per cent of Japan's

(US$40.3 billion). Australia's total active defence force is 51,000, compared to the JSDF's 240,000. The Australian Army has 25,000 personnel while the Japanese Ground Self Defense Force (GSDF) has 150,000. The Royal Australian Navy (RAN) has six submarines and only nine principal surface combatants, while the Japanese Maritime Self Defense Force (MSDF) has sixteen submarines and fifty-four principal surface combatants (destroyers and frigates).[5] Australia's annual expenditure on defence cooperation averages about A$230 million (about US$150 million) – covering the costs of combined exercises, training programs, overseas visits and various forms of defence assistance, and focused mainly on the ASEAN and Southwest Pacific areas. It also includes the cost of regional maritime surveillance operations by Australia's P-3C long-range maritime patrol (LRMP) aircraft.[6] The ADF has been operating at an extraordinary tempo since 1999, with both platforms and personnel fully committed. There are undoubtedly further areas of bilateral cooperation which might fruitfully be pursued at relatively low cost, but any substantial further enhancement of the relationship will be governed by the extent of their mutual interests in responding to larger global and regional strategic and security developments.

Intelligence exchanges

The first major field of bilateral cooperation involved respective Australian and Japanese intelligence agencies, and was instituted, at Australian initiative, in secret, in the mid-1970s. The instrumental Australian agency was the ASIS, which had established a secret station in Tokyo in 1955, and in the early 1970s began considering the possibility of entering into a liaison arrangement with the Japanese intelligence authorities. In May 1976, the Australian foreign minister approved the establishment of liaison between ASIS and the Japanese Cabinet Research Office (CRO, or *Naichō*), and formal contact was established in August 1976.[7] After the Office of National Assessments (ONA) was formed in 1977, it took over responsibility for management and oversight of the relationship with the *Naichō*. The ASIS station in Tokyo has remained one of the service's largest posts, with usually three officers engaged in intelligence liaison and exchange functions.

The intelligence cooperation was also extended to the respective defence intelligence agencies. The Australian Joint Intelligence Organisation (JIO) had also considered the development of liaison arrangements with Japanese authorities in the early 1970s, but initially made 'no progress'.[8] However, effective liaison and exchange arrangements between JIO and the JDA were established later in the 1970s. The initial exchanges mainly involved assessments concerning the strategic nuclear balance between the US and the Soviet Union and the implications of strategic arms control negotiations. By 1989, when the JIO was renamed the Defence Intelligence Organisation (DIO), the exchanges involved not only the JDA but also the intelligence directorates of the JGSDF, JMSDF and Japanese Air Self Defense Force

(ASDF), and covered a wide range of intelligence maters of mutual strategic and military interest.

The Japanese and Australian signals intelligence (SIGINT) agencies are involved in the most extensive and productive cooperative intelligence collection activities, but with little direct collaboration. Under the UKUSA arrangements of 1947–8, to which Australia is a second party and Japan a third party, Australia's Defence Signals Directorate (DSD) is responsible for the comprehensive interception of radio signals and telecommunications traffic from the eastern Indian Ocean through parts of Southeast Asia to the southwest Pacific, while US and Japanese SIGINT stations in the Japanese island chain cover a large part of Northeast Asia.[9] However, the cooperative aspects of the respective Australian and Japanese SIGINT activities are mostly managed by the US. There is almost no direct exchange of intercepted material between the Australian and Japanese SIGINT agencies, and no cooperation with respect to cryptographic matters.

Reciprocal visits by senior officials and bilateral security dialogue

Establishing mechanisms for regular official meetings and dialogues about mutual security concerns involved a fundamentally important confidence-building process. These exchanges would increase transparency, engender close personal relationships, enhance mutual understanding and increase mutual trust, but they required a certain degree of trust to be founded to begin with.

The bilateral security dialogue between Australia and Japan was initiated in March 1990, without public announcement, when an Australian party led by Paul Dibb, the Deputy Secretary (Strategy and Intelligence) of the Department of Defence, and Admiral Alan Beaumont, Vice Chief of the Defence Force (VCDF) visited Tokyo for official talks. Australia became the second country, after the US, with which Japan engages in regular bilateral security dialogues. The initial talks were hosted by Yukio Satoh, then the director-general of the Information Analysis, Research and Planning Bureau in the Ministry of Foreign Affairs (MOFA), and one of Japan's foremost official exponents of multilateralism. The discussion was limited on the Japanese side to *Gaimushō* and JDA civilians, as the JDA was at this stage unwilling to approve direct military-military talks between the JSDF and other defence forces (apart from the US). This series of exchanges, referred to as the Dibb-Beaumont talks, continued until 1995, when the Japanese side agreed to the institution of annual political-military and military-military consultations, which it hosts. (These are defined respectively as security dialogue among Foreign Ministry and defence officials at the level of director-general and deputy director-general, and dialogue among defence officials, including military officers, at that same level.) The first political-military ('pol-mil') and military-military ('mil-mil') talks were held in Tokyo in February 1996.[10]

Ministerial visits, which have been fairly regular since 1997 (averaging about once a year), have been extremely important in developing closer relations. They have been used to codify the working arrangements instituted by the senior officials, as well as for discussion of new initiatives; and they have provided the opportunity for issuance of press statements reaffirming the closeness of the relationship at the highest level and promoting public understanding of the relationship.

At the meeting in Tokyo in September 1997, the ministers (Ian McLachlan and Fumio Kyuma) agreed on 'four priority areas for cooperation'. These were:

- more frequent contact and visits by defence ministers;
- more frequent high-level contact by senior officials;
- closer contact and discussion of peacekeeping; and
- enhancing intelligence exchanges to improve understanding of security issues.[11]

Mr Kyuma visited Australia in January 1998, the second time a Japanese defence minister had visited, for talks with Minister McLachlan about 'regional security and bilateral relations'. The ministers reviewed the 'progress in security cooperation' since their Tokyo meeting, and agreed on a program for further high-level visits by and talks between senior officials (including a visit to Japan by the chiefs of the Australian Army, Navy and Air Force later in the year). They also agreed that Japan would host annual political-military talks involving defence and foreign affairs officials, as well as the military-military talks between defence personnel, and that the respective defence intelligence organisations would 'continue to expand their contacts.'[12]

In August 2002, when Gen Nakatani visited Canberra, the Australian minister for defence, Senator Robert Hill, said that Australia welcomed Japan making a more active contribution to regional security, particularly through its support for the war against terrorism and its deployment of peacekeepers to East Timor, and its legislative changes which enabled its participation in Operation *Enduring Freedom* in Afghanistan. He said:

Australia and Japan's strategic interests are closely aligned, and our defence relationship has been growing steadily in recent years. Enhanced strategic dialogue and increased interaction between our defence forces benefit both countries and the region. Cooperation in peacekeeping and the deployment of engineers from the Japanese Self Defense Force to East Timor has been a particular highlight.[13]

On 29 September 2003, when Senator Hill visited Tokyo for talks with defence minister Shigeru Ishiba and senior JDA and JSDF officials, the ministers signed a *Memorandum of Understanding [MoU] on Defence*

Exchanges between the Japan Defense Agency and the Australian Department of Defence, sometimes called the 'Australia-Japan security agreement'. The MoU recognised 'Australia and Japan's common strategic interests in the peace and stability of the Asia-Pacific region'; it affirmed the commitment of both countries 'to strengthening high level exchanges, strategic dialogue and senior visits, as well as a range of working level contacts, staff college exchanges and regular ship and aircraft visits'; and it committed both the JDA and the Australian Department of Defence 'to explore new areas of cooperation for promoting and deepening the defence relationship', including with respect to counter-terrorism and countering the proliferation of weapons of mass destruction. Senator Hill said that: 'This memorandum signals the strength of the existing bilateral defence and security relationship. It also demonstrates the increasing emphasis that Australia and Japan are placing on security cooperation.'[14]

Maritime cooperation

Among the defence forces, the closest cooperation is not surprisingly in the maritime area. Both Australia and Japan are island nations, dependent on long and vulnerable sea lines of communications (SLOCs). Australia's 'sphere of primary strategic interest', which covers more than 20 per cent of the earth's surface, extends from the mid-Indian Ocean through the Straits of Malacca and the South China Sea to the southwest Pacific.[15] This sphere encompasses Japan's longest, most important and most vulnerable SLOCs. It is neither surprising that, among the services, the closest cooperation involves the RAN, the Royal Australian Air Force's (RAAF) P-3C LRMP aircraft, and the JMSDF, nor that the closest functional cooperation involves maritime surveillance.

Both the Australian and Japanese maritime defence forces participate in the US Navy's Ocean Surveillance Information System (OSIS), a world-wide network of airborne maritime surveillance platforms, signals interception and direction finding (DF) stations, and ocean surveillance satellites which provides comprehensive coverage of ship locations and movements. In the case of airborne surveillance, both the RAAF and the JMSDF maintain P-3C *Orion* LRMP aircraft (about 20 and 80 respectively), equipped with sonar receivers, cameras, radar, infra-red sensors and electronic intelligence (ELINT) and electronic support measure (ESM) systems. The RAAF's P-3Cs cover the eastern Indian Ocean and the South China Sea, while the JMSDF's *Orions* cover the northwest Pacific down through the East China Sea. The respective P-3Cs are equipped with data links – both Link 11 and Link 16/Joint Tactical Information Distribution System (JTIDS) – allowing them to directly exchange data concerning shipping movements in areas of combined operations. Australian and Japanese SIGINT stations also contribute to the global OSIS high-frequency direction finding (HF DF) system, but through their respective arrangements with the US Navy.

Active cooperation between RAN and JMSDF elements has remained fairly modest. Minor combined exercises, called PASSEXs ('passage exercises') began in the early 1990s, involving signalling and basic manoeuvre exercises, but only when JMSDF vessels were in Australian waters. More substantive combined exercising has occurred under the auspices of the US-led RIMPAC ('rim of the Pacific') series of exercises, which are the largest, best-planned and most sophisticated joint exercises in which the RAN and JMSDF participate, together with US and South Korean Navy elements. The RIMPAC-92 exercise, in which JMSDF elements exercised against the (Orange) side commanded by an Australian rear-admiral (R. A. C. Walls), proved to be the impetus for further cooperation. The scope of the PASSEXs was expanded around 1993–4, and by the mid-1990s the two navies had implemented regular (once a year) visits by fleet elements (in the JMSDF's case, usually 2–4 ships from its training squadron) to each other's ports. Further expansion of combined exercise activities, including search and rescue exercises, were agreed in 1997.[16] And as discussed below, the war on terror, and more particularly the resultant JMSDF deployments to the Indian Ocean and the decisions by both Australia and Japan in June 2003 to participate in the US-sponsored Proliferation Security Initiative (PSI), have provided additional opportunities and rationales for combined maritime exercises.

Satellite tracking and control

An important area of cooperation that has recently developed involves Australia's support for the Japanese space program, and particularly the provision of ground facilities for tracking and controlling Japan's commercial communications and defence reconnaissance satellites. The first step in this area was purely commercial, and involved the use of the Lockheed Martin Telemetry, Tracking and Control (TT&C) station at Uralla, near Armidale, NSW, to track and control the Japanese N-SAT-110 telecommunications satellite, launched on 6 October 2000, which provides direct television broadcasting services covering Japan 'and nearby regions'.[17]

The much more important facility in terms of Australia-Japan security cooperation is the satellite ground station at Landsdale in Perth, WA. It was established in 2001–2 by Japan's National Space Development Agency (NASDA), following an agreement reached with the Australian government in October 2001, consists of two 'giant' parabolic dish antennas, and is 'operated remotely from Japan'.[18] One of the dishes is for supporting 'Japanese satellites carrying out scientific, research and commercial functions', and the other supports Japan's imaging intelligence (IMINT) or 'information-gathering' satellite program.[19]

The NASDA/JDA reconnaissance satellite program consists initially of four satellites – two with electro-optical cameras (with a 1-metre resolution) and two with microwave-radar sensors for recording images through cloud and at night (with a 1.3-metre resolution), which operate in north-south polar orbits at an altitude of about 500km. The publicised purpose of the program is to monitor North Korea, but it also collects imagery over China and Russia as well as other areas of intelligence interest. The first two satellites (one optical and the other radar-imaging) were launched on 28 March 2003; the second pair was destroyed when the launch vehicle failed in August. A new organisation, the Cabinet Satellite Intelligence Centre, was set up in Tokyo to analyse the reconnaissance data.[20] The primary role of the Landsdale station is to support the insertion of the satellites into the correct orbital position and their maintenance at the desired altitude through their operational lifetimes. The station also provides a capacity for sending tasking commands to the satellites as they proceed on south-north orbits over Australia towards their area of direct interest and for relaying imagery collected on north-south orbits back to Tokyo.

Multilateral security cooperation

At the end of the Cold War, both Australia and Japan were very concerned about the lack of any multilateral organisation for security dialogue and cooperation in the Asia-Pacific region. They had worked closely together through the 1980s to establish the Asia Pacific Economic Cooperation (APEC) process. Around 1991–2 they became the leading proponents of institutionalised multilateral security cooperation mechanisms, although their respective efforts were coincidental and mutually reinforcing rather than coordinated – and they each initially generated suspicions among some of the ASEAN countries about their motivations and their proposals.[21] Most notably, Japan played a leading role in the conception of the ASEAN Regional Forum (ARF), the centrepiece of the multilateral security cooperation architecture in the Asia-Pacific region.

The ASEAN Regional Forum

The ASEAN Regional Forum (ARF) held its first meeting in Bangkok in July 1994, but its genesis and operating modalities date back to the twenty-fourth ASEAN Post-Ministerial Meeting in Kuala Lumpur in July 1991. The Japanese Minister for Foreign Affairs, Taro Nakayama, presented a major statement at the July 1991 meeting, drafted mainly by Yukio Satoh, then the senior official in charge of research and planning in the *Gaimushō*, in which he stated:

> I believe it would be meaningful and timely to use the ASEAN Post Ministerial Conference as a process of political discussions designed to improve the sense of security among us. In order for these discussions to be effective, it might be advisable to organize a senior officials' meeting

which would then report its deliberations to the ASEAN Post
Ministerial Conference for further discussion.[22]

Dr Nakayama noted that 'a worthy topic' for regional security dialogue was
the regional anxiety about the future direction of Japanese foreign policy
concerning the region. According to Dr Nakayama:

> Expansion of the Japanese role in the Asia-Pacific region has caused
> anxiety and concern among other countries, as to how far our role
> would expand and whether or not it would take on military dimensions.
> That is why, I believe, it is increasingly important both for Japan and our
> fellow Asian nations to have opportunities on a constant basis enabling
> Japan to listen to the anxieties and concerns that other countries in Asia
> express regarding our foreign policy orientation and objectives, and, in
> turn, for Japan to provide our neighbours in Asia with direct, forthright
> explanations of our thinking. As we fulfil our political obligations in the
> Asia-Pacific region in the future, a vital part of our diplomatic activities
> will be to participate earnestly in a process which I might call 'political
> dialogue designed to increase the sense of security felt by all parties'.[23]

The ideas of extending the annual ASEAN Post-Ministerial Conferences to
include a security forum, of using senior officials' meetings (SOMs) to
support the proposed forum, and of using the forum for confidence-building
had several progenitors, among which Dr Nakayama is one of the most
prominent.[24]

Although foreign ministers and their senior officials are paramount in
the ARF process, much of its agenda has concerned defence matters and
defence officials (including military officers) formally participate in the
process. Most of the Confidence and Security Building Measures (CSBMs)
considered and implemented during the ARF's first half-decade dealt with
defence issues either directly or indirectly, such as the proposals for dialogue
on defence policy positions, publication of defence White Papers, enhanced
contacts between senior defence officials, exchanges between military
academies and staff colleges, exchanges concerning peacekeeping operations, cooperative maritime surveillance, etc.[25] The desirability of increasing
defence participation was recognised by the ARF at the outset, and by 1998
concrete steps were being taken. For example, most of the delegations at the
meetings of the ARF Inter-Sessional Group (ISG) on Confidence-building
in Honolulu in November 1998 and in Bangkok in March 1999 included
defence officials. They 'exchanged views and information on their respective
defense policies, including defense conversion, and reviewed their political-
military and defense dialogues, high-level defense contacts, joint training
and personnel exchanges with fellow ARF participants'.[26] It was also
agreed that 'participation in [the] Leaders Retreat at [the] ARF SOMs
should continue to include [the] SOM leader plus one in order to accommo-

date participation by defense officials'.[27] Meetings of the ISG now include a defence officials' lunch for informal discussions 'on issues of common interest'.[28]

Unfortunately, however, both Australia and Japan withdrew from their leadership roles later in the 1990s. Australia refocused its foreign policy priorities towards the US alliance, according somewhat less attention to regional initiatives. Japan's leadership endeavours were severely damaged by the Asian economic crisis in 1997–8, although its concerns about the proliferation of WMD (and especially North Korea's programs) and international terrorism have reinvigorated them.

The second-track security cooperation process

Japan was also at the forefront of the development of second-track security cooperation, especially in the early and mid-1990s. This was exemplified in the establishment of the Council for Security Cooperation in the Asia Pacific (CSCAP), which has emerged as the premier second-track organisation in the region. The Japanese Institute of International Relations (JIIA) was a co-sponsor of the series of meetings which led to the foundation of CSCAP in 1992–3.[29] Ambassador Nobuo Matsunaga, a former vice-minister for foreign affairs (1983–5) and ambassador to the United States (1985–9), and since March 1990 an advisor to the Minister for Foreign Affairs, served as the second non-ASEAN co-chair of CSCAP (1996–8) and played an important role in the promotion of the council. The Japanese CSCAP committee has been particularly active in the Working Group on Maritime Cooperation (of which Australia is a co-chair) and the Working Group on the North Pacific (which Japan co-chairs). Senior JMSDF officers, both retired and currently serving, regularly participate in the Working Group on Maritime Cooperation. The new chairman of CSCAP-Japan is Ambassador Yukio Satoh, former ambassador to Australia (1996–8) and to the United Nations (UN), and the *Gaimushō* official who was centrally involved in Japan's initiatives concerning multilateral security arrangements in the early 1990s. The Australian and Japanese CSCAP committees cooperated closely (together with the Canadian and Indonesian committees) in the sponsorship and organisation of a CSCAP General Conference in Jakarta in December 2003, which provided a venue for discussion (with several foreign ministers and numerous foreign ministry officials) of practical measures to enhance regional cooperation with respect to counter-terrorism.

On the defence side, the NIDS has actively promoted second-track exchanges with other defence 'think tanks' in the region, including in Australia.[30] With regard to broader conceptions of security, other Japanese organisations (such as the Japan Forum on International Relations) have played leading roles in the promotion of cooperation concerning preventive diplomacy and human security.[31]

Multilateral naval dialogue

The RAN and the JMSDF also cooperate in regional multilateral forums concerned with naval and other maritime matters. In particular, they have been prominent participants in the Western Pacific Naval Symposium (WPNS), a biennial conference initiated by the RAN in 1988, which brings together representatives of the ASEAN states, the US, Japan, the Republic of Korea, the People's Republic of China, Papua New Guinea, Australia and New Zealand for a frank exchange of views on a wide range of issues, including law of the sea and SLOC protection. It is a unique forum and has substantially improved understanding between regional navies. The JMSDF hosted the fifth WPNS in November 1996 and the eighth in October 2002. The eighth meeting focused on 'inter-operability' with specific reference to 'search and rescue, humanitarian support, disaster relief, minesweeping, refuelling, etc.'.[32] Coinciding with the WPNS, the JMSDF also organised a multilateral search and rescue exercise, in Southern Kanto waters and Sagami Bay, in which RAN elements participated.[33]

Peacekeeping operations (PKO)

The joint participation of ADF and JSDF elements in UN-sponsored multi-national peacekeeping operations (PKO) since 1992 has involved extensive and mutually beneficial cooperation between the two defence forces. The ADF has had substantial experience in UN PKO, including leadership of the largest recent PKO interventions in the region – i.e. the United Nations Transitional Authority in Cambodia (UNTAC) in 1992–3 and the UN International Force in East Timor (INTERFET) in 1999–2000 and the subsequent UN Transitional Administration in East Timor (UNTAET).

Japan's first military contribution to a UN PKO was its involvement in UNTAC. UNTAC was headed by Ambassador Yasushi Akashi, as Special Representative of the UN Secretary General. The JSDF contributed two successive non-combatant engineer battalions (each with about 600 personnel) from September 1992 to October 1993, which mainly worked on roads, bridge-building and other construction projects in the area southwest of Phnom Penh. The contingent served under the UNTAC force commander, Australian Lieutenant General John Sanderson, who evinced a strong personal interest in ensuring the success of Japan's contribution. The UNTAC success 'set the scene' for subsequent UN PKO deployments by the JSDF.[34]

In the case of East Timor, Japan provided 'prompt and substantial' financial support to INTERFET but declined military participation.[35] However, Japan decided to send JSDF personnel to East Timor in November 2001, and made a long-term foreign aid commitment, and there has been close coordination of JSDF and ADF efforts with regard to 'nation-building'. The first JGSDF contingent, an engineer battalion with 680 personnel, arrived in

East Timor in May 2002.[36] It was replaced by a second contingent (also with 680 personnel) in October 2002, which was in turn replaced by a third contingent (with 522 members) in March 2003.[37]

The US alliance

For both Japan and Australia, their respective alliances with the US are fundamental bases of their strategic policies and plans. These alliances, and the US strategic directions, affect their respective strategic priorities, force development planning and acquisition programs, and operational commitments. They also affect the scope and opportunities for important cooperative activities between Australia and Japan. The war on terror, embracing many fronts, has opened up a wide expanse of new areas for cooperation, ranging from law enforcement measures to air and marine security practices to joint participation in US-led 'coalitions of the willing' and post-war reconstruction operations. The decisions by Australia and Japan in December 2003 to participate in US ballistic missile defence (BMD) programs also raise collaborative possibilities. In June 2002, the US officially withdrew from the Anti-Ballistic Missile (ABM) Treaty and embarked on a wide-ranging program to develop and deploy both theatre and strategic/national BMD systems, but this really only codified commitments made by the Bush administration before September 11. Both Australia and Japan had also been interested in different aspects of missile defence well before September 11. However, the war on terror has provided new justifications, with the US explaining its need for defences in terms of the proliferation of WMD among 'rogue states', and, potentially, international terrorist organisations – with North Korea being prominent in this milieu.

Missile defence

The respective Japanese and Australian missile defence programs and plans provide several avenues for cooperation, such as intelligence cooperation concerning the technical details of current and prospective missile/WMD developments in the region, collaborative research and development (R&D) projects, real-time sharing of tactical early warning information (including missile launch detection and indicative flight trajectories), and the coordination of prospective BMD operations (especially those involving ship-based anti-missile systems). The extent to which any of this might be implemented is largely dependent upon Washington.

Japan has had a very limited anti-missile capability, at least against shorter-range and relatively slow missiles, since the acquisition by the JASDF of the first-generation *Patriot* missiles for high-altitude air defence in the late 1980s.[38] These were distributed among six Air Defense Missile Groups, located to protect areas of 'political, economic and strategic importance' –

the 3rd Air Defense Missile Group, based at Chitose, and protecting the central and southwestern parts of Hokkaido; the 6th, based at Misawa, covering the area around the Tsugaru Strait; the 1st, based at Iruma, protecting the Kanto area (around Tokyo); the 4th, based at Gifu, covering the Keihanshin district; the 2nd, based at Kasuga, covering the northern part of Kyushu; and the 5th, based at Naha and protecting Okinawa.[39] In 1991, following the poor performance of *Patriot* missiles of this vintage against Iraqi *Scud* ballistic missiles during the Gulf War (Operation *Desert Storm*) in January-February 1991, the JASDF decided to acquire *Patriot* Advanced Capability (PAC)-2 systems; and in 1995, following the test launch by North Korea of a *Nodong-1* medium-range ballistic missile (MRBM) on 29 May 1993, it decided to acquire twenty-four enhanced PAC-2 (so-called PAC-2 Plus) 'fire units' to protect key military installations and urban areas against missile attacks – though only by cruise missiles or ballistic missiles with slow re-entry speeds. Delivery of the PAC-2 Plus missiles began in 1998. Each of the twenty-four 'fire units' (four per Air Defense Missile Group) has eight launch stations, with four missiles per launch station, or 768 missiles.[40] Another three 'fire stations' (with ninety-six missiles) were acquired around 2000–1.

The JMSDF also acquired a limited anti-tactical ballistic missile (ATBM) capability during the 1990s, in the form of the *Standard* SM-2 (MR) Block IV surface-to-air missiles aboard its four *Kongo*-class *Aegis* destroyers, commissioned in 1993–8. (Two additional *Kongo*-class destroyers are currently under construction.) The SM-2 (MR) Block IV missiles have a range of 200 nautical miles and an operational ceiling of 95,000ft, and can be used against cruise missiles and tactical ballistic missiles.[41]

In the late 1990s, as part of the 'mid-term defense build-up plan for 2001 to 2005', and charged by North Korea's ballistic missile program, especially the launch of a *Taepodong-1* MRBM across Japan on 31 August 1998, the JDA began to formulate plans for the acquisition of more advanced versions of the *Patriot* and *Standard* systems as the basis for a nation-wide layered BMD system. Initial plans included the addition of sixteen PAC-3 'hit-to-kill' missiles to each of the twenty-four 'fire units', or 384 missiles.[42] In August 2003, the Cabinet approved the first phase of this program – a 144 billion yen (US$1.23 billion) package which included funds for nine SM-3 missiles for one of the *Aegis* destroyers (with missiles for the other five to follow), and PAC-3 missiles for the four 'fire units' in the 1st Air Defence Missile Group protecting the Kanto area, based at Narashino, Takeyama, Kasumigaura and Iruma. The JDA also announced that a new type of radar called the FPS-XX would be developed to compliment the current FPS-3 radar system and provide earlier detection and characterisation of ballistic missiles. The SM-3s (which cost 2 billion yen each) are intended to intercept incoming MRBMs during their mid-course phase beyond the Earth's atmosphere, while the PAC-3s (which cost 500 million yen each) provide a terminal defence against missiles that have eluded the SM-3s. Both systems are to be deployed in 2007.[43] It was reported in March 2004 that Japan now planned to acquire 'about 200' PAC-3s.[44]

However, Japan remains dependent upon the US for the provision of early-warning information from the US geostationary infra-red missile launch detection and tracking satellites stationed over the eastern hemisphere, which provide the first warning that launches have taken place anywhere in this enormous region. These satellites would provide the Japanese authorities with precious minutes of warning of missile launches before they could be detected by ground-based radars in Japan itself; hence the most important connection with Australia, which hosts important ground facilities for relaying early-warning information from these satellites. For two decades, the ground control station for these DSP-E (Defense Support Program – Eastern hemisphere) satellites was located at Nurrungar, South Australia, which both controlled the satellites and processed and analysed the early warning data, while at the same time relaying it to the US North American Air Defense (NORAD) complex in Colorado.[45]

The Nurrungar station ceased operations on 30 September 1999 (and was officially closed on 12 October), by which time a smaller Relay Ground Station (RGS) had been constructed at Pine Gap in central Australia for receiving and relaying early warning information from the current DSP satellites and their prospective successors, the Space-Based Infra-Red System (SBIRS) satellites.[46] The SBIRS satellites are able to detect the launches of smaller missiles (with fainter infra-red luminosity) and to track them through their flight, and hence are critical elements of any future US homeland or theatre ballistic missile defence system.

The *Nodong-1* launch on 29 May 1993 and the *Taepodong-1* launch on 31 August 1998 were both detected by the DSP-E satellites and the information processed at the Nurrungar station. Warnings were quickly communicated to the US and thence to Japan. In the case of the *Nodong-1* launch, the JDA had been informed by the US beforehand that the launch was imminent, and was told it had been detected by the early-warning satellites as soon as the HQ of the US Forces in Japan (USFJ) at Yokota air base, west of Tokyo, had been notified. But by this time the missile had already been detected and was being tracked by the JASDF air defence radar station at Waijima, on the Noto peninsula.[47] By the time of the *Taepodong* launch in August 1998, mechanisms had been established for the direct transmission of launch detection data from Colorado to the JDA HQ.[48] And by mid-2003, when the US Air Force Space Command activated a Shared Early Warning System (SEWS) Centralized Distribution Facility in Colorado, a terminal had been set up in Tokyo for the direct receipt of relayed DSP/SBIRS data.[49] By then, however, Australia's role in the control of the US satellite early warning system had substantially diminished. The SBIRS ground segment is very dispersed and highly redundant, with numerous back-up or alternative satellite control and data relay modes, and with the data about missile launches and trajectories being disseminated to multiple command posts around the world. A 60 GHz satellite-to-satellite cross-link also enables the data to be relayed to the national command centres in the US without passing through any ground facility.

The RGS at Pine Gap is staffed by only 3–4 personnel, as compared to the 400 or so staff who had maintained the Nurrungar DSP ground station. In official US terminology, it is a 'bent pipe' facility which automatically relays satellite data without any data processing or analysis.[50]

The SBIRS is certainly essential to any future US ballistic missile defence system, but particular ground elements such as the RGS at Pine Gap are really quite marginal elements. They could be removed or redeployed without significant detriment to US (or Japanese) missile defence activities.

It is possible to envisage operational cooperation in missile defence in contingencies involving ADF and JSDF elements when both forces have SM-3 anti-missile missiles. Australia plans to acquire three or four 6,000–7,500-ton Air Warfare Destroyers, the first two of which are to be in service by 2015, and to equip these with SM-3s for theatre missile defence.[51] Working together, a joint force of, say, 4–6 platforms carrying hundreds of SM-3s for exo-atmospheric interception of MRBMs and a multitude of other anti-missile systems for defence against shorter-range ballistic and cruise missiles, would provide an effective shield over ADF and JSDF elements participating in coalition operations or PKO – or even over substantial parts of their respective homelands.

The war on terror

The terrorist assault of September 11 and the resultant US-led war on terror have generated myriad opportunities for expanded cooperation – in US-led 'coalitions of the willing', regional multilateral forums, new trilateral (US-Japan-Australia) arrangements, and new fields of bilateral cooperation. The 'bilateral consultation and cooperation in the fight against terrorism' was formalised in the *Australia-Japan Joint Statement on Cooperation to Combat International Terrorism*, adopted by the foreign ministries on 16 July 2003. It reaffirmed 'our shared interest and common purpose in cooperating to fight the scourge of international terrorism', renewed 'our commitment to strength-ening cooperation in APEC, the ARF and other regional forums to disrupt terrorist networks', and recognised the 'urgent need [to] strengthen coopera-tion between us . . . to help build the capacity of countries in the region, especially in South-East Asia, to fight terrorism'.[52] It was accompanied by an 'Action Plan,' which included expanding the 'exchange of information and assessments on terrorism issues and developments, including through visits by senior officials'; improving transport security, energy security, and 'cyber secu-rity and critical infrastructure protection'; 'enhancing cooperation between law enforcement agencies in relation to both operational and counter-terrorism capacity-building issues'; and 'strengthening measures to counter the prolifera-tion of weapons of mass destruction and their delivery systems'.[53]

On the defence side, it means expanding dialogues and intelligence exchanges, intensified cooperation with regard to maritime surveillance activities, and increasing joint exercise activities. For example, in September 2003, ADF elements exercised for the first time with a Japanese coastguard vessel in Exercise *Pacific Protector* in the Coral Sea, in which a vessel 'suspected' (for training purposes) of carrying WMD was interdicted, boarded and inspected by Australian and Japanese officers, as part of the Proliferation Security Initiative (PSI). The exercise was widely regarded as being aimed at North Korea.[54] Indeed, North Korea denounced the exercise as 'a wanton violation of the sovereignty of [North Korea]' and as an 'intolerable military provocation'; it saw the manoeuvres as 'a prelude to a nuclear war' and declared that it would, in response, 'further increase its nuclear deterrent force'.[55]

It also means that there is an increasing likelihood of cooperation in operational situations, at least with respect to the provision of intelligence and logistic support, but also in interdiction operations and prospectively even joint combat operations. Australia and Japan were the only countries in East Asia to provide a military contribution to Operation *Enduring Freedom*, although only the Australian forces participated in combat operations.

Japan's support for the war in Afghanistan was both unprecedented in terms of breaking the constraints on overseas deployments of the JSDF, and also very conditional. On 19 October 2001 the Diet approved anti-terrorism legislation which authorised the JSDF to provide military support to the US-led war on terrorism – including escorts, guards, intelligence and logistics, but not direct combat services. The JMSDF moved quickly to organise a task force, consisting of a non-*Aegis* destroyer, minesweepers and supply ships, which deployed to the Indian Ocean in November – the first time Japan had assisted forces in combat since the end of the Second World War.[56] The mission of the destroyer was declared to be intelligence collection, in line with the new legislation allowing the JDA/JSDF to conduct necessary 'research' activities, rather than direct support for US operations.[57] The JASDF committed almost half of its C-130 transport aircraft in support of Operation *Enduring Freedom*, flying US military equipment and personnel to Singapore, Guam and other places in the region.[58]

In September-October 2001, the JDA/JMSDF had suggested deploying one of the new *Kongo*-class *Aegis* destroyers, equipped with the SPY-ID radar systems (allowing them to simultaneously track hundreds of targets). This proposal was welcomed by the US Navy, but 'was blocked . . . by Japanese politicians, who were concerned about upsetting Asian neighbours [i.e. China]'.[59]

In May 2002, when the six-month review of the November commitment was underway, Washington raised the question of Japanese support for a US-led attack on Iraq, and reportedly asked specifically for the deployment of *Aegis* destroyers and P-3C *Orion* long-range maritime patrol aircraft (which would replace US capabilities in the Arabian Sea if the US forces were to move to the Persian Gulf for the attack).[60] The issue was embroiled in military politics in Tokyo, with the unabashed lobbying by some Japanese naval forces for accession to the US request causing some dissatisfaction.[61]

In the case of the war in Iraq, Prime Minister Junichiro Koizumi said on 20 March 2003 that 'Japan supports the US position.'[62] However, the actual Japanese support for Operation *Iraqi Freedom* was very limited. The *Kirishima*, one of the *Aegis* destroyers, was sent to the Indian Ocean in December 2002 to protect Japanese supply ships which were refuelling US and British naval vessels, and to conduct surveillance activities in the area, in accordance with another special anti-terrorist law passed in November 2002.[63] It was widely (if only tacitly) understood that this was an indirect contribution to the forthcoming war in Iraq in that it relieved a US *Aegis* destroyer from Afghanistan operations and allowed it to move into the Gulf.[64]

Following the declared end of war in Iraq on 1 May 2003, and the passage by the Diet of the Iraq Humanitarian Reconstruction Support Special Measures Law in July, Japanese SDF have been sent to Iraq to assist the US-led coalition forces 'reconstructing' the country – the first time that Japanese SDF units have served abroad outside the UN PKO framework.[65] About 1,000 Japanese GSDF, MSDF and ASDF personnel were dispatched to Iraq in February.[66] As of March 2004, the ADF still had some 850 personnel in Iraq (a decline from about 2,000 personnel during Operation *Iraqi Freedom* a year before), performing both reconstruction and protective security duties.[67]

The prospects

There is no doubt that current and prospective geopolitical trends will lead to a further strengthening of the Australia-Japan security relationship. Given the increasing likelihood of their common involvement in US-led coalitions in the war on terror, counter-proliferation initiatives and peacekeeping operations (with and without UN mandates), as well as their mutual interest in BMD developments, it becomes increasingly likely that ADF and Japanese SDF elements will serve together in operational situations, including not only combat support activities but also actual combat. It is not difficult to envisage Australian Army and Japanese GSDF units, for example, committed to the same theatre, being embroiled in firefights in which they fight, and survive, together. But however much the direct bilateral relationship is strengthened, it will remain distinctly secondary to the respective alliances with the US. And it will be US strategic policies and defence decisions which will primarily determine the directions, pace and dimensions of the continuing expansion in cooperative activities. The degree of incoherence and unpredictability in US policies imposes considerable uncertainty on the unfolding shape of the bilateral relationship.

The possibilities can be illustrated by an imaginative leap to 2010. By then, a third of a century after the first steps were taken in secret, the intelligence relationship will be comprehensive and matured, the RAN and Japanese MSDF will be well practised in joint communications, navigational procedures and tactical manoeuvres, and substantial elements will be fully inter-operable. It will be routine for the Japanese MSDF's *Aegis* destroyers, one of which was continuously stationed in the Indian Ocean, to provide intelligence, refuelling, and air defence and anti-missile protection for RAN vessels still involved in the maintenance of political stability in the Persian Gulf. The Australian and Japanese P-3C aircraft and *Global Hawk* high-altitude unmanned aerial vehicles (UAVs) directly exchange sensor data, including electronic intercepts and imagery, concerning activities in important maritime areas, such as the South China Sea. The collaborative interdiction, boarding and inspection of vessels suspected of transporting WMD-related materials will have become fairly commonplace – despite vociferous complaints from North Korea, whose vessels bore the brunt of the searches.

Now consider a hypothetical scenario – deliberately provocative, containing some licence, but really involving only modest extrapolations from current trends. Start with the interception by the Japanese MSDF of a North Korean vessel suspected of carrying some proscribed materials – perhaps on the basis of evidence provided by Australian technical intelligence systems. During the attempted boarding, the North Korean vessel sinks, with the loss of the entire crew. North Korea retaliates by firing a *Nodong* MRBM at Japan. The launch is detected by the SBIRS satellites and the information relayed directly, through the RGS at Pine Gap, to the SEWS facility at the JDA HQ in Tokyo. At the same time, it is also relayed from Pine Gap to Australia's lead air warfare destroyer, yet to be officially declared operational, but which happens to be in the Sea of Japan, already carrying its SM-3 missiles. It has been sent to participate in a naval air defence exercise organised by the Japanese MSDF as part of the twelfth WPNS meeting and has stayed with the MSDF, which is assisting the RAN by relating some of its own extensive experience with ABM systems. The *Nodong* is successfully intercepted by an SM-3 fired from the Australian destroyer. It is later ascertained that the missile had been armed with a nuclear warhead and had been targeted at Tokyo.

Notes

1 N. Sajima, 'Japan and Australia: A new security partnership?', Working Paper no. 292, Canberra: Strategic and Defence Studies Centre, Australian National University, January 1996, p. 27.
2 Ibid., p. 1.
3 R. Dalrymple, 'Japan and Australia as anchors: Do the chains still bind?', paper presented at the Australia-Japan Symposium on Peace Building in Asia-Pacific and Australia-Japan Relations, University of Tokyo, Tokyo, 3–4 December 1994, p. 1, cited in ibid., p. 1.
4 L. Xuejiang, 'The "two anchors" of the United States', *People's Daily*, 6 April 1996, cited in Colonel M. Hoare, 'The prospects for Australian and Japanese

security cooperation in a more uncertain Asia-Pacific', Working Paper no. 123, Canberra: Land Warfare Studies Centre, September 2003, p. 15.

5 International Institute for Strategic Studies (IISS), *The Military Balance, 2002–2003*, Oxford: Oxford University Press, October 2002, pp. 142–3, 151–2, 298–9.

6 Inspector General's Division, Department of Defence, *Defence Cooperation*, Directorate of Publishing, Canberra: Defence Centre, 1995, p. 14; D. Ball and P. Kerr, *Presumptive Engagement: Australia's Asia-Pacific Security Policy in the 1990s*, Sydney: Allen and Unwin, 1996, p. 63.

7 Australian Royal Commission on Intelligence and Security, *Fifth Report*, Canberra: Australian Government Printer, 1977, Appendix E, paragraph 46.

8 Joint Intelligence Organisation (JIO), *Fourth Annual Report 1974*, Canberra: Joint Intelligence Organisation, Department of Defence, November 1974, p. 24.

9 J. T. Richelson and D. Ball, *The Ties That Bind: Intelligence Cooperation Between the UKUSA Countries – the United Kingdom, the United States of America, Canada, Australia and New Zealand*, Sydney, London and Boston: Allen and Unwin, 1985, pp. 141–4; J. T. Richelson, *Foreign Intelligence Organizations*, Cambridge MA: Ballinger, 1988, pp. 256–8.

10 Japan Defense Agency (JDA), *Defence of Japan 1997*, Tokyo: The Japan Times, 1997, p. 279; Japan Defense Agency (JDA), *Defence of Japan 2002*, Tokyo: Urban Connections, 2002, p. 243.

11 Office of the Minister for Defence, 'Australia-Japan defence ministers meeting', media release, Canberra, 8 January 1998.

12 Ibid.

13 Senator the Hon. Robert Hill, Minister for Defence, 'Australia-Japan defence talks', media release, Canberra, 20 August 2002.

14 Senator the Hon. Robert Hill, Minister for Defence, 'Australia-Japan defence relationship', media release, Canberra, 29 September 2003. See also 'Australia-Japan defence relationship', *Asian Defence Journal*, November 2003, p. 58.

15 P. Dibb, *Review of Australia's Defence Capabilities: Report to the Minister for Defence*, Canberra: Australian Government Publishing Service, March 1986, p. 37.

16 D. Greenless, 'Naval exercises to improve Japan ties', *Australian*, 26 August 1997, p. 8.

17 'N-SAT-110 on route to GEO', *SpaceDaily*, 6 October 2000, http://www.spacedaily.com/news/japan-satbiz-00c.html (accessed 8 January 2001). See also 'Lockheed Martin opens new ground station in Australia to track telecommunications satellites', 28 January 1999, http://lmms.external.lmco.com/newsbureau/pressreleases/1999/99.10.html (accessed 9 March 1999).

18 G. Taylor, 'Japan plans WA spy base', *West Australian*, 17 October 2001, p. 11.

19 B. Nicholson, 'WA stations help launch Japanese spy satellites', *Age*, 30 March 2003, p. 12.

20 E. Sekigawa and M. Mecham, 'Japan preps for its first milsat launch', *Aviation Week and Space Technology*, 27 January 2003, p. 26; E. Sekigawa, 'And so it begins', *Aviation Week and Space Technology*, 7 April 2003, p. 32.

21 Ball and Kerr, *op. cit.*, pp. 21–3.

22 His Excellency Dr Taro Nakayama, Minister for Foreign Affairs of Japan, 'Statement to the general session of the ASEAN Post Ministerial Conference', Kuala Lumpur, Malaysia, 22 July 1991, pp. 12–13. See also D. Ball, *Building Blocks for Regional Security: An Australian Perspective on Confidence and Security Building Measures (CSBMs) in the Asia-Pacific Region*, Canberra Papers of Strategy and Defence no. 83, Canberra: Strategic and Defence Studies Centre, Australian National University, 1991, pp. 53–4.

23 Nakayama, *op. cit.*, pp. 10–11.

24 Ball and Kerr, *op. cit.*, pp. 24–5.
25 Ibid., pp. 116–19.
26 Co-Chairmen's Summary Report of the Meetings of the ARF Intersessional Support Group on Confidence Building Measures, Held in Honolulu, USA, 4–6 November 1998, and in Bangkok, Thailand, 3–5 March 1999, pp. 1–2.
27 Ibid., p. 20.
28 Co-Chairmen's Summary Report of the Meetings of the ARF Intersessional Support Group on Confidence Building Measures, held in Tokyo, Japan, on 13–14 November 1999, and in Singapore, 5–6 April 2000, para. 42.
29 D. Ball, *The Council for Security Cooperation in the Asia Pacific (CSCAP): Its Record and its Prospects*, Canberra Papers of Strategy and Defence no. 139, Canberra: Strategic and Defence Studies Centre, Australian National University, 2000, pp. 5–6.
30 Sajima, *op. cit.*, p. 27; Hoare, *op. cit.*, pp. 38–9.
31 See, for example, the Japan Forum on International Relations, 'Preventive diplomacy and Japan's role: An action menu', in D. Ball and A. Acharya (eds) *The Next Stage: Preventive Diplomacy and Security Cooperation in the Asia-Pacific Region*, Canberra Papers of Strategy and Defence no. 131, Canberra: Strategic and Defence Studies Centre, Australian National University, 1999, ch. 12.
32 Japan Defense Agency (JDA), *Defense of Japan 2003*, Tokyo: Inter Group Corp., 2003, pp. 286, 299.
33 Ibid., pp. 295, 525.
34 Hoare, *op. cit.*, pp. 24–6; Japan Defense Agency (JDA), *Defense of Japan 1994*, Tokyo: The Japan Times, 1994, pp. 117–26.
35 Hoare, *op. cit.*, pp. 26–30.
36 Japan Defense Agency (JDA), *Defense of Japan 2002*, pp. 464, 467.
37 Japan Defense Agency (JDA), 2003, *op. cit.*, p. 269.
38 M. W. Chinworth, *Inside Japan's Defense: Technology, Economics and Strategy*, McLean VA: Brassey's, 1992, ch. 3.
39 Japan Defense Agency (JDA), *Defense of Japan 1996: Response to a New Era*, Tokyo: The Japan Times, 1996, pp. 92, 340.
40 K. W.Allen, J. R. East, D. M. Finkelstein, B. Garrett, B. Glaser, M. Green, M. Krepon *et al.*, *Theater Missile Defenses in the Asia-Pacific Region*, Washington DC: The Henry L. Stimson Center, Report no. 34, June 2000, pp. 4–5, 12, 75; M. Swaine, R. M. Swanger and T. Kawakami, *Japan and Ballistic Missile Defense*, Santa Monica CA: RAND Corporation, MR-1374-CAPP, 2001, p. 36.
41 N. Friedman, *The Naval Institute Guide to World Naval Weapons Systems 1997–1998*, Annapolis MD: Naval Institute Press, 1997, p. 417.
42 Allen *et al.*, *op. cit.*, p. 5; Swaine *et al.*, *op. cit.*, p. 36.
43 'Japan sets sights on $25m US missiles', *Canberra Times*, 23 August 2003, p. 19; 'World news roundup: Asia-Pacific', *Aviation Week and Space Technology*, 1 September 2003, 19; 'Japan's recent step-up in missile defense', Center for Defense Information (CDI), 10 October 2003, http://www.cdi.org/friendlyversion/printversion.cfm?documentID = 1725 (accessed 12 December 2003).
44 'Industry outlook: Japan goes ballistic', *Aviation Week and Space Technology*, 8 March 2004, p. 15.
45 D. Ball, *A Base for Debate: The US Satellite Station at Nurrungar*, Sydney: Allen and Unwin, 1987, ch. 3.
46 J. Moore, Minister for Defence, 'Early warning links strengthened', media release MIN 302/99, 12 October 1999; D. Ball, 'The strategic essence', *Australian Journal of International* Affairs, vol. 55, no. 2, 2001, pp. 239–42.
47 'Rabbits' ears and doves' dreams: Information on North Korea's missile test-firing kept secret – only bureaucrats discuss information with foreign minister and others kept in the dark', *Mainichi Shimbun*, 14 August 1994, p. 1.

48 N. Usui, 'US, Japan discuss sharing missile warnings', *Space News*, 23–9 January 1995, p. 6; N. Usui, 'Pentagon to supply early-warning data to JDA', *Space News*, 10–16 June 1996, p. 28; J. T. Richelson, *America's Space Sentinels: DSP Satellites and National Security*, Lawrence KS: University of Kansas Press, 1999, pp. 232–3.

49 F. Morring Jr, 'In orbit: Spreading the news', *Aviation Week and Space Technology*, 30 June 2003, p. 21.

50 Director, Operational Test and Evaluation, US Department of Defense, *FY 1998 Annual Report: Space-Based Infrared System (SBIRS)*, http://www.fas.org/spp/starwars/program/dote98/98sbirs.htm (accessed 12 March 1999).

51 Department of Defence, *Defence Capability Plan*, Canberra: Department of Defence, 2001, pp. 263–4; Commander Tom Mueller, RAN, 'The Royal Australian Navy and theatre ballistic missile defence', Working Paper no. 12, Canberra: Sea Power Centre Australia, 2003, pp. 18–24; S. Fruhling, *Ballistic Missile Defence for Australia: Policies, Requirements and Options*, Canberra Papers on Strategy and Defence no. 151, Canberra: Strategic and Defence Studies Centre, Australian National University, 2003, pp. 68–72.

52 Ministry of Foreign Affairs of Japan, *Australia-Japan Joint Statement on Cooperation to Combat International Terrorism*, 16 July 2003, http://www.mofa.go.jp/region/asia-paci/australia/pmv0307/terrorism.html (accessed 3 August 2003).

53 Ibid.

54 'Australia hosts military exercise in Coral Sea', *AM* (ABC Radio) 15 September 2003, transcript at http://www.abc.net.au/am/content/2003/s945883.htm (accessed 17 September 2003); 'Exercise "Pacific Protector": A special press summary', Virtual Information Center, 15 October 2003, http://www.vic-info.org/RegionsTop.nsf/0/b00d8560fb5da9fe0a256a4000ed309?OpenDocument (accessed 3 November 2003).

55 Agence France-Presse (AFP), 'N. Korea denounces US-led naval drill as "prelude to nuclear war"', 16 September 2003, http://quickstart.clari.net/qs_se/webnews/wed/bq/Qnkorea-military-drill-us.Rori_DSG.html (accessed 20 September 2003); M. Corder, 'North Korea riled by "provocation"', *Sydney Morning Herald*, 15 September 2003, http://www.smh.com.au/articles/2003/09/14/1063478067330.html (accessed 20 September 2003).

56 J. Sherman, 'U.S. seeks Japanese aid in terror fight', *Defense News*, 15–21 April 2003, p. 10.

57 'MSDF dispatch decision coming soon', *Japan Times*, 3 November 2001, http://www.japantimes.co.jp/cgi-bin/getarticle.p15?nn2001103b5.htm (accessed 2 December 2001).

58 Sherman, *op. cit.*, p. 10.

59 Ibid.

60 'U.S. eyes Japan aid in Iraq attack', *Asahi.com*, 20 April 2002, http://www.asahi.com/english/international/K2002042000252.html (accessed 22 April 2002); J. Sherman, 'Japan reluctant to join US-led attack on Iraq', *Defense News*, 6–12 May 2002, p. 4.

61 'MSDF lobbied for U.S. Aegis request', *Asahi.com*, 6 May 2002, http://www.asahi.com/english/politics/K2002050600151.html (accessed 1 June 2002).

62 'Japan supports US war on Iraq: Koizumi', *Inq7.net*, 20 March 2003, http://www.inq7.net/brk/2003/mar/20/brkafp_19-1.htm (accessed 23 March 2003).

63 A. Berkofsky, 'Japan. Aid and comfort: Japan's Aegis sets sail', *Asia Times Online*, 19 December 2002, http://www.atimes.com/atimes/Japan/DL19D01.html (accessed 8 January 2003).

64 Y. Sato, 'The GSDF will go to Iraq without a blue helmet', *PacNet*, 31 July 2003.
65 Ibid.; S. Moffett, M. Fackler, G. Fairclough and C. Hutzler, 'Japan: Marching on to a new role', *Far Eastern Economic Review*, 15 January 2004, pp.18–21.
66 'Japanese troops head to Iraq', *Canberra Times*, 4 February 2004, p. 14.
67 'Defence bid to cash in on Iraq', *Age*, 24 February 2004, p. 2.

Selected bibliography

Abuza, Z. *Militant Islam in Southeast Asia: Crucible of Terror*, Boulder CO: Lynne Rienner Publishers, 2003.

Alagappa, M. (ed.) *Asian Security Practice: Material and Ideational Influences*, Stanford CA: Stanford University Press, 1998.

Albinski, H. (ed.) *Australia and the United States*, Canberra ACT: Australian Defence Studies Centre, Australian Defence Force Academy, 1993.

Allen, K. W., East, J. R., Finkelstein, D. M., Garrett, B., Glaser, B., Green, M. J., Krepon, M. *et al. Theater Missile Defenses in the Asia-Pacific Region*, Washington DC: The Henry L. Stimson Center, report no. 34, June 2000.

Allison, G. Carter, A. Miller, S. and Zelikow, P. *Cooperative Denuclearization: From Pledges to Deeds*, CSIA Studies in International Security no. 2, Center for Science and International Affairs, Harvard University, 1993.

Anderson, A. 'Democracy and UN peacekeeping operations, 1990–1996', *International Peacekeeping,* vol. 7, no. 2, Summer 2000.

Ball, D. *A Base for Debate: The US Satellite Station at Nurrungar*, Sydney NSW: Allen & Unwin, 1987.

——'Building blocks for regional security: An Australian perspective on confidence and security building measures (CSBMs) in the Asia-Pacific region', Canberra Papers of Strategy and Defence no. 83, Canberra ACT: Strategic and Defence Studies Centre, Australian National University, 1991.

——'The Council for Security Cooperation in the Asia Pacific (CSCAP): Its record and its prospects', Canberra Papers of Strategy and Defence no. 139, Canberra ACT: Strategic and Defence Studies Centre, Australian National University, 2000.

——and Kerr, P. *Presumptive Engagement: Australia's Asia-Pacific Security Policy in the 1990s*, Sydney NSW: Allen & Unwin, 1996.

Berger, T. U. 'Alliance politics and Japan's postwar culture of antimilitarism', in M. J. Green and P. M. Cronin (eds) *The US-Japan Alliance: Past, Present, and Future*, New York: Council on Foreign Relations Press, 1999.

Blackwill, R. 'An action agenda to strengthen America's alliances in the Asia-Pacific region', in R. Blackwill and Paul Dibb (eds) *America's Asian Alliances*, Cambridge MA: MIT Press, 2000.

Blainey, G. *The Tyranny of Distance: How Distance Shaped Australia's History*, Melbourne VIC: Sun Books, 1967.

Buckley, R. *The United States in the Asia Pacific since 1945*, Cambridge/Cape Town: Cambridge University Press, 2002.

Buzan, B. 'The Asia Pacific: What sort of regionalism in what sort of world', in A. McGrew and C. Brook (eds) *Asia Pacific in the New World Order*, London and New York: Routledge, 1998.

Camilleri, J. A. *An Introduction to Australian Foreign Policy*, 2nd edn, Milton QLD: Jacaranda Press, 1975.

Chinworth, M. W. 'Inside Japan's Defense: Technology, Economics and Strategy', McLean VA: Brassey's, 1992.

Cotton, J. *Australia's East Timor Experience: Military Lessons and Security Dilemmas*, Canberra ACT: University of New South Wales, Australian Defence Force Academy, 2002.

——'Southeast Asia After September 11', in David Martin Jones, *Globalisation and the New Terror: The Asia-Pacific Dimension*, Cheltenham: Edward Elgar, 2004.

——and Ravenhill, J. (eds) *Seeking Asian Engagement: Australia in World Affairs, 1991–1995*, Melbourne VIC: Oxford University Press, 1997.

Dalrymple, R. *Continental Drift: Australia's Search for Regional Identity*, Aldershot: Ashgate, 2003.

Department of Defence, *The Defence of Australia 1987*, Canberra ACT: Australian Government Publishing Service, 1987.

Dibb, P. 'The future of Australia's defence relationship with the United States', Sydney NSW: Australian Centre for American Studies, 1993.

Dobson, H. *Japan and United Nations Peacekeeping*, London: RoutledgeCurzon, 2003.

Dupont, A. *Australia's Threat Perceptions: A Search for Security*, Canberra Papers on Strategy and Defence no. 82, Canberra ACT: Strategic and Defence Studies Centre, Australian National University, 1991.

Evans, G. *Australia's Regional Security*, ministerial statement, Canberra ACT: Department of Foreign Affairs and Trade, 1989.

——'Australia in East Asia and the Asia-Pacific: Beyond the looking glass', *Australian Journal of International Affairs*, vol. 49, no. 1, May 1995.

Frei, H. P. 'In direct alliance in the Pacific Rim: Japan-Australia relationship under the Pax Britannica and Pax Americana', trans. Toshiki Gomi, *International Relations*, vol. 68, no. 2, 1981.

Furuya, S. 'Migrants, national security and September 11: The case of Japan', *Race and Class*, vol. 44, no. 4, 2003.

Garnaut, R. *Australia and the Northeast Asian Ascendancy*, Canberra ACT: Australian Government Publishing Service, 1990.

Golding, P. *McEwen: Political Gladiator*, Melbourne VIC: Melbourne University Press, 1996.

Gorjao, P. 'Japan's foreign policy and East Timor, 1975–2002,' *Asian Survey*, vol. XLII, no. 5, September/October 2002.

Halliday, J. and McCormack, G. *Japanese Imperialism Today: Co-prosperity in Greater East Asia*, Harmondsworth: Penguin, 1973.

Hass, P. 'Introduction: epistemic communities and international policy coordination', *International Organisation*, vol. 46, no. 1, winter 1992.

Hatano, S. 'Foreign Minister Shigemitsu Mamoru and the Greater East Asian Declaration of 1943', *International Relations*, vol. 109, May 1995.

Hinton, H. *Three and a Half Powers: The New Balance in Asia*, Bloomington IN: Indiana University Press, 1975.

Hoare, M. 'The prospects for Australian and Japanese security cooperation in a more uncertain Asia-Pacific', Working Paper no. 123, Land Warfare Studies Centre, Canberra, September 2003.

Hook, G. D. Gilson, J. Hughes, C. W. and Dobson, H. *Japan's International Relations: Politics, Economics and Security*, London and New York: Routledge, 2001.

Ikenberry, G. J. and Tsuchiyama, J. 'Between balance of power and community: The future of multilateral security co-operation in the Asia Pacific', *International Relations of the Asia Pacific: A Journal of the Japan Association of International Relations*, vol. 2, no.1, 2002.

Information Office of the State Council of the People's Republic of China, *China's Non-Proliferation Policy and Measures*, Beijing: New Star Publishers, 2003.

Inoguchi, T. 'A North-east Asian perspective', *Australian Journal of International Affairs*, special issue: 'ANZUS turns 50', vol. 55, no. 2, July 2001.

——*Japan's Foreign Policy in an Era of Global Change*, London: Pinter Publishers, 1993.

International Crisis Group, 'Jemaah Islamiyah in Southeast Asia: Damaged but still dangerous', ICG Asia Report no.63, Brussels and Jakarta, 16 August 2003.

Irie, A. *Power and Culture: The Japanese-American War 1941–1945*, Cambridge MA: Harvard University Press, 1979.

Ishizuka, K. 'Peacekeeping and national interests: Positive factors influencing potential contributing states', *Kyoei University Journal*, vol. 1, no. 1, 2002.

Jain, P. and Bruni, J. 'Japan, Australia and the United States: Little NATO or shadow alliance?', *International Relations of the Asia-Pacific*, vol. 4, no. 2, 2004.

Japan Defense Agency, *Defense of Japan 2004*, Tokyo: Inter Group, 1994.

——*Defense of Japan 1996: Response to a New Era*, Tokyo: the *Japan Times*, 1996.

Juergensmeyer, M. *Terror in the Mind of God: The Global Rise of Religious Violence*, Berkeley CA: University of California Press, 2001.

——'The Religious Roots of Contemporary Terrorism', in Charles W. Kegley Jr (ed.) *The New Global Terrorism: Characteristics, Causes, Controls*, Upper Saddle River NJ, Prentice Hall, 2003.

Kingston, J. *Japan's Quiet Transformation: Global Change and Civil Society in the Twenty First Century*, London and New York: Routledge, 2004.

Korhonen, P. *Japan and Asia Pacific Integration: Pacific Romances 1968 – 1996*, London: Routledge, 1998.

Lebra, J. C. (ed.) *Japan's Greater East Asia co-prosperity sphere in World War II: Selected readings and documents*, New York: Oxford University Press, 1975.

Lifton, R. J. *Destroying the world to save it: Aum Shinrikyo, apocalyptic violence, and the new global terrorism*, New York: Henry Holt and Company, 1999.

McCormack, G. *Target North Korea: Pushing North Korea to the Brink of Nuclear Catastrophe*, Sydney NSW: Random House Australia, 2004.

Mackie, J. A. C. (ed.) *Australia in the New World Order: Foreign Policy in the 1970s*, Melbourne VIC: Nelson/Australian Institute of International Affairs, 1976.

Mann, J. *Rise of the Vulcans: The History of Bush's War Cabinet*, New York: Viking, 2004.

Martin, I. *Self-determination in East Timor: The United Nations, the Ballot, and International Intervention*, Boulder CO: Lynne Rienner, 2001.

Maswood, J. S. 'The regional context of Japanese security', in V. Selochan (ed.) *Security in the Asia-Pacific Region: The Challenge of a Changing Environment*, Canberra ACT: Australian Defence Studies Centre, Australian Defence Force Academy, 1993.

Millar, T. B. *Australia's Foreign Policy*, Sydney NSW: Angus and Robertson, 1968.
——*Australia in War and Peace*, Canberra ACT: ANU Press, 1991.
Milner, A. (ed.) 'Perceiving "National Security",' *Australian-Asian Perceptions Project Working Paper no. 5*, Academy of the Social Sciences in Australia, Canberra, 1994.
Nakagawa, Y. 'The WEPTO option', *Asian Survey*, vol. 24, no. 8, August 1984.
Newman, A. 'Cooperative threat reduction: "locking in" tomorrow's security', *Contemporary Security Policy*, vol. 22, April 2001.
Nishihara, M. *The Japanese and Sukarno's Indonesia*, Honolulu: University of Hawaii Press, 1976.
Nye, J. S. Jnr 'US National Interest and Global Public Goods', *International Affairs*, vol. 78, no. 2, April 2002.
——'Limits of American Power', *Political Science Quarterly*, vol. 117, no. 4, 2001–2.
O'Hanlon, M. and Mochizuki, M. *Crisis on the Korean Peninsula*, New York: McGraw-Hill, 2003.
Olsen, E. A. 'The evolution of Japan's security policy options,' in Y. W. Kihl and L. E. Grinter (eds) *Security, Strategy, and Policy Responses in the Pacific Rim*, Boulder CO: Lynne Rienner, 1989.
Olson, L. *Japan in Postwar Asia*, London: Pall Mall Press/Council on Foreign Relations, 1970.
Pillar, P. R. *Terrorism and US Foreign Policy*, Washington DC: Brookings Institution Press, 2001.
Polomka, P. *Japan as Peacekeeper: Samurai State, or New Civilian Power?*, Canberra Papers on Strategy and Defence no.97, Canberra ACT: Strategic and Defence Studies Centre, Australian National University, 1991.
Porter, B. D. *War and the Rise of the State: The Military Foundations of Modern Politics*, New York: Macmillan, 1994.
Ramakrishna, K. and Tan, S. S. 'Is Southeast Asia a terrorist haven?', in Kumar Ramakrishna and See Seng Tan (eds) *After Bali: The Threat of Terrorism in Southeast Asia*, Singapore: Institute of Defence and Strategic Studies, 2003.
Renouf, A. *The Frightened Country*, Melbourne VIC: Macmillan, 1979.
Richardson, M. *A Time Bomb for Global Trade: Maritime-related Terrorism in an Age of Weapons of Mass Destruction*, Singapore: Institute of Southeast Asian Studies, 2004.
Richelson, J. T. and Ball, D. *The Ties That Bind: Intelligence Cooperation Between the UKUSA Countries – the United Kingdom, the United States of America, Canada, Australia and New Zealand*, Sydney NSW, London and Boston MA: Allen & Unwin, 1985.
Rix, A. *The Australia-Japan Political Alignment: 1952 to the Present*, London: Routledge, 1999.
Sajima, N. 'Changing ANZUS: The future of northern and southern anchors', *International Affairs*, no. 446, May 1996.
——'Japan and Australia: a new security partnership?', Working Paper no. 292, Canberra: Strategic and Defence Studies Centre, Australian National University, 1996.
——'Japan: Strategic culture at a crossroads', in K. Booth and R. Trood (eds) *Strategic Cultures in the Asia-Pacific Region*, London: Macmillan, 1999.

Searle, A. and Kamae, I. 'Anchoring trilateralism: Can Australia-Japan-US security relations work?', *Australian Journal of International Affairs*, vol. 58, no. 4, December 2004.

The Japan Association of International Relations (ed.) *The Historical Evolution of Australia-Japan Relations*, International Relations no.68, Tokyo: Yuhikaku, 1981.

Sakai, K. '11 September and the clash of civilizations: The role of the Japanese media and public discourse', *Arab Studies Quarterly*, vol. 25, nos.1 and 2, 2003.

Sakai, T. 'The political economy of the new East Asian Declaration of 1943', *International Relations*, vol. 97, May 1991.

Swaine, M., Swanger, R. M. and Kawakami, T. *Japan and Ballistic Missile Defense*, Santa Monica CA: RAND Corporation, MR-1374-CAPP, 2001.

Takai, S. 'Japan's contribution to UN peacekeeping', *Social Science Japan*, no. 6, February 1996, Institute of Social Science, University of Tokyo, http://web.iss.u-tokyo.ac.jp/newslet/SSJ6/takai.html (date accessed: 20/05/03).

Shinoda, T. 'Koizumi's top-down leadership in the anti-terrorism legislation: The impact of political institutional changes', *SAIS Review*, 2003.

Simon, S. W. 'East Asian security: The playing field has changed', *Asian Survey*, vol. XXXIV, no.12, December 1994.

Smith, H. (ed.) *International Peacekeeping: Asian and Regional Perspectives*, Canberra ACT: Australian Defence Studies Centre, Australian Defence Force Academy, 1993.

Sissons, D. 'Australia and Japan, 1961–1965', in G. Greenwood and N. Harper (eds) *Australia in World Affairs*, Melbourne VIC: F. W. Cheshire, 1967.

Squassoni, S. A. 'Weapons of mass destruction; trade between North Korea and Pakistan', *CSR Report for Congress*, 11 March 2004.

Stockwin, A. 'Negotiating the Basic Treaty between Australia and Japan, 1973–1976', *Japanese Studies*, vol. 24, no. 2, September 2004.

The Japan Forum on International Relations, 'Preventive diplomacy and Japan's role: An action menu', in D. Ball and A. Acharya (eds) *The Next Stage: Preventive Diplomacy and Security Cooperation in the Asia-Pacific Region*, Canberra Papers of Strategy and Defence no. 131, Canberra ACT: Strategic and Defence Studies Centre, Australian National University, 1999.

Timperlake, E. and Triplett II, W. C. *Red Dragon Rising: Communist China's Military Threat to America*, Washington DC: Regnery Publishing Inc., 1999.

Tow, W. T. 'The Janzus option: A key to Asian/Pacific security', *Asian Survey*, vol. 2, no. 4, March 1981,

——'Reshaping Asia-Pacific security', *Journal of East Asian Affairs*, vol. 8, no. 1, winter/spring 1994.

——'Deputy sheriff or independent ally? Evolving Australian-American ties in an ambiguous world order', *The Pacific Review*, vol. 17, no. 2, June 2004.

——and R. Trood, *Power Shift: Challenges for Australia in Northeast Asia*, Canberra ACT: Australian Strategic Policy Institute, June 2004.

Uchiyama, M. 'The Sino-Japanese War (1894–95): A re-evaluation after 100 years', *International Relations: Japan's Wartime Diplomacy and the Post-war Visions*, vol. 109, May 1995.

United States Department of Defense, Office of International Security Affairs, *United States Security Strategy for the East Asia-Pacific Region*, Washington DC: US Government Printing Office, February 1995.

——'United States Security Strategy for the East Asia-Pacific Region', Washington DC: USGPO, February 1995.

Verrier, J. R. 'Australia's self image as a regional and international security actor: Some implications of the Iraq war', *Australian Journal of International Affairs*, vol. 57, no. 3, November 2003.

Walton, D. 'Japan and East Timor: Implications for the Australia-Japan relationship', *Japanese Studies*, vol. 24, no. 2, September 2004.

Watanabe, A. 'Japan and Australia: A comparison of their strategies for coexistence with Asia and America', in P. King and Y. Kibata (eds) *Peace Building in Asia-Pacific Region*, St Leonards NSW: Allen and Unwin, 1996.

Watt, A. *The Evolution of Australian Foreign Policy*, Cambridge: Cambridge University Press, 1967.

Wheeler, N. J. and Dunne, T. 'East Timor and the new humanitarian intervention', *International Affairs*, vol. 77, no. 4, 2001.

White House, *The National Security Strategy of the United States of America*, Washington DC, September 2002.

——*National Strategy to Combat Weapons of Mass Destruction*, Washington DC, December 2002.

Williams, B. 'Japan, North Korea and the "war on terror",' in M. Vicziany, D. Wright-Neville and P. Lentini (eds) *Regional Security in the Asia Pacific: 9/11 and After*, Cheltenham: Edward Elgar, 2004.

Woodman, S. 'A question of priorities: Australian and New Zealand security planning in the 1990s', Working Paper no. 260, Canberra ACT: Strategic and Defence Studies Centre, Australian National University, 1992.

Index

For Product Safety Concerns and Information please contact our EU
representative GPSR@taylorandfrancis.com
Taylor & Francis Verlag GmbH, Kaufingerstraße 24, 80331 München, Germany